THE NEXT MVE

FOR BUSINESS OWNERS

The Transition, Growth and
Exit Planning Strategies
You **NEED** to Know

D1251359

Nick Niemann, ESQ

BRIEFBACK
BUSINESS
INSTITUTE

Omaha, Nebraska

Copyright © 2009 Nicholas K. Niemann – All rights reserved.

Legal Notice/Disclaimer and Circular 230 Disclosure information on following page within this book. This publication may not be reproduced, stored in a retrieval system, or transmitted in whole or in part, in any form or by any means, electronic, mechanical, photocopying, recording, or otherwise, without the prior written permission of Nicholas K. Niemann. Brief quotations may be used in professional articles or reviews if proper credit is awarded.

Published by:
BriefBack Business Institute LLC
Nicholas K. Niemann
1601 Dodge Street
Suite 3700
Omaha, NE 68102
(402) 633-1489
nniemann@mcgrathnorth.com

The Next Move For Business Owners™ trademark is owned by BriefBack Business Institute LLC.

First Softcover Edition 2009

ISBN 10: 0-9796195-7-2
ISBN 13: 978-0-9796195-7-1
LCCN: 2009927594

www.OwnersNextMove.com

Printed in the United States of America
10 9 8 7 6 5 4 3

Legal Notice/Disclaimer

While the examples mentioned in this book are based on actual clients' situations, the names and certain facts have been changed in order to protect their privacy. This publication should not be considered as legal, tax, business or financial advice. This publication is designed to provide information about the subject matter covered. It is provided with the understanding that neither Nicholas K. Niemann nor his firm has been engaged by the reader to render legal, tax, business or financial advice or other professional service (unless a specific engagement letter has been executed). If legal, tax, business or financial advice or other expert assistance is required by the reader, the services of a competent professional should be sought. Neither Nicholas K. Niemann nor his firm nor BriefBack Business Institute LLC shall have any liability or responsibility to any person or entity with respect to any loss or damage caused, or alleged to be caused, directly or indirectly, by the information contained in this book. While this book contains information which is intended to be thorough, we do not presume to address every conceivable matter which could impact a particular business owner's transition or exit situation. Use of this book by the reader constitutes agreement to these terms.

Circular 230 Disclosure

The following statement is provided pursuant to U.S. Treasury Department Regulations: Any U.S. tax advice contained in this communication (including any attachments) is not intended or written to be used, and cannot be used, for the purpose of avoiding penalties under the Internal Revenue Code, nor should such advice be used or referred to in the promoting, marketing or recommending of any entity, investment plan or arrangement.

Contact Information

Nicholas K. Niemann
1601 Dodge Street
Suite 3700
Omaha, NE 68102
(402) 633-1489
nniemann@mcgrathnorth.com

An Introduction To Transition Growth And Exit Planning

Dear Business Owner:

Transitioning and exiting successfully from a closely held company or family business has never been quick or easy. It requires that certain specific actions be taken over a period of time by you, your management team and selected advisors.

Many opportunities exist for enhancing your business, financial, tax, personal, and legacy outcomes -- in particular, if proper transition and exit strategies are put in place up to 10 to 15 years ahead of your expected exit. This is why I created The Next Move For Business Owners™ Program.

A successful outcome depends on evaluating and addressing 12 Critical Building Block components during the Transition Growth and Exit Planning process.

Decide

1. Decide What I Want
2. Decide What I've Got

Protect

3. Protect My Family
4. Protect My Business
5. Protect My Ownership

Grow

6. Grow My Investments
7. Grow My Business

Prepare

8. Prepare My Management
9. Prepare My Company
10. Prepare My Tax Savings Plans

Exit

11. Plan My Inside Route Exit
12. Plan My Outside Route Exit

Using The Next Move Program described in this book, my team and I work with business owners and their advisors around the country to determine, prioritize and take the actions needed now and over time.

I hope this book provides you with some insights into what you need to do to successfully accomplish the outcome and legacy you hope to achieve.

Sincerely,

Nicholas K. Niemann

Dedication

This book is dedicated to:

My parents, Ferd and Rita – for being great parents and for teaching me all of the essentials of how to own, operate and innovate successful business ventures.

My wife, Ann – the love of my life, for being a great wife and a great mother to our six children, Katie, Becky, Christine, David, Lisa and Tricia.

Acknowledgements

I work with an ever increasing number of professional advisors as part of a number of Transition Growth and Exit Planning teams to assist business owners. This includes private bankers, financial advisors, CPAs, insurance advisors, merger and acquisition ("M&A") advisors, corporate attorneys, investment bankers, management consultants, bank officers, business appraisers, and compensation specialists.

These advisors have come to realize the benefit of Transition Growth and Exit Planning both to the business owners they work with and to their own professional responsibilities. I want to thank you for your input and ideas from each of your perspectives in how to assist business owners with a successful transition and exit from their businesses.

I also want to thank my partners at McGrath North, with whom I've worked for over 25 years, for the insights, creativity and strategies I've learned from you in assisting business owners.

Profile

Nicholas K. Niemann began his business career helping his family build and manage their various business interests in restaurants, supermarkets, real estate, ranching, farming, construction and retail merchandising.

As a practicing Transition Growth and Exit Planning advisor, he and his team work with business owners and their advisors around the country to help them develop and implement plans to transition and exit from active duty and ownership of their businesses. A properly prepared Transition Growth Plan will help owners achieve the personal, family, business and financial legacies they want to achieve during their transition and upon their eventual exit from their business.

Nick has advised business owners for over 27 years and is a frequent speaker at national and regional business owner transition and exit planning programs to business, industry and professional groups. He is a member of the Business Enterprise Institute, the leading exit planning advisor organization in the country. He is also the founder and president of BriefBack Business Institute LLC which publishes transition and exit planning guidance for business owners.

He has provided Transition Growth and Exit Planning guidance for companies in many business sectors, including Consumer Product Manufacturing, Industrial Manufacturing, Business Services, Food and Beverage, Construction, Engineering, Health Care, Agribusiness, Real Estate, Distribution, Financial Services, Retail, Human Resources, Franchise, and Consumer Services.

Nick is a partner in the Omaha, Nebraska law firm of McGrath North. He has an AV rating from the Martindale-Hubbell National Law Directory (the highest rating for legal ability, ethics, professional reliability and diligence) and has been awarded Fellow status by the Nebraska State Bar.

Nick is the principal designer and drafter of Nebraska's main business economic development legislation (e.g. 1987 LB775 and 2005 LB312). These programs have resulted in over 100,000 new jobs and $20 billion of new capital investment in over 600 business growth expansion projects throughout Nebraska. This business growth and business owner exit legislation has for over 20 years helped growing Nebraska businesses to expand effectively exempt from Nebraska income and sales taxes and has enabled Nebraska business owners to exit and sell their company exempt from Nebraska capital gain taxes.

He graduated from Creighton University's College of Business in 1978, summa cum laude, with a degree in accounting and has a CPA certificate. He received his J.D. from Creighton's School of Law in 1981, magna cum laude. He has served on the adjunct faculty of Creighton's School of Law, teaching transition and exit planning, taxation, business valuation and estate planning. He serves on the Advisory Board for the Creighton University Center For Family Business. He also serves on the Headquarters Target Advisory Group for the Omaha Chamber of Commerce.

Nick and his wife Ann have been married for 28 years and have six children and four grandchildren.

Preface

This book has been written in response to the frustrations I have witnessed from business owners who have spent years building a business, only to run into roadblocks when you start to consider your eventual exit.

There has been a lack of credible, thorough information published that takes on all the aspects of what you need to do today to successfully accomplish your transition and exit, whether this is next year or in five, ten, or fifteen years, and whether your "exit" means an exit from active duty or ownership, or both. This book is intended to provide a thorough approach to the Transition Growth and Exit Planning needs of you as a business owner.

This book is a successor to my earlier book on exit planning titled "Exit on Your Terms". It is written for business owners. I have intentionally kept it non-technical. Time permitting, I may do a technical version of the book for advisors.

Nicholas K. Niemann

"Just the facts, maam."

Sgt. Joe Friday
from the 1960's television
show "Dragnet"

"I hear the train a comin', it's rollin 'round the bend."

Johnny Cash
"Folsom Prison Blues"
Columbia Records

Table of Contents

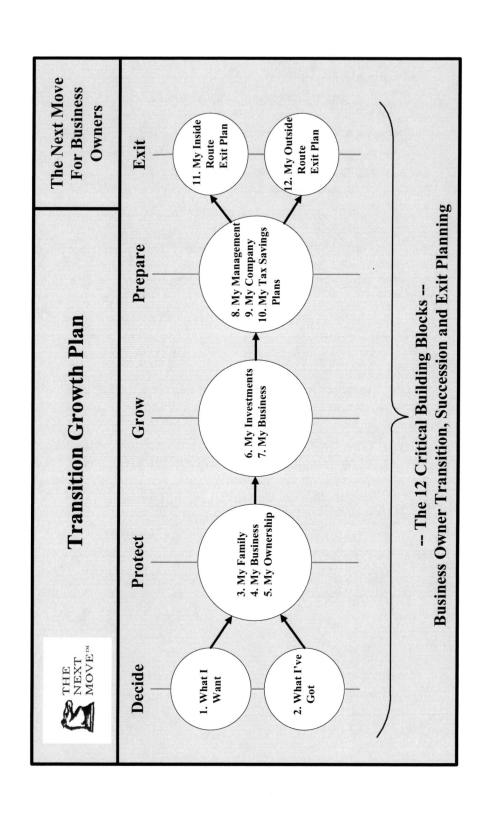

Introduction

Chapter 1

Introduction To Transition Growth And Exit Planning

It was supposed to be a simple plan. However, as Jim, Jr. explained it, he described a scenario that was all too familiar to me. His father Jim, Sr., had founded a very successful business-to-business service company thirty years earlier that had been extremely successful during his father's lifetime. Jim Sr. was an extremely effective innovator as well as a strong manager and motivator. He was the driving force behind his company. Jim Sr. had always expected his son Jim would step in upon his death. However, Jim Sr. had unexpectedly died a few months earlier. Jim Jr. was now finding the company was slipping away from him. He admitted he lacked his father's talents and drive and that he had really never felt comfortable taking over the company (but he couldn't tell his father that). Since his father hadn't developed a strong management team, Jim was concerned the company wasn't going to be worth even the estate taxes still due on it, much less provide the income he needed.

Over the course of 25 years, Josh had built a great niche manufacturing business, and he was now ready to take his chips off the table. He was willing to stay active in the company for a couple years but he was running out of steam, and his family wanted to see him more. His business was producing consistently strong cash flow at a level that is normally very attractive to most private equity group buyers. Yet he and his M & A intermediary found that none would touch him. When he came to see me about this, it became clear he had made six of the common mistakes business owners and their advisors commonly overlook. And he was running out of time for a course correction.

Do The Things Necessary To Make It Happen

Eventually, every business owner will exit his or her business – whether voluntarily or otherwise. At that time, every owner wants to accomplish certain personal, financial, business and estate planning goals. Most fail to do so.

We have all heard the statistics on how few family businesses make it to the second or third generation and how many implode in the first generation. Thirty-four percent of businesses fail in their first two years. Less than 50% are still operating after six years. Of those, that make it, only 30% to 35% survive to the second generation. Only 12% to 15% make it to the third generation, while 3% make it to the fourth generation. These statistics have been widely reported, e.g. by USA Today (2001) and the Small Business Administration (2003). The Small Business Administration reports that the "primary cause for failure . . . is lack of planning."

Efforts by business owners to exit their businesses have been, on average, less than satisfying. Some studies show that over 75% of former business owners regretted the decision to sell their company because the sale did not accomplish their personal or business objectives. What was the reason the business owners gave? They did not understand all of their options, so they didn't make informed decisions.

Create Opportunities Now So You Have Options Later

Over the years, we have worked with hundreds of business owners to help them overcome these odds and achieve a successful outcome for the time and capital they have invested in their businesses. This book is intended to help you to learn about the transition growth and exit planning process which will help you to create and understand your options and will provide the active steps which you need to take today so you can successfully exit tomorrow.

What Will Be Your Future Exit Outcome?

What do you hope will be the future outcome of the time and financial investment you've made in your business? Based on over 27 years of working with owners of small, medium-sized and large family businesses, we've found the answers to this question tend to be very similar. Most owners of family businesses have some or all of the following hopes or wishes:

- That your income from the business will continue to grow and provide an increasing standard of living for you and your family.

- That your business will help you accumulate sufficient financial resources for a comfortable retirement.

- That your business will not suffer or be lost through the negative influence of either internal or external adversities or claims.

- That both your business and your family can financially survive your unexpected, premature disability or death.

- That you can retire upon your own terms, while leaving your business in the good hands of successor management which you have selected and groomed.

- That ultimately you can either pass on a successful and valuable business to your family, or sell your business to your fellow owners, management or an outside buyer of your choice at a full and fair price, while minimizing potential federal and state taxes.

- That you can accomplish all of this with minimal shareholder, management and family squabbles.

- That your advisors will help you understand your options to help you make informed decisions.

These tend to be common family business owner wishes, whether you own all or part of your business, whether your business is small or large, whether you are in the business of selling products or services, and whether you started the business yourself or inherited or bought it from someone else.

The Present Atmosphere

This is no small issue for business owners and their families in our country. Fortune Magazine recently reported (June 26, 2006) that the largest intergenerational transfer of wealth in history is now underway, totaling $45 trillion, which it says will be transferred over a 55-year period through 2052. It says about one third of this will pass to baby boomers, while the rest will go mainly to baby boomer children. Cornell University economist and demographic expert Robert Avery has predicted that baby boomers themselves will transfer $10 trillion to later generations. The Exit Planning Institute reports that the vast majority of this wealth is stock in more than 12 million closely held companies and that during the next ten to fifteen years more than 70% of these businesses are expected to be transferred. A recent study by Boston College has projected that over the next 50 years $41 trillion of American wealth will transfer from the current generation to the next generation.

A recent 2006 survey of thousands of business owners by Capital Solutions found that 43% planned to exit their business within the next 5 years, 70% within the next 10 years and 90% within the next 15 years. They found that many owners were uncertain of their exit route and were considering multiple options. The top 3 responses were: put up for sale (45%), move ownership to children (35%) and sell to management/key employees (30%). The top five concerns listed by business owners regarding their transition were: developing a smooth transition plan, determining company value, addressing tax impact, having a capable successor and post-exit employee security.

How Do You Achieve The Future Outcome You Want?

Almost all of the business owners that we have worked with over the years are very good at what they do. They also all realize that a business is not successful or profitable simply because they might wish it to be so. It's a basic and well understood principle of business – to be profitable and successful, you need to actively take the steps needed to efficiently provide, at a competitive price, products or services that a significant segment of the consumer or business public needs or wants.

You know you can not simply wish or hope this will happen on its own. The successful family business requires years of hard work, planning, dedication, and good business decisions. Likewise, you can't simply wish for your transition and exit to be successful and then expect it to be. You need to actively cause your transition and exit to be successful.

Over the years, I've had the opportunity to work with my own family in a number of their business operations, which have included restaurants, supermarkets, ranching, farming, retail merchandising, construction and real estate. They have provided good examples of the "entrepreneur's work ethic," not just by working hard in their businesses, but also by working hard on their businesses.

I've also had the opportunity to get to know many business owners. Most business owners whom we've worked with tend to realize, some sooner than others, that the future outcome they want for their business (and family) will be realized only if they apply the same skills to work ON their business as they have applied to working IN their business.

How is this done? It's done by realizing that your business should not rule your life. It's done by realizing that you need to take the steps necessary to rule one of the most important but too frequently overlooked aspects of being a business owner – the proactive, successful transition and exit process. It's done by asking two fundamental questions and then taking decisive action based on the answers.

Question 1: What Will Be The Probable, Almost Certain, Future Exit Outcome Of Your Present Course, If Left Unchanged?

You should take some time to answer this. What will be the outcome of your present course? The probable almost certain future outcome of a business owner's investment of time and capital depends on how well you understand this.

What we attempt to do through Transition Growth and Exit Planning is to help you to work ON your business through various business Transition Growth and Exit Planning tools and techniques which have a proven track record of producing a better outcome for those who utilize them.

Learn From The Past And Create Your Future

So, where do we begin? The first step is to understand the "probable, almost certain, future outcome of your present course, if left unchanged." Will you be able to sell your business? Will your business be in a position to be sold at top dollar and minimized taxes when you are ready to depart. Will you have a capable successor, whether amongst your family or key employees or recruitable from outside the company? Are you prepared for the unexpected? Since you have read this far, you obviously intend to find out – and to do something about it before your exit arrives and the future is over.

Understand What Is Right. Deal With What Is Wrong

We begin this review by making certain, as advisors, that we both have a solid understanding of your business and personal situation. A good physician will not make a diagnosis or recommendation without first doing a thorough "Patient History and Physical" (known in the medical field as an "H and P"). Likewise, a good business Transition Growth and Exit Planning advisor first needs to do a brief "History and Physical." Like a medical History and Physical, this typically reveals the areas of most concern which need to be addressed.

What we have found over the years is that to the extent this reveals that certain tools are missing, the probable almost certain future outcome for your business investment will be less than that hoped for. This "History and Physical" leads to the next question.

Question 2: What's Missing, The Presence Of Which Would Make A Substantial Difference In Producing A Better Exit Outcome?

There are over 100 different Transition Growth and Exit Planning tools and techniques utilized as part of approximately 40 exit strategies which business owners are very successfully using to provide the missing components, the presence of which equips you and your business for achieving a substantially better future exit from your business. These tools and techniques can help assure that you can successfully enhance and protect your current and future business profits and value, as well as successfully pass on or sell your business upon your retirement, disability or death.

Stop, Look Both Ways, Proceed With Care

My purpose, as a Transition Growth and Exit Planning advisor, is to help you determine which of these tools and strategies can best assist you. Based on your particular needs as a business owner, this process requires a certain amount of detailed discussions and planning over a period of time with one or more other professionals working together.

I'll Wait Until…

"I'll wait until… the economy bounces back… or until we reach our next revenue milestone… or until my family pushes a bit harder about my plans…" or until this, that or the next thing. This is what we call the "Wait and See" Exit Plan. It is a recipe for failure.

Don't Overdo It or Underdo It

Don't overdo it by spending so much time planning for your transition and exit that you neglect the continuing needs of running your Company. Likewise, don't underdo it by neglecting to determine and take the actions needed to be successful in protecting, transitioning and exiting from your Company. What good is it to reach third base with no one on deck to bring you home.

Triage

A medical professional will, after an assessment of the situation, prioritize the most immediate and secondary needs of the patient and then address the most critical needs first. Likewise, we find that in the Transition Growth and Exit Planning process, a similar triage is often necessary or appropriate. While we advocate the need to address all 12 building blocks described in this book, this does not mean they need to be addressed in the same order described in this book.

The Key To Success

Our firm has helped plan ahead for, design, negotiate and implement the purchase, sale or transfer of hundreds of businesses with selling prices ranging from a few hundred thousand dollars to several hundred million dollars. Each transaction presents unique objectives, hurdles and opportunities. And each business owner's success was dependent on the focus on transition and exit planning which occurred well in advance of the sale or transfer of the business.

The key to success is to get started well in advance. As a business owner, you need to become engaged in the Transition Growth and Exit Planning process. Don't wait like Jim and Josh until your options disappear.

Chapter 2

What Is The Essence Of Transition Growth And Exit Planning?

Why Should Owners Bother?

Most of us would never invest in a publicly held company on the stock market if no process existed for fairly valuing that investment and being able to exit that investment at fair value at a time of our choosing. What's more, most of us would never continue to pour more and more money and effort into that investment, year after year, never knowing what the company is worth and never knowing how you could eventually cash out from it or pass it along to your family. Most of us would view investing and operating under that scenario as insanity.

Yet, this is exactly the situation in which business owners often find themselves. They have spent years investing time, money and effort into their closely held company, only to be stymied and frustrated as they begin to think about how they can eventually exit their business.

The SBA reports that up to 90% of the net worth of small business owners is tied up in their business. Most business owners want their exit to result in the continuation and success of the business, while at the same time, they want this net worth to obtain financial security and freedom for themselves and their families.

What Is Transition Growth and Exit Planning?

Transition Growth and Exit Planning is the deliberate, adaptable and customized process for assisting business owners with a successful transition and eventual exit from their company. Ideally, this transition and exit will occur on the business owner's terms and timetable. However, sometimes unforeseen events (such as the owner's unexpected death or disability or the loss of key employees) will frustrate the best laid plans. For this reason, Transition Growth and Exit Planning addresses not only your planned, foreseeable exit, but also provides back up plans in the event of an unexpected owner, partner or key employee death, disability, departure, dispute, divorce or business downturn.

Transition Growth and Exit Planning helps you to avoid the "entrepreneur's curse" of being in "wealth prison". It helps you to convert your business equity into liquid investments to help achieve the "freedom" element of financial freedom.

The Essence Of Transition Growth and Exit Planning

Transition Growth and Exit Planning, in its essence, is designed to help the business owner achieve the following:

* Piece of mind rather than confusion

* Reaching for the stars rather than being amongst the fallen stars

* Charting your own route rather than going where the wind blows you

* Navigating your specific, charted course rather than running blindly through a maze of dead ends

* Family accord rather than family discord

* Accomplishing hopes and dreams rather than living through a nightmare

* Creating leaders to succeed you rather than simply creating managers who will run the train off the tracks

* Achieving future financial security rather than ending up in financial uncertainty

* Leaving a legacy rather than leaving a mess

* Maintaining control rather than being out of control

* Creating your own seller's market for your business rather than settling for whatever comes along

* Overcoming your exit roadblocks rather than being steamrolled.

Your Next Move Needs Versatility

Transition Growth and Exit Planning is intended to enable the business owner to have the option to move in several directions, depending on future events and circumstances. This is the rationale behind the Chess Board piece of the Knight chosen as the logo for The Next Move program. The Knight is the most versatile piece on the Chess Board. Unlike all other Chess Board pieces, the Knight can move in eight different directions and can 'jump over' all other chess pieces (of either player) to reach its destination. Transition Growth and Exit Planning, when properly designed and implemented, likewise will provide the business owner with several alternatives for achieving his or her goal and with the ability to 'jump over' what may be roadblocks for others.

Due to its versatility, a Knight in Chess should always be close to where the action is. This piece is generally more powerful when placed near the center of the board where its flexibility is the greatest. The Knight is also the only piece that can move at the beginning of the game before a pawn or any other piece. It also is the only piece that can be in a position to attack a king, queen, bishop or rook without being reciprocally attacked by that piece.

Likewise, a Transition Growth Plan provides a business owner with a versatile and effective plan which can be used throughout the course of a business owner's "Next Move" towards his or her transition and future exit.

Transition Growth and Exit Planning Dynamics

Transition Growth and Exit Planning needs to deal with the interaction of three key dynamics involved with the closely held family business. This is the intersection where the company's business dynamics meet the family's personal dynamics and the owner's financial dynamics. Unless all three are addressed, a successful exit is less than likely.

I have often found it necessary or helpful to act in a mediator's role in helping the family members or other partners decide how they will work together in the future. Transition and exit planning truly presents a situation where the intersection of the business, family and ownership dynamics needs to be carefully, thoughtfully and skillfully addressed.

The Transition Growth and Exit Planning Dynamics Intersection

Chapter 3

Overcoming Transition Roadblocks

Overcoming Your Transition Roadblocks And Bottlenecks

Every business owner faces a number of roadblocks when exiting his or her business. These roadblocks exist whether your exit is anticipated or unexpected. These roadblocks can collectively create an exit bottleneck which delays, diminishes or dooms your successful exit. Exit roadblocks prevent the vast majority of exits from being successful or from accomplishing the results that business owners want to see. An exit roadblock is any obstruction which prevents or slows down your eventual successful exit from your business.

15 Common Owner Transition and Exit Roadblocks

The essence of Transition Growth and Exit Planning includes overcoming your transition and exit roadblocks. Some of these are from internal forces. Some are from external forces. Fifteen common roadblocks are:

- **Hanging On Too Long.** You simply want to keep owning and/or working for personal, non-economic reasons. You aren't ready to retire or you aren't ready to move on to a new venture. You may have accomplished all of your economic goals and all of your other roadblocks to a successful exit have all been dealt with. However, you simply want to keep working and you aren't ready to pass on ownership. This may be fine. Or it may become destructive, either to your health, your family well-being, and the goals and objectives of your key employees (who may decide to move out to a company with leadership opportunities). Or it might cause you to miss a selling opportunity that won't be there later. Not understanding how to move on and how to take on new personal and family objectives post-exit, i.e. "hanging on too long", can become a roadblock to a successful exit that ought to be occurring sooner rather than later.

- **Tax Hit.** If you haven't planned at least five to ten years ahead of your exit to address the tax issues that you will face upon your lifetime exit or your death exit, then your exit is unlikely to be as successful as you'd like because of the "tax hit" roadblock.

- **Price Mis-Expectation.** If you don't know or can't achieve a reasonable, realistic value for your business, then "price mis-expectation" becomes a roadblock that will bottleneck your exit.

- **Leadership Void.** If you haven't worked on grooming one or more potential leaders (not simply managers) or if you don't have the likelihood for recruiting a successful leader from the outside upon your exit, "leadership void" is a roadblock to a successful exit.

- **Objectives Chaos.** If your personal, financial and prime exit objectives conflict with each other, then "objectives chaos" is a roadblock to your successful exit.

- **The Missing Buyer.** If your business in its present or likely future make-up is not marketable (or is not marketable at a fair price) to an insider or outside third party, then "the missing buyer" is an exit roadblock.

- **Management Shallowness.** The absence of sufficient, capable business managers, i.e. "management shallowness," is a roadblock to a successful exit.

- **Financing Gap.** Insufficient or unwilling outside bank or other third party lender financing can create a "financing gap" roadblock which means you need to carry back part of the sale price.

- **Financial Dependence.** If your company's outside third party ongoing operations financing requires your ongoing, post-exit personal guarantee or other financial support, then "financial dependence" is a roadblock to your exit.

- **Third Party Consents.** If outside consents (e.g. from a lender, franchisor, or licensor) are needed and will be difficult to obtain, then "third party consents" can delay and sometimes sidetrack an exit.

- **Co-Owner Disputes.** If co-owner disputes can't be resolved (resulting in the loss of business value), or if you can't require other owners to sell or to buy (when you are ready to exit), then "co-owner disputes" can become a roadblock to your exit.

- **Family Disputes.** Family disputes (usually over money or management roles) tend to doom many businesses and owner exits.

- **Insufficient Cash Flow.** If your business doesn't generate sufficient, predictable cash flow, then "insufficient cash flow" will mean neither a sale to an insider nor to an outsider will likely meet your objectives.

- **Non-Credible Accounting.** A "non-credible accounting" system which can't be relied on by a potential inside or outside buyer, can delay or prevent a successful exit indefinitely.

- **Unexpected Adversity.** An "unexpected adversity", such as a downturn in your business or the loss of key employees (including yourself), can delay or prevent a successful exit.

Be The Shortstop

Exiting your business is easy. Anyone could exit their business today and be on a beach in the Cayman Islands tomorrow. The trick, however, is to exit successfully, with your goals (personal and financial) intact and accomplished. In baseball, the shortstop is one of the most highly skilled players. To be a successful play maker he needs to be able to quickly move to the left or to the right, to charge forward, or to fade back into the outfield. The same is true of the successful business owner planning his or her future exit.

Overcome The Biggest Roadblock - Do Something Today To Make It Happen

The biggest roadblock in Transition Growth and Exit Planning is actually the mental block. It is the reliance on a misplaced belief that everything will just be ok without my effort to make it so. However, that's not the world we live in. Just as in your business operations, you need to make it happen if you want to be successful in your transition and exit.

This book will help you learn how to move and how to recognize and overcome your transition and exit roadblocks and bottlenecks. You will learn specifically what you need to do today to help make your transition and future exit successful tomorrow.

Chapter 4

The Exit Factor

Often The "Elephant In The Corner"

An "elephant in the corner" is, of course, any situation which is very obvious to a group of persons but which is not being openly discussed. The "elephant in the corner" in many closely held businesses is the question of what will happen to the business when its present key executive/owner(s) moves on, whether planned or unplanned.

Regardless of the extent to which this topic is discussed, it is nevertheless on the minds of the many constituencies impacted by the success and operations of your business. These constituencies typically include yourself, your spouse, your children, your other key employees, most of your employment staff, your franchisor, your banker, your main customers, your key suppliers, your key advisors, and your local community.

How well you have dealt with, planned for, openly discussed and specifically addressed the various concerns of these constituencies regarding your future exit has significant direct impact not only on yourself and your immediate family, but also on your business today and into the future. This is due to the differentiated concerns each of these constituencies consciously or subconsciously bring into your business.

The Exit Factor

We refer to the collective seen and unseen impact of the exit concern on how these constituencies deal with your business and with you as the "Exit Factor". Just as the saying goes "all politics are local," it is equally true that "all business is personal." Each of these constituencies have their own personal reasons for their concern with your future succession or exit. This does not mean they are concerned only with themselves, but simply that they will have an interest in your business that will reflect their unique circumstance.

For example, your spouse may be interested, among other things, in the impact of the business on your continuing good health, on your ability to spend time together, on the future role of one or more of your children in the business, as well as a salary continuation or other economic impact regarding your expected or unexpected exit. Your children may be interested, among other things, on who will run the company and the impact this would have on other members of your family, as well as the financial impact of the business to them.

A key employee may be interested, among other things, on whether he or she will have the opportunity to reach full potential for leadership in your company or whether he or she might be passed over in favor of a less competent family member – whether with regard to being able to manage the company or to being an owner in the company. The failure to deal with this can, of course, lead to the loss of key employees to other competing companies who are more willing to address this. Your other employees will often be concerned, among other things, with the continuation of the success of the company (and therefore, their employment potential), as well as the potential for a change in company culture upon your exit.

If you are a franchise business, your franchisor will be concerned with the continued viability of your franchise upon your planned or unexpected exit. This impacts not only the franchisor's income, but as importantly, the integrity and reputation of its franchise system.

Your banker or other business lender will, among other things, be concerned both personally with the loss of a close personal relationship that a good banker will have developed with you, as well as a concern for the viability of the business if your exit transition is not properly handled.

Your local Chamber of Commerce, besides being interested in the continuing success of the company, is concerned with whether new ownership might move the business to a different community.

Your co-owners, in addition to the loss of a personal business associate, will be concerned with whether they, you, or a third party will ultimately own the business in a planned exit, or with their ability to work with your family through a transition upon your unexpected exit. And so on.

Your concerns as a key owner will typically span all of these interests, which is fine, because you are the one who has the best opportunity to deal with the Exit Factor.

Even Tiger Has A Coach

The fact that you are reading this book about how to exit your business would normally mean you had a lot of success in building, owning and operating a business from which you have the potential to exit from. Running any business today involves a high degree of specialized knowledge, intestinal fortitude, mediation skills, insight and vision. Yet, this does not mean you are an expert in everything. Transition Growth Planning tends to be one of those areas for which business owners look for assistance.

Like all successful sports figures, even Tiger Woods has a coach. Reading a book on how to play golf may help you to play and understand the game better, but it won't make you a professional golfer. Likewise, reading this book will help you understand the exit game. Don't expect it to mean you should "go it alone" in planning to address your Exit Factor. This book would be a disservice to business owners if it gave you that expectation. The Next Move For Business Owners Transition Growth Program provides you the coaching you need during each step in this process.

Uncoordinated Actions

The problem which business owners have faced in the past is that it is very difficult to find professional advice or a professional approach which touches on all of the steps and considerations which need to be dealt with to plan an owner's exit.

As a result, business owners tend to take uncoordinated action over the course of several years, perhaps based on the isolated advice of differing advisors who are comfortable only with their specific, relatively narrow field of expertise. Perhaps your CPA has talked about some tax planning. Maybe your corporate attorney has talked about a buy-sell agreement to deal with certain contingencies. Perhaps your financial planner has talked about your retirement goals. Perhaps your insurance advisor has sold you some life insurance policies that you are not sure anymore what they really cover. Perhaps your estate planning attorney has talked about a "succession plan." Perhaps you received an unsolicited letter in the mail (and most likely, many such letters) from a business broker, claiming how he or she can sell your business (typically based only on the knowledge that your name came up on a mailing list that the broker uses).

The result of all of these isolated, uncoordinated efforts between you and your advisors is that you have started and stopped, and probably started and stopped several times since, in attempting to think through some plan for your exit. The most likely result is that you now have a "financial junk drawer" and have become frustrated with the process because you instinctively know that you have not solved the Exit Factor.

The Need For Exit "Outpatient Care"

A large reason for these unsatisfactory results amongst the efforts of business owners is because planning for an exit is outside the expertise for most business owners, and it is something that most professional advisors only deal with one or two facets of.

By and large, most professional organizations still fail to address the full range of business owner exit planning needs. The Bar Association is still teaching courses isolating on simply "succession planning" or "estate planning" for business owners. The Society of CPAs is still teaching courses just on succession tax strategies, and most insurance and financial advisors attend programs dealing simply with how to place financial products. The result is a general lack of the in depth transition and exit planning service needed by business owners.

The Next Move Transition Growth Program

This is why I've developed The Next Move For Business Owners Transition Growth Program. Using this program, a Transition Growth Plan can be prepared and tailored for business owners. Each plan is the result of a review of the Transition Growth and Exit Planning process. This plan consists of the 12 building blocks detailed in this book.

Chapter 5

The Top 12 Reasons Owner Transitions Are Not Successful

Over the past several years, I have spoken with business owners around the country who had decided they had reached the point of being ready to leave their businesses. However, no one was stepping up to provide them the exit results they wanted. These owners had spent all of their time aggressively working in their business, but had spent little time aggressively working on how they would eventually exit their business. They found themselves late in the game with few options to achieve their exit objectives. Simply put, they were too late.

What follows are the top 12 reasons I've seen for why business owner exits often fail. Each of these reasons impacts the company's ongoing profitability as well as an owner's future exit results.

1.   **Unclear and Conflicting Owner Objectives.** Your financial, personal, transition and exit objectives are not determined or conflict with each other (or with the objectives of your partners, key employees, spouse or other family members).

2.   **Cash Flow Impact On Company Price Misunderstood.** You haven't understood your exit is dependent upon an inside buyer's or third-party buyer's expectations and needs regarding your company future cash flow and you haven't uncovered or understood how your company's exit-appropriate buyer-specific valuation is to be determined.

3.   **No Business Owner Estate Plan.** You have not realized the difference between a regular and business owner Estate Plan, and you have failed to adequately protect your family and address your family's needs and desires relative to your business.

4.   **Insufficient Company Structure and Key Asset Protection.** Your company is not properly structured to protect assets or to deal with contingencies, and you have failed to identify your key intangible assets or to adopt the legal safeguards to protect your key intangible assets (such as your key employees and intellectual property rights).

5. **Co-Owner Issues and Disputes.** You have failed to utilize a Buy-Sell Agreement and a Business Continuity Agreement to pre-decide how ownership will be bought and sold (and funded) between partners upon death, disability, divorce, disputes, and retirement and how to avoid or resolve co-owner disputes due to future disagreements.

6. **Mismanagement of Personal Wealth.** You have failed to properly manage your personal (non-company) wealth, resulting in an indefinite and extended need to draw on company resources and a disruption to your transition timing and to your successor's expectations.

7. **Nonsustainable Business Growth.** Your company lacks an effective transition period Strategic Growth Plan and Continuous Business Model Innovation Program for sustaining continued product and service innovation, brand recognition, customer engagement, business growth and profitability, all of which impacts your company's present growth and survival, and therefore your future exit pricing and feasibility.

8. **Lack of Capable Leadership Management Successors.** A process for replacing you and other key management or leadership (either internally or externally) has not been identified or developed, and you have failed to properly develop, incent and retain key personnel.

9. **Not Keeping the Business Always Ready for Sale.** You fail to realize your company should always be ready to be sold. The future can quickly change (for the better or worse) your presently expected business exit timing.

10. **Missing Pre-Exit Tax Tools.** Pre-Exit tax minimization steps haven't been taken in time or at all.

11. **No Capable Inside Buyer Exists.** You haven't groomed a capable inside buyer (such as a partner, key employee or family member) to be ready to buy when you're ready to sell, and you haven't designed an economically and financially feasible, mutually beneficial, tax efficient sale structure to an inside buyer.

12. **Misunderstanding the M & A Market.** You are unable to sell to a third party due to not understanding, addressing, and managing toward the expectations of the mergers and acquisition market for your company in your industry.

The 12 critical building blocks identified in this book were developed to specifically overcome these 12 principal reasons for why business owners have been failing.

The purpose of Transition Growth and Exit Planning is to lay out a systematic approach which helps assure that you timely and thoroughly take the steps needed to achieve success in accomplishing your personal, financial, transition and exit objectives.

The Transition Growth and Exit Planning process provides a means for business owners to help see the status of their own transition and exit situation and will show you the steps needed to actively do something about it. This is not a plan to read and then put on the shelf. It's a plan that is intended to help business owners address the call-to-action every business owner needs to undertake.

A Transition Growth Plan will address the above 12 problem areas and will help you avoid these pitfalls and mistakes. This plan provides you with a tailored roadmap for how you will achieve your transition and exit successfully, on your terms and on your timetable.

The Top 12 Reasons Business Owners Transitions Are Not Successful

1.   Unclear and Conflicting Owner Objectives.

2.   Cash Flow Impact On Company Price Misunderstood.

3.   No Business Owner Estate Plan.

4.   Insufficient Company Structure and Key Asset Protection.

5.   Co-Owner Issues and Disputes.

6.   Mismanagement of Personal Wealth.

7.   Nonsustainable Business Growth.

8.   Lack of Capable Leadership Management Successors.

9.   Not Keeping the Business Always Ready for Sale.

10.   Missing Pre-Exit Tax Tools.

11.   No Capable Inside Buyer Exists.

12.   Misunderstanding the M & A Market.

Chapter 6

Why A Transition Growth Plan If You Don't Plan To Exit Soon

Beginning the Transition Growth and Exit Planning process does not mean that you must carve in stone a departure date from your business or the terms and conditions of your departure. If you are like most business owners, you have played one of the most crucial roles in establishing the past success and future potential for your company. Only you and your spouse (and sometimes your children) should be telling you when or how you must leave your business.

Instead, Transition Growth and Exit Planning recognizes the fact that you will actually exit your business eventually. Perhaps you plan to manage your business until your death or disability. Perhaps you plan to retire before your death or disability, but intend to own your company until your death or disability. Your plans might also include one or more of the following:

- You plan to keep working on growing your business for some time yet, and want to take the steps needed now to preserve and protect your business so it is thriving when you do eventually exit.

- You plan to keep working on growing your business for some time yet, but want it structured right for your eventual retirement or unexpected exit.

- You aren't ready to exit yet, but recognize the need to have a plan in place.

- You would like to still run your business for a while, but want to start developing a successor so you can spend more time traveling with your spouse and/or other family members.

- You've achieved your goals as a business owner and would like to leave when and if the best opportunity comes up.

- You would like to give an adult child or key employee the opportunity to start leading the company (and perhaps be able to coach them for a while).

- You are ready to retire as soon as feasible.

- You would like to spend more time with your children or grandchildren.

- Your spouse would like you to retire.

- Your children would like you to retire.

- You would like to retire from most active duties, but remain as owner.

- You are not sure whether you are able or willing to keep up or catch up with the new technologies demanded in your industry.

- You are not sure you want to fight another economic down cycle.

- You may recognize that valuation multiples today may present a temporary window of opportunity for your exit.

- Taking your company to the next level will require a new level of debt or equity which may or may not be feasible.

- As you've reached this point in your life, you have a decreasing tolerance for risk and a desire to remove some financial chips from the table.

- Fatigue and boredom may be starting to set in.

- Perhaps you are ready to start a new chapter in your life or have just lost the "fire in the belly" to continue pursuing your business.

- Perhaps you never thought you would sell, but someone is offering you the right price and the right terms.

- Perhaps you or your spouse or other family member are starting to encounter some health concerns or you want to take some steps to head off the development of health concerns.

- Perhaps you have some adult children or key employees who are starting to insist on ownership if they are to remain with the company.

- Perhaps you want to exit this company and invest in a new venture.

- Perhaps you want to take some time to test the market for the sale of your company.

- Perhaps you have come to realize that the best course for your family, your long term employees, and your valued customers, is for you to lay in the ground work and the planning for your exit, whether this occurs sooner or later, so that you have best provided for the continuity of the business, the continuity of employment for your valued employees and the continuity of products and services for your valued customers.

Pre-Exit Timeframes

Certain exit results, which are addressed in the Transition Growth and Exit Planning process, require that actions be taken years ahead of your exit to be fully effective. Some examples include the following (with pre-exit time estimates):

- Elect Subchapter "S" tax status to avoid double tax on sale of business (10 years).

- Utilize credible, buyer-acceptable, reviewed/audited financial statements (3-5 years).

- Bridge gap between exit "cash-in-pocket" retirement needs and your company's exit value (5-10 + years).

- Build a management leadership team depth chart (5-15 years).

- Identify and develop specific capable successor(s) (5-10 years).

- Acquire adequate financial gap contingency funding (such as life and disability insurance) while in good health and insurable (10-15 years).

- Implement gifting program to reduce death taxes (10-20 years).

- Determine and implement key employee buy-in (5-10 years).

- Determine and utilize key employee retention incentive (5-15 years).

- Bring company up to industry level financial and business benchmarks to help attain desired exit pricing (5-10 years).

- Implement pre-exit business entity restructuring (2-5 years).

- Develop outside Board of Director members to help guide the company in the event of your unexpected death or disability (5-10 years).

- Find acceptable outside buyer at right time in business and economic cycle (2-5 years).

Regardless of your present plans or intentions, putting the proper cornerstones into place now - ahead of your exit - increases the odds of a successful and more profitable exit, whether your exit occurs according to your timetable or is prompted by unexpected circumstances.

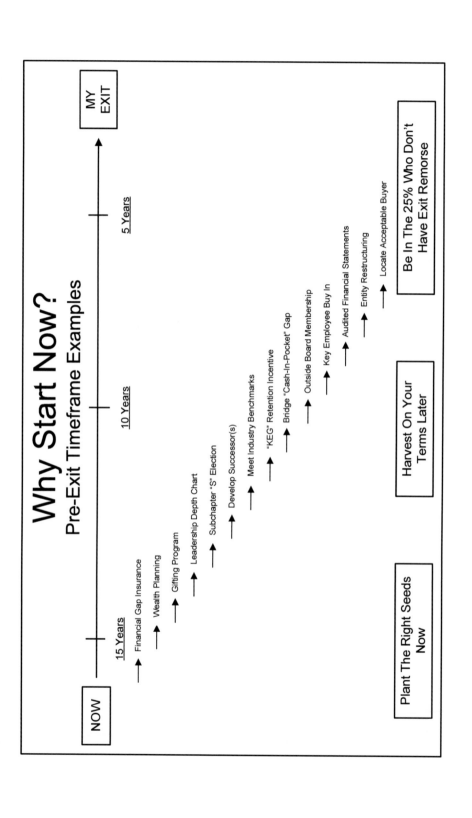

Why Start Now?
Pre-Exit Timeframe Examples

NOW

15 Years

10 Years

5 Years

MY EXIT

Financial Gap Insurance

Wealth Planning

Gifting Program

Leadership Depth Chart

Subchapter "S" Election

Develop Successor(s)

Meet Industry Benchmarks

"KEG" Retention Incentive

Bridge "Cash-In-Pocket" Gap

Outside Board Membership

Key Employee Buy In

Audited Financial Statements

Entity Restructuring

Locate Acceptable Buyer

Plant The Right Seeds Now

Harvest On Your Terms Later

Be In The 25% Who Don't Have Exit Remorse

Chapter 7

You Already Have An "Exit Plan"

Whether you realize it or not, you as a business owner already have some type of "transition plan", "succession plan" or "exit plan." You may or may not have given much thought to this plan. You may or may not have written down the components of this plan. Parts of this exit plan might be scattered throughout various documents or actions which you have taken at various times over the course of your business life.

This exit plan might be partially reflected in a Will or a Trust which you executed several years ago. It might be partially reflected in the components of a life insurance or disability insurance policy which you established either through the company or on your own in the past. It might be reflected in some verbal statements that you've made to family members or to key employees or key advisors. Or, a large portion of your exit plan might be reflected in those steps which you haven't taken.

Over the years I've dealt with a variety of these kinds of "exit plans". We've done this either after the fact, once a business owner has died or become disabled or often a business owner has seen key employees picked off by other companies. Or we've reviewed the elements of the exit plan which the business owner had at the time we were engaged to create a more specific, comprehensive Transition Growth Plan.

I've given some names to 15 of these types of partial, informal exit plans. As you read this book, you should consider what type of exit plan you think you have in place today and which of the various exit strategies discussed in this book would provide you and your family with a better exit outcome in the future.

1.   **The "Wishes Are Horses" Exit Plan**

As the old saying goes, "If wishes were horses, then beggars would ride." This type of exit plan is by the owner who believes that wishes are actually horses and that a good exit outcome will occur just by wishing it to be so.

2. **The "Uncle Sam" Exit Plan**

Under this type of exit plan, which is highly favored by your Uncle Sam, your exit will result in the highest amount of tax obligations to federal and state governments on account of your decision not to implement tax-saving strategies.

3. **The "Ostrich" Exit Plan**

Under this exit plan, the business owner has decided to put the head in the sand by not proactively addressing issues and disputes which he or she knows will occur or need to be dealt with on account of his or her planned or unexpected exit.

4. **The "Backwards K" Exit Plan**

In baseball, if a batter strikes out on a called third strike, without swinging, then the strikeout is marked in the scorekeeper's record as a backwards "K". This type of exit plan is present when the business owner decides to not even take a swing at attempting to put together a written exit plan. This is also known as the "Let My Surviving Spouse Deal With It" Exit Plan.

5. **The "Mulligan" Exit Plan**

In a casual game of golf, the players can, of course, take a shot over, which is called a "mulligan." This doesn't work in professional golf. It seldom works in Transition Growth and Exit Planning. For example, if you are disabled or die, without the proper strategies and funding in place to deal with your unexpected exit, you (or your family) don't have the opportunity to do this over. Or, if you've lost the key employee you thought was going to be your successor, because he or she grew tired of your uncertain future plans, you don't get a do over.

6. **The "Wait and See" Exit Plan**

Under this type of exit plan, the business owner is forever and forever unwilling to make a decision about how to proceed. The paralysis that results from always wanting to "wait and see" how things turn out tomorrow before making a decision can be very detrimental. In Transition Growth Planning, we operate under the principle that "all plans are firm until changed." This means that it's generally best to establish a plan and then revise and adjust it as needed depending on what happens tomorrow.

7.   **The "Flea-Flicker" Exit Plan**

American football has a play known as the flea-flicker in which the ball is hiked, handed off or lateralled to a running back, who fakes a run and then flicks the ball back to the quarterback who throws a long pass. The runner gives up the likelihood of a reasonable yardage gain and in exchange the team is betting on the low percentage long pass. The flea-flicker is generally viewed as an extremely high-risk play that results in either a big gain, a turnover or a loss. In this type of exit plan, the business owner gives up a profitable and reasonable exit outcome, always shooting for the extraordinary outcome with the low percentage occurrence.

8.   **The "Return to Sender" Exit Plan**

In this type of exit plan, a lack of pre-sale planning results in a business owner selling the business to an incapable buyer for an installment note payable who ultimately defaults on the payments, resulting in the business being sent back to the seller, typically in a lesser condition, to attempt to exit from again.

9.   **The "Scorched Earth" Exit Plan**

In this type of exit plan, the business owner or owners decide they will deplete the business of all of the cash resource potential, leaving a business which is incapable of surviving. If the business was destined for liquidation anyway, perhaps this is the proper outcome. However, if it works to the detriment of the key employees, loyal employment staff and valued customers who have relied on you and the business, then in the end it's an approach that business owners will likely regret.

10.   **The "Last Man Standing" Exit Plan**

In this type of exit plan, a dominant owner forces out his or her co-owners on terms that are unfair, resulting in the dominant personality holding entire ownership of the company which in large part has been purchased at a discount. This type of exit plan is obviously not favorable for the business owner that was bought out at a huge discount.

11.   **The "Holding The Bag" Exit Plan**

In this exit plan, the business owner is too naïve or generous in buying out his or her partners, and therefore, overpays because of a misconception as to real value. The owner is left owning the company, having paid a price which he or she can never realize and may, in fact, be left going under or with trying to pay off purchase debt long past the time when he or she also wishes to exit.

12.   **The Exit Plan "In a Box"**

This is an exit plan which a business owner has bought into from an advisor who has failed to tailor the particular objectives of the business owner to the particular circumstances of the business and the family by simply imposing a "cookie cutter" approach.

13.   **The "Deathbed" Exit Plan**

This type of exit plan is literally developed on the business owner's deathbed which, of course, is generally too late to implement sound decisions.

14.   **The "Junk Drawer" Exit Plan**

The junk drawer exit plan is the result of the uncoordinated actions of the business owner and his or her advisors over a period of time. It consists, for example, of a life insurance policy bought ten years ago, a buy-sell agreement executed fifteen years ago, a Will signed when the owner's first child was born, scribbled notes in the owner's desk attempting to start, and start again, to focus on the beginnings of an exit strategy, etc. This "plan" rarely works.

15.   **The "Iceberg" Exit Plan**

This is perhaps the most common type of exit plan. Here the owner believes he or she has dealt with the steps needed to be prepared for a future exit, but has only envisioned the tip of the iceberg without realizing the depth of other matters that need to be dealt with. This is also known as the "Ignorance Is Bliss" Exit Plan.

What Kind Of Exit Plan Do You Have?

The purpose of the Transition Growth and Exit Planning process described in this book is to help provide you a roadmap for first of all recognizing and secondly avoiding each of the above types of exit plans. A Transition Growth Plan should be designed to provide a plan that is fully effective for both you and others impacted by your exit.

Chapter 8

Recent Transition Growth and Exit Planning Activity

I have been helping business owners address a variety of Transition Growth and Exit Planning needs and objectives in a variety of business sectors. A summary of some of these may help illustrate the steps that other business owners are taking to protect and promote their interests. These are for clients around the country and are described in insufficient detail so as to prevent identifying any particular private matter.

Consumer Product Manufacturers

- Consumer marine product manufacturer - Corporate Reorganization and Management Transition Program.
- Fuel producer and distributor – Mediate ownership transition.
- Food production company – State Incentive Growth Plan.

Industrial Manufacturers

- Tool manufacturer – Transition Growth Plan.
- Industrial product manufacturer – Design Sale to ESOP with Stock Appreciation Rights Plan for key management.
- Commercial equipment manufacturer – Design and implement Inside Route Exit to partner.
- Injection molding company – Transition Growth Plan for transfer to family.
- Tool and die company – Transition Growth Plan for transfer to key employees.

Agribusiness

- Cattle feedlot – Buy-Sell Agreement and Business Continuity Agreement.
- Cattle ranch – Business Owner Estate Plan.
- Horse ranch – Transition company from father to son.
- Family farming operation – Transfer of farm operations to son.
- Farm operation – Mediate ownership dispute.

Real Estate

- Commercial building general contractor – Strategic Growth Plan.
- Residential developer – Transition Growth Plan.
- Commercial construction company – Partner Buy-Out.
- Residential real estate brokers – Buy-Sell Agreement between partners.

Personal Services

- Outdoor recreation services – Funded Buy-Sell Agreement between partners.
- Senior care services – Design Inside Route Exit to son.
- Tax preparation services – Transition Growth Plan with Inside Route Exit to founder's children.
- Personal hair care system – Company reorganization and Estate Tax Plan.
- CPA firm – Transition Buy-Out by new partners.

Financial Services

- Bank holding company – ESOP Feasibility Study.
- Investment advisory firm – Federal Income Tax Plan.
- Financial management firm – Business Model Innovation Program.
- Life insurance advisors – Company Reorganization Plan, Buy-Sell Agreement and Non-Compete Agreement in transition from founder to key personnel.

Retail

- Retail clothing chain – Design and Implement Outside Sale.
- Retail home furnishing company – Outside Route Exit Plan to supplier.
- Retail tractor franchisee – Transition Growth Plan to key employee.
- Retail jewelry store – Inside Route Exit from father to son.
- Retail store chain – Mediate ownership dispute.
- Consumer product retailer – State Income Tax Plan.

Food and Beverage

- Supermarket chain – Design and implement sale of minority owner's stock to majority owner.
- Discount Supermarket chain – Sale of company to key management.
- Sports restaurant – Transition Growth Plan to transfer to key employee.

Construction and Engineering

- Heavy equipment contractor – Business Asset Protection Plan.
- Construction engineering firm – House-In-Order Plan and Design sale to Private Equity Group.
- Storage facility contractor – Business Owner Estate Plan.
- Electrical contractor – Sale of company to key employees.
- Utility Contractor – Leadership Team Development Program.
- Construction Firm – Personal Asset Protection Plan and Insured Contingency Plan.

Healthcare

- Surgical hospital – Physician Joint Venture Agreement with future Exit Plan.
- Imaging center – Investor and physician Joint Venture with Buy-Out Agreement.
- Ambulatory surgical center – Physician-hospital system joint venture with Buy-Sell and Business Continuity Agreements.

Physicians

- Family practice – Sale of practice to employee physicians.
- Radiologists – Establish Professional Corporation with Buy-Sell Agreement.
- Orthopedic surgeon – Corporate Redemption and Employment Agreements.
- Ophthalmologist – Shareholder Agreement.
- Eye surgeon – New physician Buy-In.

Franchise

- Restaurant franchisee – Sale by partner.

- Restaurant franchisee – Corporate Reorganization to achieve parents' transition.
- Restaurant franchisee – Business Owner Estate Plan and Estate Tax Plan.

Product Development and Technology Licensing

- Product development company – Business Model Innovation Program.
- Bank institution software licensing – State Incentive Growth Plan.
- Technology licensing company – State Incentive Growth Plan

Human Resources

- Human resource placement firm – Establish ESOP for transition by founder to employees.
- Executive recruiter – Design and implement Key Employee Incentive Agreement and Inside Route Exit.

Consumer Services

- Veterinary firm – Design Installment Sale to key employee.
- Home remodeling firm – Corporate Structure Design.
- Airline service provider – State Incentive Growth Plan.

Business Services

- Business-to-business services – Monetize Intellectual Property for founders and license back to company.
- Telecommunication solution firm – Buy-Sell and Employment Agreements.
- Professional printer – Transition Growth Plan.

Leasing and Management

- Real estate management firm – Design and implement Partner Buy-Out.
- Real estate leasing company – Buy-Sell Agreement.
- Restaurant management firm – Inside Route Exit Plan and Insurance Plan.

Sample Transition Growth Plan

Decide ⇒	Protect ⇒	Grow ⇒	Prepare ⇒	Exit
1. **What I Want** • Legacy Statement • Transition Growth & Exit Objectives Statement • Advisor Team	3. **My Family** • Business Owner Estate Plan • Insurance Plan • Education Funding Plan • Personal Asset Protection Plan	6. **My Investments** • Comprehensive Wealth Plan	8. **My Management** • Leadership Team Development Program • Management Transition Program • Key Employee Incentive Agreement	11. **Inside Route Exit** • Inside Route Assessment • Inside Route Exit Plan • Inside Transfer Implementation
2. **What I've Got** • Pre-Exit Fitness Test • Report Card • Business Valuation • Personal Financial Statement	4. **My Business** • Business Asset Protection Plan • Insured Contingency Plan • Funded Stay Bonus Plan	7. **My Business** • Business Model Innovation Program • Strategic Growth Plan	9. **My Company** • Entity Restructure Plan • House-In-Order Plan	12. **Outside Route Exit** • Outside Route Assessment • Outside Route Exit Plan • Outside Sale Implementation
	5. **My Ownership** • Funded Buy-Sell Agreement • Business Continuity Agreement		10. **My Tax Savings Plans** • Estate Tax Plan • Federal Income Tax Plan • State Income Tax Plan • State Incentive Growth Plan	

© Copyright 2009 Nicholas K. Niemann. All Rights Reserved.

Chapter 9

Transition Growth and Exit Planning In Economic Uncertain Times

We always live in economic uncertain times. As this book goes to print, the country and the world are in the midst of a particularly major economic recession. Many business owners are struggling to just keep their doors open, to keep revenues intact, and to address an overall economic climate where fear and panic are resulting in a wait-and-see attitude among many.

This could prompt a question "Why should I take the time now to look at my transition and exit plan? I have my hands full just trying to get my business through this recession."

It's important to understand that most of what we work on in Transition Growth and Exit Planning should be addressed regardless of the point we are at in any economic cycle. The building blocks we address represent best practices for protecting and growing your business and address always having your business ready for a planned and expected transition and exit as well as for an unexpected exit, which can occur at any time.

Let's take a look at some of our Transition Growth and Exit Planning building blocks to illustrate this:

- **Protect My Family**. Regardless of the current economy, you need to make sure your family is protected, e.g. by having the proper business owner estate plan and adequate financial resources (which may also prompt a need to enhance your life and disability coverages in case you and your family won't be able to realize in the near term the income or value you may have expected from your company).

- **Protect My Business**. When your company's ongoing capabilities are being challenged by an economic recession that is outside your control, the last thing you need is to compound that challenge with further adversity which was within your control to avoid. This is addressed in this building block. In an off economy it is even more important to protect what you have. This building block shows you how.

- **Protect My Ownership**. When times are tough, you and your partners may be more prone to disputes, both as to operating issues and valuation issues. It's important to have a well-constructed Business Continuity Agreement and Buy-Sell Agreement and to have the right metrics addressed in the chosen company valuation method within the agreement.

- **Grow My Investments**. As of the beginning of 2009, not a lot of this has been occurring recently. What does that mean you should be doing. Recent portfolio losses in the overall massive stock market decline does not necessarily mean that you should be changing investment advisors. However, it may prompt a desire to address if you have the right personal investment strategy and advisor team in place. This building block addresses this.

- **Grow My Business**. This building block will help you address whether the business logic of how your business makes money (your Business Model) and your strategic actions to accomplish this (your Strategic Growth Plan) are current, effective, innovative and profitable. This is also the time to look at business acquisition opportunities.

- **Prepare My Management**. If you think you may be feeling uncertain about your company's future prospects, consider how your key personnel and other members of your work force are coping with this. Now is exactly the time to assure them of their role in your vision for the company and of your ongoing transition and future exit vision. If your focus ignores this and instead is simply on how to meet revenue goals and cut costs, you run the risk that you view your team's concerns as important only when the times are good for you. When the company is hurting, can you afford to lose any key members of your team. Have you fully considered their need to become more engaged in your long term vision for your company. Are you taking this opportunity to find top talent at other companies who would want to become part of your vision.

- **Prepare My Company**. Your corporate structure. Your accounting system and controls. Your corporate housekeeping. Your control of the company's ability to freely act. The actions in this building block are critical regardless of the stage of the economy.

- **Prepare My Tax Savings Plans.** Many tax saving strategies need to be implemented well in advance of your exit to be fully effective. Some of these strategies are actually more effective when initiated in a down economy, especially where values and interest rates are low (e.g. a family stock gifting program, IDGTs, GRATs). Certain state tax incentive programs need to be (or are more effective when) engaged ahead of your growth, so initiating these in an economic downturn can actually work out better.

- **Plan My Inside Route Exit.** This building block will help you decide how to incent your key personnel to stay and help you to take the steps needed now for them to potentially become the future buyer of your company. When company values are low, this can present your key personnel with the opportunity to become invested ahead of your next value move.

- **Plan My Outside Route Exit.** When your company's market value is down, this is the time to be critically addressing what really builds company value in the M & A marketplace.

Keep Looking Ahead

By continuing to look down the highway through a clear windshield while keeping an eye on the important information available on the dashboard, you will see and be able to pursue the next opportunities that are coming your way. The last thing you want to have happen is to only catch them in the rear view mirror after you have passed them by. This is true of both how you work **in** your business (by making adjustments to your company operations) as well as how you work **on** your business (by addressing your transition growth and exit planning needs). Neither can cease simply because of the point in time we are all at in the economic cycle.

Chapter 10

Twelve Building Blocks To A Successful Transition

We have seen too many half-way attempts by other professionals at transition or exit planning, often in a truncated format called "succession planning". These attempts have the same thing in common – they seek to apply the professional's narrow specialty to a situation that demands multiple areas of knowledge.

Exiting a closely held company successfully has never been quick or easy. Given the many unforeseen events which can occur before you exit, we have found that a successful exit from your business needs to rest on a 12 building block design process (which involves eight key areas of professional advisor capabilities). This is an experience-based, proven step-by-step process that has been leading business owners to their ultimate success — the profitable sale or transfer of their businesses.

This process is tailored to meet the particular exit objectives of a business owner. This process helps to keep the train on the tracks and to successfully hand the controls to the next conductor. The Transition Growth and Exit Planning process is a planning process designed for success rather than failure.

Building Block 1 – Decide What I Want

The first action is to identify your personal, financial and exit objectives and then to make sure they fit together. This begins with an understanding of six prime transition questions that, once answered, enable you to move forward with clarity and purpose.

1. Who – Who do you want to transfer your business and duties to?
2. What – What part of the business do you want to transfer or keep?
3. Where – Where do you want to reside after your exit?
4. When – When do you want to exit from active duty and/or ownership?
5. Why – Why do you want to exit?
6. How Much – How much net cash-in-pocket do you need or want to receive from exiting your business?

Other objectives impact your Transition Growth and Exit Planning choices. These personal and financial objectives, which can impact you, your family and your business, are addressed in this process as well.

During this step you should begin to visualize your life post-exit, to focus on your other personal or life goals, whether this is to begin or buy a new business, to take on charitable endeavors, to begin a new career, or to just retire. Many business owners find it difficult to just move directly from being active sixty to eighty hours per week immediately into complete retirement, so its important to start to address your post-exit plans.

Building Block 2 – Decide What I've Got

This step requires that you look at both your personal (nonbusiness) wealth and your business value. It also entails a review as to where you stand on the other critical Building Blocks.

Every business has a value, either to you as the owner, or to someone else as a potential future owner. Building Block 2 in the process helps you to uncover what you have - how much your business is actually worth. This is a critical step in the Transition Growth and Exit Planning process. It cannot be skipped while you go on to other parts of the process. You must uncover the value of your business and you must do it at the start of the Transition Growth Planning process.

This is because your transition objectives can only be met in light of the net value you can expect upon leaving the business. This interaction between establishing transition objectives and obtaining a business valuation can not be answered in a vacuum. Selling your business to an outside financial buyer is very different than selling your business to a strategic buyer, just as selling your business to an outside third party is very different than selling or transferring your business to a family member, employee or co-owner ("insider"). The valuation approaches used are dramatically different.

If you've first identified your transition objectives and determined the likely type of buyer for your business, a business valuation can make a substantial difference in helping to produce a better outcome for you.

Building Block 3 – Protect My Family

Have you established your family's financial security if the unexpected happens to you? Depending on your personal situation, you may have financial and personal goals and objectives that include ongoing financial support for your spouse and family, education funding for your children and grandchildren, charitable funding for your favorite charities, and helping to assure that your assets are transferred to your family members upon your death as quickly and simply as possible.

You may also have personal financial objectives which involve protection of your assets against unwarranted and unexpected, but potential future creditor claims, either from business operation exposures, personal accidents, personal injury or other casualties and contingencies. In addition, you may want to assure that your estate, including your business interests, is arranged in a fashion to minimize potential death taxes. Lastly, you may want to address certain objectives for determining which family members would be responsible for running your business if something happened to you before your planned exit. This step addresses these needs.

Building Block 4 – Protect My Business

You can't transition from your business if you haven't protected it along the way. This Building Block, is concerted with operating under the safest business entity structure, planning to avoid disputes, protecting intangible assets, and being prepared for an unexpected departure, death or disability to a key employee or owner.

Building Block 5 –Protect My Ownership

Have you created a business contingency plan if the unexpected happens to you or to another key owner? Certainly, death, permanent incapacity, divorce (each as to either you or a co-owner) or a dispute among co-owners are probably not your intended exit routes. However, these contingencies exist as possibilities in every business and therefore, need to be addressed as part of the Transition Growth Planning process. Without proper contingency planning, your business can implode.

Business continuity is more than simply determining who will be the owner or seller upon certain events. A Transition Growth Plan also needs to focus on producing a better outcome by re-examining together your existing contingency plan and revising it to reflect proper trigger events, pricing, and spousal salary continuation, as well as family and co-owner dispute avoidance and resolution techniques, all consistent with your present transition exit objectives.

Building Block 6 – Grow My Investments

This Building Block will address a comprehensive wealth program for you and your family. It looks at the investment options available and helps you focus on the optimum investment strategies.

Building Block 7 – Grow My Business

For a moment, think of what you would do if you were rebuilding your company from scratch today from the ground up. What would you include to attract buyers (or professional buy-out funds) to look at your company? What features or characteristics would be necessary to make your business more valuable to you (while you own it) and more saleable and valuable to others (when you are ready to sell)? What features would you include to help protect and build your tangible and intangible assets?

These features are called "value drivers." They are characteristics that either reduce the risk associated with owning your business or enhance the prospects that your business will grow significantly in the future. Business buyers look for certain value drivers. The Next Move Program addresses the value drivers you will need to improve and protect in the Transition Growth and Exit Planning context to produce a better exit outcome.

Building Block 8 – Prepare My Management

This step includes an analysis of what is needed to help attract and retain key employees. You should normally be grooming one or more key persons to be able to be your successor. That type of person will usually be attracted to company ownership. We will typically want to look at one or more types of key employee equity ownership incentives which not only address this need, but which also keep all of your future exit alternatives available to you.

Imagine trying to run a sports team without a depth chart for each of the key positions. Even a simple high school football team has someone ready to go in for the quarterback if the first string quarterback is injured or becomes sick.

The same basic principle applies for running a business. This is especially the case when you are in the process of planning for your own succession, whether through a transfer to insiders or a transfer to an outside third party.

Building Block 9 – Prepare My Company

Most of us would not attempt to sell our home unless we first took certain steps to "fix the place up" so it's ready for sale. Generally, however, it's best to continually keep your "home" fixed up as if it is ready for sale. Not only does this allow you to enjoy your home better, but it also helps to prevent small problems from becoming big problems, from preventing small maintenance jobs from becoming major mechanical breakdowns. Likewise, in business, it's important to address certain pre-exit readiness initiatives ahead of the time of your actual exit. This improves your chances of being prepared for an unexpected event or an unexpected opportunity, and also helps you to keep your business operational in a more profitable format.

Pre-exit readiness initiatives include securing the pre-exit outside consents that will be needed, having a credible accounting system, avoiding inside and outside disputes, having the ability to control the sale of your company, and accomplishing a "house-in-order" due diligence check-off before an actual sale or transfer.

Building Block 10 – Prepare My Tax Savings Plans

Much of our United States tax system is based on how tax is imposed or not imposed on individuals and businesses, depending on the degree to which you have implemented tax savings strategies. Advance planning and advance actions can impact your tax situation dramatically. This Building Block will show you how.

Building Block 11 – Plan My Inside Route Exit

Do you know whether your business can be transferred to an inside buyer? Do you know how to transfer your business in an affordable manner to family members, co-owners or key employees, while enjoying maximum financial security and paying the least possible taxes?

If your exit route is a transfer to co-owners, employees or family, you must do so in a way that keeps the new owner from crashing the train (your company) until the final payment is made. In Transition Growth Planning, that means addressing at least two fundamental conditions which are present in this type of a transfer. First, the income tax consequences of the transfer must be minimized for <u>both</u> the seller and the buyer. Second, the departing owner must concentrate on acquiring maximum security for payment of the purchase price.

It is important to address both of these conditions because they are based on one of the overriding concerns with a transfer to "insiders". This is, that the future conductor of your train — children or key employees — has little or no cash. Since cash is at a premium, effective Transition Growth Planning means designing methods to help guarantee that you receive the company's future cash flow at the lowest possible tax cost — both to you as seller and to the insider buyer.

There are several alternative design techniques to plan for a sale to an insider. Each of these can help produce a better outcome.

Building Block 12 – Plan My Outside Route Exit

Do you know whether a third party buyer will be interested in your business? Do you know how to find such a buyer? Do you know how to sell your business to a third party, at optimal pricing while paying the least possible taxes? To help attain a better outcome for your exit, this step involves specific pre-sale planning to address what to do and not to do to find a buyer and to know how to withdraw a certain amount of value before sale in a tax efficient manner.

There are seven possible overall routes to exit from ownership of your business. Sale to a third party is one of them (which typically is accomplished through either a negotiated sale or controlled auction).

When you actually sell your business, your silent partners (the IRS and your state Department of Revenue) will want to take their shares of the selling price. The size of their shares, however, depends on both your tax planning and your company tax structure. Without addressing both of these, the tax bite may be twice as large.

Conclusion

These 12 Building Blocks form the cornerstone of Transition Growth and Exit Planning and are accomplished through review and utilization of the various transition and exit strategies detailed throughout this book.

Building Block 1 - Decide What I Want

Chapter 11

Synchronize Owner Transition Growth Objectives

The first step listed in a famous rabbit stew recipe is "Catch rabbit". Likewise, as you and your advisors begin the Transition Growth Planning process, don't overlook the obvious. Every business owner must begin the Transition Growth and Exit Planning process by reviewing his or her primary personal, financial and exit objectives. Once established, your objectives become the final destination towards which your Transition Growth Plan needs to advance.

The Transition Growth and Exit Planning process, whether you intend to sell the business to an outside party or to transfer it internally to a family member or an employee, cannot proceed until the owner's objectives are thoroughly analyzed, understood and internally consistent.

Define Your Universe

This review of the owner's objectives needs to be thorough, specific and forthright. A successful exit will involve help from a number of advisors. If these advisors don't understand the mission, they won't be working in a coordinated effort. If the team quarterback isn't clear if the play is a run to the left or a pass to the right, the likelihood of successfully scoring is remote.

Before addressing your primary exit objectives, the Transition Growth and Exit Planning process needs to begin with an understanding of your personal and financial objectives.

This review of your objectives is the time to consider what you want to do post-exit and to address the type of legacy you want to leave to your family, your business and your community.

Prime Transition Growth Objectives

In the Transition Growth and Exit Planning process, your Transition Growth Plan and the various component Transition Growth

Planning tools are dependant on six prime objectives. These in effect represent different forks in the road. While a good Transition Growth Plan includes fall back plans, it is critical that you and your advisors begin by having a keen understanding of the following six prime exit objectives:

1. Who – Who do you want to transfer your business and duties to?

2. What – What part of the business do you want to transfer or keep?

3. Where – Where do you want to reside after your exit?

4. When – When do you want to exit from active duty and/or ownership?

5. Why – Why do you want to exit?

6. How Much – How much net cash-in-pocket do you need or want to receive from exiting your business?

First, it's necessary to start to identify your primary and fallback exit routes. Your options normally include a sale to outside third parties, or sale to inside key employees, a sale or transfer to family members, or a sale to your partners. This is developed further under Building Blocks 11 and 12.

Second, its necessary to know what part of your business you intend to transfer or keep. This can entail a review of personal, business, investment and tax objectives.

The third prime objective is to determine where you want to reside after your exit. If you are considering a move to another State upon your retirement and if you presently are a resident in a State which will tax the gain on the sale of your business, then you should consider whether a move to a State which doesn't impose a tax should be considered before your sale. Certain actions are needed ahead of your sale to establish your new legal residency in another State.

The fourth prime objective is to determine approximately when you want to exit your business. This addresses not simply your desire to transfer ownership, but also the time you desire to reduce or retire from your active management.

The fifth prime objective considers why you want to exit. This will help you to address who you want to benefit from your transition.

The sixth prime objective is to determine your "Cash-In-Pocket Composite Index," as explained in more detail in Building Block 1. If the "Cash Needed From Sale of Business Today" is more than the net cash which can be realized from selling your business today, then your Transition Growth Objectives need to be coordinated accordingly.

Family Retreats and Conferences

Transition Growth and Exit Planning needs to address the interaction of business dynamics, family dynamics and other financial dynamics. As you begin to consider your personal, financial and exit objectives, you should schedule one or more family retreats or conferences where you (and your lead Transition Growth and Exit Advisor, as appropriate) can discuss, evaluate and consider your objectives in light of the wishes and expectations of your loved ones.

Chapter 12

Understand Potential Exit Routes

When we talk about transitioning or exiting from your business, our focus is on two types of exits:

- Active Duty Exit.

- Ownership Exit.

This chapter focuses on these alternatives.

Active Duty Exit Routes

As the company's principal leader, you have a number of ways to leave active duty. These are, for the most part, obvious, but need to still be considered, generally decided upon in advance, and communicated to your exit advisor team so there is an understanding as to precisely what your objectives are. It is important in the exit process to eliminate as many wrong assumptions between yourself as the owner and your advisors who are seeking to help in your transition. In addition, it is helpful to avoid incorrect assumptions between you and the other members of your key management team.

Your "active duty" exits include the following:

- **Complete Retirement.** This is at a designated date or age.

- **Leadership Phase-Out.** For example, if you are presently the Chairman, CEO and President, a leadership phase-out would include handing off your President duties and/or CEO duties to a successor and retaining your duties as Chairman for some period of time.

- **Active Consultant.** – Here you agree to stay on in an active consulting role while handing off all officer and director duties to your successor. This status as an active consultant might be for a pre-agreed period of time, or be set up for a date to be established in the future.

- **Retainer.** This involves being an inactive consultant, but you agree to remain available as an advisor to your successors if and as needed.

- **Disability.** In this case you have decided to work and retain your positions of leadership until you are no longer able to productively continue.

- **Death.** You have decided that you really have no intention of retiring at all and would be content to literally "die at your desk," as they say.

Each of these alternatives involves personal as well as business and financial considerations. If you are ready to move on and hand over the reigns, you are going to pick one of these, or some combination of these alternatives, depending on what is best for you, your family, your business, and the perceptions and objections of your key management team. Good leaders on your team, if in fact they are as good as you believe, will typically want to have the opportunity to take over one of the top positions. Nothing in business is static. If your key management does not see this opportunity as a possibility, you may face the prospect of losing a key management performer as a tradeoff to your personal desire to remain fully active longer than perhaps you should.

When these active duty exits are viewed in the context of your ownership exit options, you may or may not have the freedom of choice. Your buyer of your business may well insist on one or the other of these options. This, of course, varies from business to business, and from situation to situation. A strategic buyer may well be purchasing your business without a need for you to continue for any period of time, or perhaps, to continue only in a retainer capacity. On the other hand, a financial buyer might insist that you stay for a period of time to help transition management duties, in particular, depending on the management depth in place behind you.

Ownership Exit Routes

As the ancient philosopher Seneca stated, "When a man does not know which harbor he is heading for, no wind is the right wind."

It is important in the Transition Growth and Exit Planning process to understand where you, as an owner, want to end up. In the context of Transition Growth Planning, this revolves largely around six principal objectives, as stated in a previous chapter.

It is the "Who" objective that is considered now. This objective, however, cannot be considered in isolation. Depending on "what" you want to transfer or keep, and depending on "when" you want to transfer ownership, the objective of "to whom" may well need to be dependent.

If you were to take a trip from Omaha, Nebraska to northern Minnesota, you could travel via a number of routes to arrive at the same destination. You could take Interstate 80 east to Des Moines, then turn north to Duluth, Minnesota on Interstate 35, then take Hwy. 61 to Lutsen. Or, you could take any of a number of diagonal routes through various small towns in Iowa and Minnesota.

You also could have chosen from a variety of methods of transportation. You could walk any of these routes and eventually arrive. You could ride a bicycle and arrive in about two weeks. You could travel by car and make the trip in less than a day, or you could charter a plane and be there in a couple of hours. You also could have chosen some combination of these and other routes and methods, including travel by train or boat.

With each of these routes and methods of travel, you can achieve your destination. However, each involves a different combination of cost, time, comfort, satisfaction, and personal preference.

Choosing an exit route and exit method to depart from ownership of my business is a similar process. There are seven main exit **routes** for exiting ownership from your business. There are at least 30 exit **methods** for exiting all or part of your business ownership. It is with that understanding that the following discussion of "ownership exit routes" needs to be considered.

Exit Route: Employees

Your employees may be the most natural fit as a buyer of your business. They will typically have a good understanding of how the business works, as well as some motivation to see the business continue after your departure, with the possibility of it continuing under their control. Whether they are financially capable of purchasing your business, and how this might be structured to address financial capabilities, is covered elsewhere in this book. Some of the methods by which employees could acquire your business would include a purchase by a key employee group (with third-party lender financing or seller financing), a purchase by an employee stock ownership plan (possibly leveraged through bank financing), or a sale to just one key employee (either with bank financing or seller financing).

Exit Route: Family

Your family is a second, natural, potential exit route for your business ownership. Often, for estate planning and other financial reasons, an owner may have already transferred a sizable portion of ownership to a spouse, children and grandchildren.

If your objective is to retain ownership and continue to profit and oversee the business until your death, then your ownership exit may be through the bequest that you leave to your family, via your estate plan upon your death. Of course, you may decide to simply own the company until your final, literal exit. Here, you might have resigned from your active duties years in advance and simply remained as a passive owner as you mentored a key employee or family member to take over your management duties, or you might have continued to retain your management duties until your death.

Assuming instead that you would like to transfer your ownership in exchange for some cash with which to retire on, the exit methods to accomplish this could include a direct, negotiated sale to family for the full price, or a part sale/part gift for less than the full price.

Exit Route: Co-Owner

Another natural, possible purchaser of your business is one or more co-owners. Whether this makes sense depends on the exit objectives and financial capabilities of your co-owners. The method of purchase by a co-owner would typically be either through a negotiated direct sale transaction, or through a previously agreed trigger event under a Buy-Sell Agreement. Depending on the independent means available to the co-owner(s), this type of sale would either be self-financed by the co-owner, bank financed, or seller financed and may or may not include "earn-out" provisions.

Exit Route: Third Party Strategic Or Financial Buyer

A strategic buyer is a person who is interested in your business because of the synergies which it can add to the buyer's business. This may be a competitor or similar business looking to expand into your area, or it may be a person looking to add market share who is already in your area. The strategic buyer might be specifically interested in certain parts of your business, such as your distribution network, your customer base, your intellectual property, or your product or service lines. Besides being a competitor, the strategic buyer may be a supplier or customer, or someone who is looking to actively become involved in managing your specific type of business. The exit methods can include a direct, negotiated purchase or a limited auction.

A financial buyer is a person who is interested in owning and profiting from distributions or from the future sale of your business, but who is typically not interested in having to manage your business. This can include an individual investor, a group of investors or a private equity fund. The exit methods for this type of buyer can include a direct negotiated purchase or a limited auction.

Exit Route: Public Market

Another type of financial buyer would be the public stock market. The exit method for this route would typically be through an initial public offering (based on a number of different pricing options, such as a best efforts or a Dutch auction offering).

Exit Route: Liquidation Buyer

This route would be chosen when the liquidation value of your business exceeds its going concern value. In other words, if you can receive more from liquidating and selling the parts of your business than you can from trying to sell it as a going concern, then this route makes sense. Potential buyers can range from equipment dealers to real estate developers to technology licensors and to competitors or others in the business interested in some or all of the parts of your business. The exit method would either be an auction or a directly-negotiated sale, in either case, with the expectation of this being a cash transaction.

Exit Route: Partial (Or Twice)

Redemption/Refinance. This route leads you to a partial ownership exit. One exit method is a refinancing of your business to add debt borrowing to your balance sheet from a third-party lender, such as a bank or other financial institution, with the objective of using the loan proceeds to redeem part of your ownership. This, in essence, lets you take some of your chips off the table while keeping control of the company as you move forward. This route, of course, only works if you have a balance sheet and a net cash flow which is strong enough to support the debt service payments.

Recapitalization. Another partial exit route is to sell part ownership to a third party and retain either a majority or minority position for sale at a later date. The most common method is a recapitalization leveraged buyout by a private equity firm. Typically a private equity firm will not be interested unless you have annual EBITDA (Earnings Before Interest, Taxes, Depreciation and Amortization) of at least $2 million to $10 million. A private equity firm will typically want at least 80% ownership, leaving you 20%, and will want you to remain to run the company for a certain period. The firm will also want to have about 10% ownership available to issue to new or existing key employees, which will either be dilutive to both you and the private equity firm, or not dilutive to you, depending on the terms which can be negotiated. A sizable portion of the price will be financed with debt. The recapitalization gives you the opportunity to continue to still achieve some later equity upside from the sale of your retained 20% and to "stay in the game" to continue to manage the company, while you have taken the balance of your chips off the table.

Franchise. If you have developed your business systems so they can be efficiently replicated and if you have a highly profitable niche which many others would like to own, then you can consider franchising the business. This involves a close review of about a dozen key factors.

Joint Venture. Lastly, you may consider forming a joint venture with another company as a step towards your eventual exit.

Impact Of Exit Route Decision

Regardless of which exit route you choose, the remaining steps in the Transition Growth and Exit Planning process need to be addressed. This is because they either apply to specifically carry out the exit route you have chosen, or because they may apply as a backup for which you want to be prepared, should you choose or need to change exit routes into the future.

Ownership Exit Alternatives

Exit Routes	Exit Method

Inside

Key Employee Group	⟹

- ☐ Management Buyout (MBO)
- ☐ Leveraged Management Buyout (LBO
- ☐ Stock Option/Purchase
- ☐ Stock Bonus/Purchase
- ☐ Employee Stock Ownership Plan

Family Members	⟹

- ☐ Part Sale/Part Gift
- ☐ Lifetime Gifts
- ☐ Private Annuity Sale
- ☐ Grantor Retained Annuity Trust
- ☐ Installment Sale
- ☐ Inheritance
- ☐ Negotiated Sale

Co-Owners	⟹

- ☐ Buy-Sell Agreement "Put"
- ☐ Texas Shoot Out
- ☐ Right of First Refusal
- ☐ Event Trigger (Death, Disability)
- ☐ Negotiated Sale

Outside

Third Party (Financial or Strategic)	⟹

- ☐ Negotiated Sale
- ☐ Controlled, Limited Auction
- ☐ Unsolicited Offer

Public Market	⟹

- ☐ Initial Public Offering (IPO)
- ☐ Dutch Auction
- ☐ Reverse Merger
- ☐ Direct Public Offering

Liquidation	⟹

- ☐ Partial Liquidation
- ☐ Controlled Liquidation
- ☐ Fire Sale

Partial	⟹

- ☐ Sell Partial Stake
- ☐ Sell Control Stake
- ☐ Redemption/Refinance
- ☐ Franchise
- ☐ Joint Venture

Chapter 13

Establish Your Cash-In-Pocket Composite Index

You can more effectively start to think about and discuss in detail your eventual exit if you know this number. The question is what is your number.

The Cash-In-Pocket Composite Index is the sum total of the following:

- Cash needed or wanted to support you and spouse for the rest of your lives if you completely retired today.

- Cash needed or wanted to support your dependent children until adulthood if you completely retired today.

- Cash needed or wanted for children and grandchildren education.

- Cash in pocket you'd like to leave your children and grandchildren upon your death.

- Cash in pocket you'd like to leave for special causes (such as child and grandchild education funding and favorite charities).

This index takes into account not just the capital you need to maintain your standard of living, but also the excess capital above your needs to address the additional family, charitable and community objectives you wish to achieve. Depending on the precision you want, this step may also entail having your financial planner or CPA perform a Financial Needs Analysis for you, as well as preparing a Comprehensive Wealth Plan (detailed under Building Block 6) to best utilize and project the growth of your business and non-business investable capital.

Cash Needed Or Wanted From Sale Of Business

Once you've determined your "Cash-In-Pocket Composite Index" number you can determine the net cash needed from the sale of your business. This looks at not only the liquid assets you presently have on hand, but also the amount you (and your spouse) need from your business after you exit to achieve financial independence. The realistic amount you can expect from the sale or transfer of your business is discussed in at Building Block 2. This is key to starting to determine how you can meet your prime objectives.

My Cash-In-Pocket Composite Index (Estimated)

A determination of my Cash-In-Pocket Composite Index begins with an understanding of those who I want to benefit <u>financially</u> by my exit:

Family	**Other Persons/Plans**
☐ Myself	☐ Charities
☐ My Spouse	☐ Employees
☐ My Children	☐ Community
☐ My Grandchildren	☐ Other _____

My objectives can only be addressed if I have estimated the "cash-in-pocket" I'd <u>like</u> or <u>need</u> following my exit from my business. This consists of:

- Cash Needed/Wanted For Me And My Spouse Until Death $_____
- Cash Needed/Wanted To Support Children $_____
- Cash Needed/Wanted For Child/Grandchild Education $_____
- Cash I'd Like To Leave To Children At My/Our Death $_____
- Cash Needed For Charitable/Other Plans $_____

           Total Cash-In-Pocket Composite Index $_____

Chapter 14

Understand The Potential Sale Models

As you consider what you want to achieve, you need to begin to consider the various potential selling models which exist for selling your Company. Several different models exist for selling your Company in an inside sale (e.g. to your key employees, family, partners or ESOP) as well as in an outside sale (e.g. to an investor, private equity group, competitor, supplier, customer or industry roll up). These can best be considered by addressing the principal components of the transaction.

Transaction Structure

The principal choices to overall structure include:

- **Asset Sale**. Sale of the Company assets to a new entity set up by the buyer(s).

- **Stock Sale**. Sale of the stock you own in the Company to the buyer(s).

- **Joint Venture**. Transfer of all or part of the Company assets to a newly formed limited liability company or corporation which you (or your Company) will own along with the buyer(s).

- **Franchise**. Franchise your business and sell franchise's to selected qualified buyers.

- **Equity Rollover**. This enables you to keep a portion of your ownership equity invested in the buyer's company. This may be some form of full tax deferred merger or a partial rollover (e.g. utilizing an LLC "drop-down" or a so-called S corporation "inversion" transaction).

Pricing

The principal choices to the pricing for the sale of your Company include:

- **Fixed Price**. The price here is determined and fixed under the terms of your sale agreement.

- **Contingent Or Earn Out**. The price here would be adjusted based on the Company's performance after the sale. This could be dependent, for example, on the Company's future revenue, EBITDA (earnings before interest, taxes, depreciation and amortization), net cash flow, net earnings, or key customer retention. Certain collars could be used to set a floor and ceiling on the price adjustments.

- **Combination**. Some combination of fixed price and contingent price.

Valuation

The valuation of the Company on which the price will be based depends on the parties' negotiations and could include the following factors:

- **Appraisal**. An appraisal can be obtained by one or both parties.

- **EBITDA Multiple**. The parties may determine pricing based on a multiple (e.g. 4 to 8) of past (e.g. 1 to 3 year weighted or simple average) or projected earnings.

- **Earnings Multiple**. The parties may determine pricing based on a multiple of past or projected net earnings.

- **Discounted Future Cash Flow**. The parties may determine pricing based on the present, discounted value of future expected cash flows.

- **Sales Multiple**. The parties may determine pricing as a multiple of past or projected revenue.

Payment

The principal alternatives for payment of the purchase price include the following:

- **Cash**. You may require full cash paid at the time of closing of the sale.

- **Installment Note**. You may be willing to accept an installment note from the buyer for the price (typically secured by the assets of the Company or the purchased stock as collateral).

- **Equity**. You may accept equity in the buyer as payment.

- **Combination**. You may agree to the receipt of a combination of cash, a promissory note and equity.

Other Agreed Payments

You may decide to accept some part of your overall payments in other items of compensation such as:

- **No Compete**. You might decide to be paid to agree not to compete in the future.

- **Consulting**. You might agree to an ongoing fee to consult with the buyer about the business.

- **Employment**. You might agree to continue to be employed after the sale for some period of time for an agreed compensation package.

- **Lease**. If you presently own or decide in the transaction to retain real estate or equipment that has been used in the business, you can agree to lease this to the buyer.

- **Intellectual Property**. If you presently own or decide in the transaction to retain intellectual property that has been used in the business, you can agree to license this to the buyer.

Portion of Stock Transferred

You may choose in a stock transfer from the following as to the amount of stock sold:

- **100% Transfer**. The sale of 100% of your stock now to fully exit ownership.

- **Less than 100%**. The sale of less than 100% of your stock to enable you to remain a part owner with the objective of continuing to achieve equity growth with the possible sale of the balance in the future.

- **Multiple Phase Transfer**. Particularly in the sale of your stock to your key employees, family or ESOP, you may choose to sell or transfer just some of your stock now, with the balance over several steps (and in each case leaving you the option to change course in the future as to the sale of the balance of your stock).

Management Retention Incentive

In order to properly compensate your key employees, as well as to incent them to remain with the Company upon a sale, you will want to consider providing one or more of the following:

- **Stock Bonus**. Bonusing key management shares of stock in the Company.

- **Stock Purchase**. Allowing key management to purchase shares in the Company at a full or bargain element price.

- **Stock Option**. Granting key management stock options in the Company.

- **Phantom Stock**. Providing key management what is known as synthetic equity in the form of phantom stock.

- **Stock Appreciation Right**. Providing key management synthetic equity in the form of a stock appreciation right.

- **Deferred Compensation**. Providing key management with a deferred compensation plan (unfunded or funded, e.g. with one of several insurance products).

- **Stay Bonus**. Providing key management with a cash Stay Bonus for agreeing to remain with the Company for a certain period after the sale (paid by the seller or buyer).

- **Employment Commitment**. Providing key management with an employment agreement and/or position commitment for a certain period of time.

Chapter 15

Engage The Advisor Team You Want

Transition Growth Team

Depending on the degree of complexity of your situation, the design and implementation of your Transition Growth Plan to assist you in successfully navigating an exit from your business may require eight key areas of advisor knowledge. Some individuals may possess more than one of these eight areas, so your transition team might not necessarily require eight different individuals. These areas of advisor knowledge include the following:

1. Transition Growth and Exit Planning Advisor
2. Banker/Wealth Management Advisor
3. Financial Planning/Insurance Advisor
4. Corporate and Estate Planning Legal Counsel
5. Certified Public Accountant
6. Mergers & Acquisitions Market Analyst
7. Business Appraiser
8. Business Management Advisor

As a Transition Growth and Exit Planning Advisor, I've designed the Next Move For Business Owners Transition Growth Program in such a way as to enable you, as well as your other advisors, to address the Transition Growth Planning design and implementation process utilizing your business knowledge and their regular expertise, regardless of their actual Transition Growth Planning experience.

The Touch Football Doctrine – Choosing Your Team

For example, a CPA who has little experience in Transition Growth and Exit Planning nevertheless is invaluable due to his or her knowledge of you, your family and your company and of the tax planning, cash flow projections, and accounting systems issues which impact Transition Growth and Exit Planning.

If you have a regular corporate attorney and a regular estate planning attorney, we likewise want them on the Transition Growth Planning team. They provide their professional and personal insights regarding you, your family and your company, often gained over the course of several years, which enable me as a Transition Growth and Exit Advisor to more quickly and accurately pinpoint the best Transition Growth Planning tools and techniques to utilize. Attorneys from different law firms routinely work together today, each bringing their particular area of expertise to bear on the task to be accomplished.

If you regularly work with your company banker to help grow your business (which you should be doing), we want that banker on the Transition Growth Planning team. The Transition Growth and Exit Planning process needs to be conducted within the reality of your current banking relationship and future financing options, which is best accomplished when your banker is involved in the process. In addition, your banker brings a number of Transition Growth and Exit Planning tools and services to the table which can be critical to success.

Business owners unfortunately often view financial planning and insurance advisors as simply product salesmen. Some may deserve this. However, many financial and insurance advisors are committed to developing specialized knowledge in areas which directly impact Transition Growth and Exit Planning. An increasing number of such advisors are working hard to assist business owners with addressing their specific Transition Growth and Exit Planning needs.

You may or may not have ever utilized a Mergers & Acquisitions Market Analyst, a Business Appraiser, or a Business Management Advisor. We often want to utilize a Business Appraiser to help address Building Block 2 – Decide What I've Got. We often want the M&A Market Analyst involved in the Transition Growth Planning process to help assess the Building Block 12 – Plan My Outside Route Exit and to assist in implementing an outside sale. We bring one or more Business Management Advisors to the process, depending on your particular needs under Building Block 7 – Grow My Business.

Our approach has been designed to enable your regular or new advisors to "plug into" this Transition Growth and Exit Planning process to assist in designing the right Transition Growth Plan for you.

So What Now? - Working On Your Business

If you stayed with me up to this point in the book, hopefully I have provided you with a little information that you didn't have and have answered a few questions that you did have, as well as perhaps provided a little motivation and direction for taking the steps needed to "always being ready to exit." At this point in the book, you have a simple decision to make. From here forward, your main objective shouldn't be to just learn additional information about Transition Growth and Exit Planning. I've covered what I think business owners need to know in order to be effective and successful in accomplishing their own personal exit.

Put A Stake In The Ground

The balance of this book is now focused specifically on the actions you need to take if you want to actually put this knowledge to effective use for you, your spouse, your family and your business constituencies. If a little information was all you were after, then simply put this book back on the bookshelf and go back to working 60 – 80 hours a week working in your business. You could try to convince yourself that everything will just work out and everyone will just get along without specific actions or direction by you.

However, I doubt that that approach is what has brought you this far in owning, developing and operating a successful business.

To be successful with your eventual exit, it's up to you to do something to actually cause this success. The first step is for you to decide that you are going to cause a given result to occur. The second step is to take the actions that will help you make this happen.

As a business owner you need to be committed to taking the steps needed to accomplish the Transition Growth process with success.

Coaching From Third Base To Home

Your years of successfully running your business have gotten you to third base. However, you still haven't really won the game until you reach home plate. The Transition Growth and Exit Planning process serves as a coach, helping you to decide when and how to successfully reach home (including who to put up to the plate and the on deck circle to get the hit to bring you home).

Building Block 2 -
Decide What I've Got

Chapter 16

Take The Pre-Exit Fitness Test

What's Your State Of Exit-Readiness

We all go through life in a constant state of either being ready or not for the events and circumstances which we will face. This is equally true for our immediate, ultimate, or unexpected exit from our business, as the case may be. The fact is we really don't know when we will be exiting our business. We may think it is going to be in 10 or 15 years, however, the reality is that even the best laid plans can change quickly (or at least more quickly than we anticipated), due to unforeseen business, financial, personal, health and family changes in circumstances (whether good or bad).

The Boy Scout motto is "be prepared". It is good advice, and it is particularly applicable in business owner Transition Growth and Exit Planning. Just as you would not normally venture into a new market or a new product line without adequate preparation, you wouldn't want to venture into your foreseeable or unforeseeable exit without adequate preparation.

So. Where do you stand? How ready are you for the expected and the unexpected? What follows is a test which we've designed to help you to answer that question. At the end of this test you should have a better idea of the answers to the following two fundamental questions:

• What will be the probable, almost certain, future outcome of your present course, if left unchanged?

• What's missing, the presence of which would make a substantial difference in producing a better outcome?

Read the questions carefully. These questions are part of the "History and Physical" we utilize in the Transition Growth and Exit Planning process. Be honest with yourself. This test measures your readiness **today**. After you've gone through the Transition Growth Planning process, you can take the test again to review what will typically be substantially better exit readiness results. If you don't know an answer for sure, it should be answered "no". A few questions might be "not applicable" to you. Answer them "yes".

PRE-EXIT FITNESS TEST

Building Block 1 – Decide What I Want	YES	NO
1. Do I know for sure who I want to transfer my duties and my business to e.g. to an insider (family member, key employee or co-owner) or to an outside third party?	☐	☐
2. Do I know for sure whether I <u>can</u> transfer my business to an insider or to an outside third party?	☐	☐
3. Have I determined which parts of my business assets (real estate, equipment, intangible property, certain divisions) will be retained by me and leased/licensed to the company (rather than sold to the buyer)?	☐	☐
4. Do I know in which State I want to reside after I exit from active duty?	☐	☐
5. Have I decided for sure when I want to start transitioning some of my duties to enable me to leave the business for an extended period of time and when I want to transition all of my duties to a successor permanently?	☐	☐
6. Have I decided for sure when I want to begin transferring ownership of my company and when I want to have completed the transfer of all of my ownership in my company in return for financial independence?	☐	☐
7. Do I know why I want to exit (and who I want to benefit from my exit)?	☐	☐
8. Do I know for sure how much cash-in-pocket I need or want upon my retirement to achieve financial independence?	☐	☐

9.   Do I know for sure how much net after tax cash I need or want from the sale of my business today in order to achieve financial independence? ☐ ☐

Building Block 2 – Decide What I've Got YES NO

10.   Do I know whether my business financial results and value are understated (and if so by how much) because compensation, real estate rental, equipment rental and intangible licensing between myself and my company are not at normalized market levels? ☐ ☐

11.   Do I know how much my company is actually worth to the type of buyer I intend to transfer to, in after tax realizable cash? ☐ ☐

12.   Has the value of my business been estimated recently by a valuation expert or M&A transition specialist? ☐ ☐

Building Block 3 – Protect My Family YES NO

13.   Have I executed a durable financial power of attorney which is a "present power" which designates a capable person (and capable successors) to handle my financial affairs upon my disability? ☐ ☐

14.   Have I executed a durable health care power of attorney which designates a capable individual (and capable successors) to handle my medical affairs upon my disability and which is HIPAA compliant? ☐ ☐

15.   Have I executed a health care directive (living will) which specifies proper guidelines for utilizing or maintaining health care procedures in extraordinary circumstances? ☐ ☐

16.   Have I executed a pour-over will to designate a capable personal representative (executor) and capable successors to handle my estate (including business matters) upon my death? ☐ ☐

17.   Have I executed a living trust which protects my spouse and which protects my children and ☐ ☐

grandchildren until designated ages?

18.   Have I re-titled my assets into my living trust "bucket" (including my business assets) in order to avoid probate court intervention with regard to my business? □ □

19.   Have I appointed capable successor trustees to my living trust who understand my business operations? □ □

20.   Have I addressed my charitable giving objectives, in particular from a pre-exit tax favored perspective? □ □

21.   Have I addressed my education funding objectives, in particular from a pre-exit tax favored perspective? □ □

22.   Have I implemented the applicable personal Asset Protection Plan tools, given an assessment of my personal exposure to business and personal contingent liability risks? □ □

23.   Have I addressed specific bequests and equalization to and amongst children who are active or inactive in the business? □ □

24.   Have I designated in my Estate Plan how my personal representative (executor), family business representative or trustee is to manage or sell my business upon my death or disability? □ □

25.   Have I included in my Estate Plan a dispute resolution provision which prevents a dissatisfied child from disrupting business operations? □ □

26.   Have I recently evaluated my personal life and disability insurance needs and implemented the insurance coverages appropriate to addressing my financial gaps, needs and objectives? □ □

27.   Have I established a funded salary continuation plan or agreement to provide ongoing support to my spouse and family upon my death or

disability?

Building Block 4 – Protect My Business   YES   NO

28.   Is my financial reporting and accounting   ☐   ☐
control system providing a high degree of protection
and assurance for my financial systems credibility and
tax law compliance through CPA reviewed or audited
financial statements (to both protect my profits today
and to demonstrate my earnings track record to a
potential buyer of my business)?

29.   Have I recently done an intellectual property   ☐   ☐
audit to help assure my business has a high degree of
protection for my intangible assets (such as trade
secrets, trade names, trademarks, service marks, and
patents)?

30.   Are both my company entity structure <u>and</u> risk   ☐   ☐
management program set up to best protect certain
assets or business segments from the risk of liabilities
or risks from another business segment? In particular,
have I recently completed a thorough risk management
assessment to identify and reduce property, casualty
and business risk exposures of emerging liabilities that
could otherwise jeopardize company profitability and
ability to sell at full price?

31.   Is the company able to retain key employees,   ☐   ☐
customers, suppliers and franchisor relationships upon
my death or disability?

32.   Will I be able to avoid a family dispute that   ☐   ☐
would be detrimental to my business upon my death or
disability?

33.   Is my company financially prepared to deal   ☐   ☐
with the loss of a key employee?

34.   Have I developed a contingency notification   ☐   ☐
letter to customers/patients, lenders, suppliers,
franchisor and employees for immediate release upon
my death or disability?

35. Do I have contingency shareholder and board of director resolutions for directing board of director actions upon my death or disability? ☐ ☐

36. Do I have contingency board of director instructions for the process for selecting an interim and permanent successor (or confirming my pre-designated successor) and/or taking contingency options to manage the company upon my death or disability? ☐ ☐

37. Have I determined whether I need a "stay bonus plan" to help retain key personnel from departing a "potentially sinking ship" upon my death or disability? ☐ ☐

38. Have I addressed already existing or potential disputes or disagreements which will surface on account of my unplanned exit from the business involving co-owners, family, customers, creditors, franchisor, vendors, employees and managers? ☐ ☐

39. Have I minimized the financial hit to my company due to the loss of key personnel (including yourself), by having performed key employee valuations, backed up by key employee life and disability insurance coverage payable to the company? ☐ ☐

Building Block 5 – Protect My Ownership YES NO

40. Will my spouse or family be able to receive cash for the full value of my stock upon my death or disability? ☐ ☐

41. Is my company able to resolve continuing ownership by one or more partners pursuant to a pre-determined written, contractual method upon an irreconcilable dispute? ☐ ☐

42. Is my company able to contractually control retention of ownership amongst key owners upon a divorce? ☐ ☐

43. Is my company able to continue to obtain bank or other third party financing upon the loss of me (or another owner) as a financial resource, guarantor or ☐ ☐

lender?

44. Is my company financially and operationally prepared to deal with the loss of my key services? ☐ ☐

45. Do I have an exit plan letter to my family, with written instructions to my spouse and family for handling business matters upon my death or disability? ☐ ☐

46. Do I have pre-written guidelines for assisting my spouse, family and advisers in selling the company to a third party or insiders upon my death or disability? ☐ ☐

47. Do I have pre-written designation to my spouse, family and/or board of directors naming principal exit plan advisors to assist in advising family and my board of directors on the transition of business matters upon my death or disability? ☐ ☐

48. Have I established a Business Continuity Agreement to help avoid or resolve disputes (in such areas as dividend distributions, compensation setting, stock redemption policy, voting agreements and competing activities)? ☐ ☐

49. Have I established a Buy-Sell Agreement which establishes must/may buy obligations on death, disability, employment termination, retirement, bankruptcy and divorce of all shareholders? ☐ ☐

50. Have I established Buy-Sell Agreement provisions giving the majority owner "drag along" rights to sell all stock (including the minority) in a company sale? ☐ ☐

51. Have I established a Buy-Sell Agreement which establishes the right type of stock pricing? ☐ ☐

52. Have I provided sufficient funding for the Buy-Sell obligations under our Buy-Sell agreement? ☐ ☐

53. Have I established in our Buy-Sell Agreement key provisions for addressing non-competition and non-solicitation, as well as Subchapter "S" protection, as applicable? ☐ ☐

Building Block 6 – Grow My Investments	YES	NO
54. Do I have a professionally prepared Comprehensive Wealth Plan?	☐	☐

Building Block 7 – Grow My Business	YES	NO
55. Is my facility appearance and efficiency up to industry standards?	☐	☐
56. Have I recently benchmarked my business operations to determine if I am deploying my financial and human capital as efficiently as others in my industry (in order to achieve better cash flow for the business owners and a better price and cash flow upon my exit)?	☐	☐
57. Do I have a current written Strategic Growth Plan for my business?	☐	☐
58. Do I have a written Business Model Innovation Program?	☐	☐
59. Is my business cash flow predictable, steady and growing?	☐	☐
60. Have I addressed the "Porter Forces" impacting my business and have I assessed the presence and duration of the "economic moats" impacting or benefiting my business?	☐	☐

Building Block 8 – Prepare My Management	YES	NO
61. Does my business have a high degree of protection designed to keep key employees from being hired away or utilizing company know how for other employers?	☐	☐
62. Have I recently completed a thorough human resource audit to assure my compensation plans and employee benefits programs are competitive with optimal benefit mix, my policies and procedures are legally compliant and my retention of employees is equal to or better than industry average?	☐	☐

63.   Have I built a Leadership Team Development Program with a key management team which is capable today of leading my business in my absence (and leading my business when owned by a third party buyer)? ☐ ☐

64.   Is my key management team engaged to the degree that they see themselves as having a possibility of owning my company and therefore being less inclined to jump ship for a competitor? ☐ ☐

65.   Do I have an effective Key Employee Incentive plan which is either equity-based or cash-based and which provides a rolling-vesting performance commitment? ☐ ☐

66.   Do I have a Management Transition Program in which I have targeted specific inside successors to top management (or have retained an outside management recruiting firm to hire a successor from outside the company)? ☐ ☐

Building Block 9 – Prepare My Company   YES   NO

67.   Is my company entity structure set up to best help me separate in advance those assets or business segments I may wish to retain or to sell separately upon my exit? ☐ ☐

68.   Have I resolved all litigation or other "skeletons in the closet" which could impair my ability to sell or the pricing I might receive? ☐ ☐

69.   Do I have sole control to cause the sale of my company (and to require fellow shareholders to sell)? ☐ ☐

70.   Do I have the ability to sell my company without the need for franchisor approval, licensing agency approval, or lender approval and have necessary approvals been obtained? ☐ ☐

71.   Do I know whether I can sell my company without incurring penalties or prohibitions under production, supply, and incentive agreements? ☐ ☐

72.   Have I completed a due diligence buyer ☐ ☐
checklist to flush out those aspects which need to be
placed in order before a sale can occur?

73.   Are my corporate organization chart and ☐ ☐
corporate minute book up-to-date?

Building Block 10 – Prepare My Tax Savings Plans   YES   NO

74.   Have I determined whether my business needs ☐ ☐
to be restructured in order to minimize taxation both
in company operations and upon sale of the company
and has this restructuring been implemented?

75.   Have I determined whether advanced tax ☐ ☐
elections can minimize taxation to me and the
company upon sale and have such elections been
implemented?

76.   Have I determined how I am going to avoid ☐ ☐
state capital gain taxes upon my sale and am I in a
position now to do so?

77.   Do I have a plan for obtaining all available ☐ ☐
state and local tax and nontax incentives for my
business and employment growth and expansion?

78.   Have I executed a living trust which properly ☐ ☐
establishes the appropriate marital deduction
provisions and federal estate tax exemption utilization
for both spouses?

79.   Have I implemented appropriate estate tax ☐ ☐
reduction tools, such as annual exemption gifting,
family limited liability partnership, lifetime exemption
gifting, a gifting power of attorney and irrevocable life
insurance trust, as applicable?

Building Block 11 – Plan My Inside Route Exit   YES   NO

80.   Have I determined whether an actual potential ☐ ☐
inside buyer exists for my company who will be in a
position to pay me the price I am expecting?

81.   Have I determined the reasons why my ☐ ☐
business would be attractive to an inside buyer and

whether my business presently has those characteristics?

82. Do I have a present program in place for beginning to provide ownership (through either stock grants or stock purchases) to key employees as a retention tool and as a means to improve the likelihood of a sale to insiders as I exit? ☐ ☐

83. Have I decided whether I will provide seller-assisted financing on a sale to an insider and whether this will provide the financial security which I need or want? ☐ ☐

84. Have I decided whether I am willing to receive, as part of the compensation for a sale to an insider, deferred compensation, a consulting fee or payment for a no-compete? ☐ ☐

85. Have I decided whether a sale to an insider needs to be accomplished through transfer of part of the ownership now and the balance later? ☐ ☐

86. Have I determined the estimated tax impact to myself on the sale of my business to an insider under my present business structure and taken the steps to minimize the tax impact? ☐ ☐

87. Have I determined the estimated buyer tax impact on the purchase of my business by an insider under the present business structure and how to make the purchase more tax effective for the buyer (which may also increase the chances of selling at a better price)? ☐ ☐

88. Have I determined whether the bank will finance my sale to insiders and whether I am willing to take back the company should the buyer default on the purchase? ☐ ☐

89. Have I determined the employee stock ownership restrictions and buy-back obligations which need to exist as to stock owned by key-employees if I am still an owner in the company? ☐ ☐

90.   Have I determined whether a sale to an
Employee Stock Ownership Plan is feasible (and if
bank financing would be necessary, whether this would
be available)?

☐   ☐

Building Block 12 – Plan My Outside Route Exit   YES   NO

91.   Have I decided whether a sale to an outside
third party is my primary or backup plan for exiting my
business and if so whether this would be a financial
buyer or a strategic buyer?

☐   ☐

92.   Have I determined the specific reasons my
business would be attractive to a third party buyer (as
either my primary or backup plan) and whether my
business presently has those characteristics?

☐   ☐

93.   Have I investigated the M&A market for my
specific business to determine whether my business is
marketable to an outside third party buyer at a decent
price?

☐   ☐

94.   Have I identified specific potential outside
third party buyers (such as competitors, customers,
investors, suppliers, similar businesses, private equity
funds, franchisor, etc.)?

☐   ☐

95.   Have I established my anticipated deal terms
for selling to an outside third party buyer?

☐   ☐

96.   Have I established the estimated seller tax
impact on the sale of my business to an outside buyer
under my present business structure and taken the
steps to minimize the tax impact?

☐   ☐

97.   Have I estimated the buyer tax impact on the
purchase of my business under my present business
structure and determined how to make the purchase
more tax effective for the buyer (which may also
increase the chances of selling at a better price)?

☐   ☐

98.   Have I determined whether partial payment
for my business in the form of items other than sale
price (e.g. deferred compensation, salary continuation,
etc.) will be more tax effective for either me or for

both the seller and the buyer?

Transition Growth Plan and Implementation	YES	NO
99. Do I have a written Transition Growth Plan (and has this been thoroughly communicated to key employees, family members, key advisors and my banker who need to know this)?	☐	☐
100. Do I believe I am as prepared as I should be for both my planned and unexpected exit?	☐	☐

TOTALS

(YES)	(NO)
Ready	Not Ready

Test Results – Confront The Facts

How well did you do? The following table provides an estimate of your "State Of Pre-Exit Fitness" for your planned or unplanned exit:

0-10	"No" answers –	You are reasonably ready to exit.
11-20	"No" answers –	Your present plan needs to be developed further.
21 or more	"No" answers –	You are seriously unprepared for your transition or exit.

Chapter 17

Develop Your Transition Growth Report Card

The Report Card Concept

We have all grown up being accustomed to the Report Card concept. All school systems utilize it as a means for grading the level of your progress towards achieving a pre-determined set of important goals, objectives or measurements.

Report Cards, of course, typically use a letter grade measurement, where "A" is the best (or very good), followed by "B" (good), "C" (average), "D" (below average) and "F" (failing).

Other systems use a number measurement where "A" = 4, "B" = 3, "C" = 2, "D" = 1 and "F" = 0. In such a System the grades in all courses are averaged together, with a 4.0 average being a straight "A" average, 3.0 a "B" average, and so on.

The Transition Growth Report Card

We have adopted and adapted the Report Card concept to the Transition Growth and Exit Planning process. A sample is included below.

This enables you to self-evaluate which grade you believe you have achieved so far in your Transition Growth Planning. Just as you had a Report Card at the end of each school semester, you can re-grade your progress as you proceed through each of the 12 Building Blocks in the Next Move Transition Growth Program. The objective should be to achieve a straight "A" or 4.0 result.

TRANSITION GROWTH REPORT CARD

DATE: _____

Building Block 1 – Decide What I Want   Grade

▮ **Who**. I know who I will transfer my duties to and whether I will transfer my Company to an outside third party, key employee(s), partner, family or ESOP.   _____

▮ **What**. I know what portion of my Company will be transferred, kept, or kept and leased back.   _____

▮ **Where**. I know where I want to reside after I exit my Company.   _____

▮ **When**. I know when I want to exit from active duty and ownership.   _____

▮ **Why**. I know why I want to exit and who I want to benefit.   _____

▮ **How Much**. I know how much net cash-in-pocket I need or want to receive from exiting my Company   _____

Building Block 2 – Decide What I've Got   Grade

▮ **Company Fair Value**. I know the fair market value of my Company.   _____

▮ **Intangible Assets**. I have identified my valuable transferable intangible properties.   _____

▮ **Normalized Accounting**. My financial statements have been normalized to reflect fair market compensation, related party rentals and industry accounting standards.   _____

▮ **Nonbusiness Net Worth**. I know the value of my financial net worth outside of my Company.   _____

▮ **Target achieved**. The net after tax realizable value from my Company plus my personal net worth equals or exceeds my Cash-In-Pocket Composite Index.   _____

Building Block 3 – Protect My Family   Grade

▮ **My Spouse**. My Estate Plan and Asset Protection Plan financially protect my spouse.   _____

- **Myself.** My Estate Plan and Asset Protection Plan financially protect me. _____

- **My Children/Grandchildren.** My Estate Plan and Asset Protection Plan financially protect my children and grandchildren. _____

- **Education.** My Estate Plan achieves my family education objectives. _____

- **Charity.** My Estate Plan achieves my family charitable objectives. _____

- **Personal Insurance Plan.** My Personal life and disability insurance coverage is up-to-date and fully covers my family's needs and objectives. _____

Building Block 4 – Protect My Business   Grade

- **Asset Protection.** My Company corporate structure protects my business from disastrous litigation exposure. _____

- **Casualty Protection.** My Company safety program/casualty insurance program and business interruption insurance program sufficiently protect and insure my business from incurring unexpected costs or disastrous litigation exposure. _____

- **Employment.** My Company employment policy/ programs protect my Company from unnecessary employment litigation/claims. _____

- **Internal Controls.** My accounting system has sufficient internal protective controls. _____

- **Intellectual Property.** My Company's intellectual property protection program covers my human capital and proprietary capital. _____

- **Disaster Alert.** My disaster alert program sufficiently informs employees, customers and other constituents of Company direction upon my or other key owner death/disability. _____

- **Proprietary Capital.** My Key Employee Group has executed employment agreements which address nonsolicitation of customers and other employees and protection of Company intellectual and proprietary data. _____

Building Block 5 – Protect My Ownership   Grade

▌ **Corporate Governance**. We have a working Board of Directors with the optimum representation of qualified inside and outside directors.

_____

▌ **Business Continuity**. Our Business Continuity Agreement sufficiently addresses Company operational issues due to financial, corporate and business contingencies.

_____

▌ **The 5 D's**. Our Buy-Sell Agreement sufficiently addresses unexpected key owner death, disability, divorce, departure and disputes.

_____

▌ **Funding**. Our Buy-Sell Agreement trigger events are fully funded with insurance and/or Company reserves.

_____

Building Block 6 – Grow My Investments   Grade

▌ **Wealth Plan**. My Comprehensive Wealth Plan is diverse, effective and actively managed by an outside investment professional.

_____

Building Block 7 – Grow My Business   Grade

▌ **Sales Growth**. My rate of sales growth would be considered attractive to an outside investor.

_____

▌ **Cash Flow Growth**. My rate of cash flow growth would be considered attractive to an outside investor.

_____

▌ **Business Model Innovation Program**. My Business Model Innovation Program is well designed and continuously utilized to keep my business model ahead of competition and to find new and developing opportunities to sustain and grow my company.

_____

▌ **Strategic Growth Plan**. My Strategic Growth Plan demonstrates an effective Company growth strategy without my presence; it addresses the "Porter Forces" impacting my business and assesses the presence and duration of my "economic moats".

_____

▌ **Acquisition Program**. My ongoing site acquisition and business acquisition program is engaged and effective.

_____

▌ **Product Development**. My product/service development program is highly effective and competitive. _____

▌ **Employee Engagement**. My employees are highly engaged and exceed industry performance standards. _____

Building Block 8 – Prepare My Management   Grade

▌ **Leadership**. Without counting current transitioning owners, my Company has one or more leaders capable of running the Company for at least 5 – 10 years. _____

▌ **Development**. We have an effective Leadership Team Development Program for each key management position. _____

▌ **Depth Chart**. Our management depth chart is sufficient to run the Company without existing transitioning owners. _____

▌ **KEG Engagement**. Our Key Employee Group receives sufficient equity or cash incentive compensation to see themselves invested long term in the outcome of the Company. _____

Building Block 9 – Prepare My Company   Grade

▌ **Consents**. We have obtained the necessary pre-exit outside consents. _____

▌ **Internal Controls**. We have accounting system credibility. _____

▌ **Sale Control**. We have assured pre-exit inside control to sell company. _____

▌ **Check-Off**. We have accomplished our pre-exit house-in-order check-off. _____

Building Block 10 – Prepare My Tax Savings Plans   Grade

▌ **Operating Taxes**. We operate under a Company structure and operational system which minimizes State income, sales and property taxes. _____

▌ **Incentives**. Our site selection and expansion program maximizes the use of available State and local site _____ selection incentives.

▌ **Ownership Exit**. Our capital gain taxes upon ownership exit will be minimized through proper corporate structure and tax elections. _____

▌ **State Capital Gain**. State capital gain tax upon my ownership exit will be minimized or avoided due to proper exemption planning or State residency planning. _____

▌ **Estate Taxes**. My estate taxes will be minimized or avoided due to advance planning and/or funding. _____

Building Block 11 – Plan My Inside Route Exit Grade

▌ **Outlook**. I have determined (and planned for) my inside sale outlook. _____

▌ **Terms**. I have established tax efficient, bankable sale to insider terms. _____

▌ **Method**. I have determined whether a stock bonus, a direct purchase, an ESOP, or a combination is the best way to transfer to our employees. _____

Building Block 12 – Plan My Outside Route Exit Grade

▌ **Outside**. I have determined (and planned for) my outside sale outlook. _____

▌ **Terms**. I have established tax efficient sale to outsider terms. _____

▌ **Method**. I have determined the best exit route method for a sale to an outside third party. _____

Transition Growth Plan Grade

▌ **Plan**. My written Transition Growth Plan has been updated within the past 2 years and the implementation of the Action Plan items has been occurring on schedule. _____

Grade Average _____

Chapter 18

Identify Valuable, Transferable Intangible Assets

Tangible assets are easy enough to identify. These are typically reflected on the asset side of a company's financial statements. Under generally accepted accounting principles, the value of such assets is typically identified (with certain exceptions) at historical cost. These assets include cash, inventories, equipment and buildings, to name a few. Generally speaking, a company's financial statement does not reflect the true market value of these tangible assets, nor does it reflect the degree to which you are efficiently utilizing all of the tangible parts of your business to produce profit or to produce a predictable, sustainable, growing cash flow.

Less apparent from reading any company's financial statements is the presence or type of intangible assets which the company has assembled and put into operation to produce that profit and cash flow. While certain intangible assets may have a cost allocated to them when they have been purchased, a balance sheet very likely does not include a recorded list of intangible assets.

Instead, the presence of intangible assets within a company is typically identified by a potential purchaser in the due diligence process when a potential acquisition candidate is being evaluated for purchase. Even when identified, the value of these intangible assets is often determinable only indirectly, for example, by considering the extent to which a company's profit exceeds a reasonable rate of return on the value of its tangible assets.

This evaluation by a potential buyer can include the type of business benchmarking addressed at Building Block 7. However, if you expect to be able to realize a better price for your business, you should expect to identify the valuable, transferable intangible assets you've built as part of your business.

Various types of intangible assets exist in a successful company. By identifying those intangible assets which are truly creating your company's earning capacity, and by carefully protecting them so they remain intact when you are negotiating your exit transaction, you can improve your exit outcome.

Workforce In Place

The first intangible is your "workforce in place". Quite simply, does your company have talent? It includes the composition of a workforce (for example, the experience, education or training of a workforce), the terms and conditions of employment, whether contractual or otherwise, and any other value placed on employees or any of their attributes. To the extent that your company has invested in the skills and training of your workforce, you have helped to develop one of your most important assets and created an intangible asset which adds value to a purchase price.

In a recent study by McKinsey & Company of 13,000 executives from 120 companies and case studies of 27 leading corporations, to learn the key to developing higher financial returns for shareholders, McKinsey found that the most important corporate resource over the next 20 years will be "talent." In "War For Talent", published by Harvard Business School Press, the authors concluded that the factor which made the most difference to higher shareholder returns (a 22% higher return in their studies) was a "pervasive talent mindset".

Watson, Wyatt Worldwide's ("WWW") "Human Capital Index" ("HCI") quantified the people management practices which a company must implement or avoid to maximize shareholder value. Based on studies conducted by WWW, the book "The Human Capital Edge – 21 People Management Practices Your Company Must Implement (Or Avoid) To Maximize Shareholder Return" provides compelling evidence as to how specific human capital practices drive financial results. The numbers are impressive and highly relevant as you consider your company's exit value to you. They demonstrate that companies which adopt and combine the human resource practices they studied can experience up to a 47% increase in shareholder value.

What is your level of workforce talent in the right place? What is your workforce satisfaction, morale, and retention (or turnover) rate? To the extent you are better than your industry average and you've documented these aspects of your business, you've demonstrated a favorable workplace, which makes your business of more interest and value to a potential buyer. One example, amongst several, of the management tools utilized in this area is Predictive Index®. Initially developed to assist the military in World War II to help determine the best candidates to serve as military spies, it became the grandfather to the employee recruitment and measurement tools in use today. Besides helping companies to get the "right people in the right seats on the bus", it also enables employers to periodically assess the morale of the workforce – something of key interest to an owner looking to grow a company and to a buyer looking to acquire it.

Such measurement tools provide a powerful combination of education, consulting and assessment, offering a better understanding of what makes people work, and which help you learn how to motivate them to work better. These tools help you build new leaders at every level of your company and, most importantly to your exit, they help you hire and retain talented people who are crucial to the success, and exit value, of your company.

Information Base

The intangible asset "information base" includes business books and records, operating systems and any other information base (regardless of the method of recording the information). This includes a customer-related information base, which is any information base that includes lists or other information with respect to current or prospective customers. This also includes accounting or inventory control systems, customer lists, subscription lists, insurance expirations, patient or client files, or lists of newspaper, magazine, radio or television advertisers (each depending on your type of business). A common example is the McDonald's restaurant operating system. Typically the "information base" should be well-developed and of significant value in most franchise operations.

To the extent that you have systematized your business operations, you have generally added value in which a purchaser should be interested. Systematic operations not only have the benefit of providing a consistent and efficient means of producing a profit, but also provides a consistent, predictable and expected product or service for your customers or clients. Every business, by definition, has some degree of systematized processes for producing and selling products or services. However, not all businesses have developed and documented their system to the extent of meeting the expectations which a potential buyer of that business would like to see intact and functioning.

If you have developed and documented your operating systems to such an extent that you could franchise your business, you've added value, which makes your business of more interest and value to a potential buyer.

Know-How

This type of intangible includes any patent, copyright, formula, process, design, pattern, know-how format, package design, computer software or other similar property which reflects past and present intellectual capital of the business. The rights to this type of intangible asset can often be one of the most valuable assets within a business operation, particularly if it has been suitably documented.

Customer-Based Intangibles

A "customer-based intangible" is any composition of market, market share, or other value resulting from the future provision of goods or services pursuant to contractual or other relationships in the ordinary course of business with customers. This can include the existence of a customer base, a circulation base, an undeveloped market or market growth, insurance in force, the existence of a qualification to supply goods or services to a particular customer, a mortgage servicing contract, an investment management contract, or other similar relationships with customers involving the future provision of goods or services.

Have you ever quantified your customer "engagement" or turnover? To the extent this is favorable or exceeds industry average and you've documented this, you've added potential value which a buyer should be interested in.

Supplier-Based Intangibles

A "supplier-based intangible" is the value resulting from the future acquisition, pursuant to contractual or other relationships with suppliers in the ordinary course of business, of goods or services that will be sold or used by the taxpayer. This intangible exists to the extent that the company has a favorable relationship with persons providing distribution services (such as favorable shelf or display space at a retail outlet), the existence of a favorable credit rating, or the existence of favorable supply contracts.

Government Licenses And Permits

Any license, permit or other right granted by a governmental unit is an intangible asset, even if the right is granted for an indefinite period or is reasonably expected to be renewed for an indefinite period. This includes, for example, a liquor license, a taxi-cab medallion, an airport landing or takeoff right (sometimes referred to as a slot), a regulated airline route, or a television or radio broadcasting license.

Covenants Not To Compete

This type of intangible includes any covenant not to compete, or agreement having substantially the same effect, entered into in connection with the direct or indirect acquisition of an interest in a trade or business or a substantial portion of a trade or business. For example, if your company is the beneficiary of such a covenant not to compete, which effectively keeps another company out of your market place, this represents an intangible value to your business.

Franchises, Trademarks And Trade Names

Franchises, trademarks and trade names all represent potentially valuable intangible assets. A "franchise" includes any agreement giving one of the parties to the agreement the right to distribute, sell, or provide goods, services, or facilities within a specified area. The term "trademark" includes any work, name, symbol or device, or any combination of these, which has been adopted and used to identify goods or services and to distinguish them from those provided by others. The term "trade names" includes any name used to identify or designate a particular trade or business or the name or title used by a person or organization engaged in a trade or business. A trademark or trade name can include any trademark or trade name which arises under statute or applicable common law or under any similar right granted by contract. These intangible assets are potentially very valuable in a franchise business.

Going Concern Value

The intangible "going concern value" is the additional value that attaches to property by the reason of its existence as an integral part of an ongoing business activity. Going concern value includes the value attributable to the ability of a trade or business (or any part of a trade or business) to continue functioning or generating income without interruption, despite a change in ownership.

Absence of Contingent Liabilities

The absence of pending litigation, tax audits, environmental exposure, contract breaches, negligence claims, product liability claims and other contingent liabilities is in effect an intangible asset which can enhance the value of your business.

Goodwill

The intangible of "goodwill is the value of the trade or business which is attributable to the expectancy of continued customer patronage. This expectancy can be due, for example, to the name or reputation of the trade or business or any other factor.

What is the public perception of your business? Have you ever independently surveyed this? Are you well known, trusted, respected, looked to for solutions, etc.? To the extent you've documented this, you've added an element of value which a buyer should be interested in buying.

Identify And Then Protect

Once identified, the Transition Growth and Exit Planning process will address whether you've taken the steps to protect the intangible assets you've developed.

Chapter 19

Normalize Your Financial Results

Business owners of privately-held companies typically receive income from their companies other than through simply dividends or the eventual capital gain on the sale of their stock. Specifically, most active owners receive a salary and other compensation for their services. In addition, those who own real estate, equipment or intangible assets utilized by the company will also receive rental and royalty income from the lease or license of this property to the company.

Often, the true fair value of such services or the use of such property is a range, rather than one fixed number. This is because the value of these services or property is not necessarily precisely determinable. Often, the width of this range can be several tens of thousands of dollars between the low end and the high end.

Depending on the tax structure of the company, business owners will frequently find it more tax advantageous to pay this compensation, rent and royalties from the company to the individual owners at the high end, rather than the low end. This is particularly true if the company is organized as a "C" corporation.

While this may present tax planning opportunities during the normal life cycle of business ownership, it can present a detriment to the selling price during the Transition Growth and Exit Planning process. This is because when compensation, rent and royalties are paid by the company at the high end, this results in less net income and less net operating cash flow being reflected as earned by the company.

Since a buyer will typically determine a purchase price in reference to some multiple of net income and/or net operating cash flow, the above practice can have a detrimental, downward impact on the selling price opportunity available (which greatly exceeds the tax benefits the owner felt he or she was receiving).

Business owners often attempt to overcome this during the selling process by contending that these company expensed amounts should be "normalized" to reflect a more realistic value as to what an unrelated company would have negotiated with an owner-employee, lessor or licensor for the actual market compensation, rent and royalty. During the selling process, this puts the business owner in the awkward position of contending that he or she has been overpaid. This can also put the business owner in a compromised position should tax authorities seek to contend that the overpaid amounts represented nondeductible "constructive dividends" paid by the company, resulting in a retroactive tax liability.

Another issue which can arise if these amounts are at the high end of the market range is that minority shareholders of the company, if any, could complain that the payment of these amounts is a breach of a fiduciary duty owed to them. Since a business owner's Transition Growth Plan will often involve the beginning of selling part of the company (or awarding stock bonuses for shares in the company) to key employees, this raises the potential of a shareholder dispute going forward through this process (in particular if this has not been agreed to ahead of time).

Proper tax and corporate planning during the Transition Growth and Exit Planning process can help to optimize and resolve these competing objectives.

By beginning to move the company's payments to the owners for compensation, rent and royalties more to the mid-level range of fair value, the opportunity arises to better reflect a realistic company valuation and better selling price.

The Transition Growth and Exit Planning process will guide a business owner through this normalization process step-by-step.

Chapter 20

Determine Business Exit-Specific Value

Why Do You Need To Know Business Value?

A universal ownership objective is to secure the income stream you will need to support the lifestyle you and your family plan to enjoy. Knowing the value of your business is critical if you are to successfully complete the Transition Growth and Exit Planning process. Knowing this value - and knowing how this value is determined – becomes important for the following reasons:

- Your business is generally your most valuable asset. Financial security depends on maximizing its value and converting that asset to cash (with minimum tax consequences). (Building Block 1).

- If you plan to transfer your business to an "insider," you need to know the relationship between business value, tax consequences of transfer, and cash flow requirements of the buyer. (Building Blocks 8 and 11).

- To find out whether your business is actually marketable to a third party buyer (and at what price). (Building Block 12).

- To find out which type of third party buyer will likely be interested in your business — and what specific features incent that type of buyer to buy at the best price. (Building Block 12).

- To provide guidance as to what areas of improvement in your business could best impact price. (Building Block 7).

- The type of buyer you sell to determines whether the "sale price" (at least for your "ownership" interest) should be high or low and whether other (more tax effective) ways to realize value from your business should be utilized. (Building Blocks 10, 11 and 12).

Why Does Your Transition Growth and Exit Advisor Team Need To Know This?

Your Transition Growth and Exit advisors need to have a solid understanding of your company's valuation for a number of reasons:

- It impacts Building Block 1 – Whether your objectives can be met.

- It impacts Building Blocks 4 and 10 – Determining whether you are operating under the optimal tax and legal business entity format.

- It impacts Building Block 11 – If your business growth, stability and eventual exit can benefit from beginning to transfer some ownership to key employees.

- It impacts Building Block 12 – To help gain an understanding of a realistic selling price (and terms) to a third party.

- It impacts Building Blocks 11 and 12 – To develop the cash flow model and type of sale techniques to help make a sale to insiders feasible and most attractive as to tax impact for both the seller and buyer.

- It impacts Building Block 5 – To understand how to define and determine value upon contingencies (upon death, disability, divorce, disputes and casualty loss), as well as how to fund a purchase upon these trigger events.

- It impacts Building Blocks 3 and 10 – To understand expected estate consequences (relating to tax matters and family equalization).

Case Study – Price Mis-Expectation

Howard was the owner of a west coast equipment manufacturing and distribution company, Howard Co. He had a close relationship with one of the banks with which we work. Both were interested in establishing a Transition Growth Plan for his eventual exit from active duty and ownership of Howard Co.

Howard anticipated selling the company to one or more of his key employees. As a basis for his pricing, he had supplied us with a recent appraisal of the company which indicated a company valuation of approximately $22 million. At this price, Howard estimated that a transfer of his stock would net him approximately $16 million after taxes, which reflected the "cash-in-pocket" which he wanted to walk away from the business with. He asked us about the feasibility of transferring his company to his key employees, and the bank was interested in the feasibility of financing the transaction.

Upon review of the appraisal, we noted that the appraiser had arrived at the $22 million company valuation by averaging four different business valuation techniques. These included a straight book value (which was approximately $30 million), along with a price/earnings valuation, a discounted cash flow valuation and an EBITDA multiple valuation (each of which indicated a valuation of approximately $15 million). In arriving at the estimated value for the company, the appraiser, incorrectly, primarily weighted the book value and gave a lesser weighted average amount to the other three valuation techniques. Based on consultation with our M &A market analyst, as well as a further valuation review, we estimated that the true value of the company was presently in the range of $16 million and that the bank financing as well as inside buyer price capability was in that range as well. Based on our financial benchmark analysis, we were able to identify areas in which the company was not performing up to industry average, which was impacting net income and net cash flow and was therefore the reason for the relatively higher book value valuation compared to the other valuation techniques. Howard decided to postpone his exit to allow him to work on addressing the improvements needed to the company to achieve the walkaway number he was after.

Various Types Of Valuations

During the transition process, a number of different types of business valuations are often discussed. These different types of valuations all tend to have the same objective, which is to establish a value for your ownership interest in the business which you (or your family in your absence) expect to receive, or would be satisfied to receive, in full exchange for your ownership interest. These differing types of valuations can come into play at or during various parts of the exit process.

Your business valuation initially provides some idea as to what your company is worth, as a means not only to provide you with an estimate of the value which your efforts have achieved, but also to provide your advisors with a valuation estimate for their planning purposes in helping you to achieve your objectives. Differing types of valuations can also be used in determining the price to be established for a transfer to insiders, the price to be established for a transfer to outsiders, and the price to be used in a Buy-Sell Agreement in the event something happens to you prior to your planned exit.

Some of the different types of valuation approaches include the following:

- **Preliminary Valuation.** This is a rough estimate of the value of your business, which can be determined relatively quickly, but which lacks much of the due diligence and analysis which would be part of a full business appraisal. This type of preliminary valuation can be performed by a financial advisor, a CPA, or an attorney, with the proviso, however, that it represents only a guide, but should not be viewed as a full, documented valuation of your business.

- **Walk-Away Value.** This is simply the value which you have determined you need at this point in time as a price to walk away from your business. This valuation may be significantly higher or lower than the true value of your business, and it simply represents the number you would be happy with.

- **Lowest Defensible Value.** It may seem odd that a seller should be looking to establish the lowest defensible value. However, this counterintuitive valuation approach is extremely useful when planning for an exit in which you are looking to minimize the total tax impact on both the seller and the buyer. To the extent that the total tax impact is minimized, this provides additional dollars on the table, which can either be provided as part of the compensation paid to the seller, or as a reduction in the total cash flow needs that the buyer must come up with in order to be able to accomplish the purchase. In essence, the objective of the lowest defensible value is to provide the ability to transfer actual ownership at a lesser price (defensible for tax purposes), while at the same time providing the seller with other exit compensation (e.g., deferred compensation for past services that have not yet been fully compensated). Because of the interplay of tax rates imposed on a seller to exit, as compared to the tax rates imposed on a buyer who is earning taxable cash with which to pay the seller, a combination of different types of compensation (e.g., sales price, consulting fees, deferred compensation, no-compete payments), can result in a more favorable overall outcome for both parties.

- **Appraised Value.** This represents the valuation of your business, based on a careful analysis of your company's historical results and the projected future results, with the application of current valuation principles and economic factors to reach an estimated value, documented in a written appraisal by a qualified business appraiser. This valuation typically represents the appraiser's determination of that price which a hypothetical buyer would pay to a hypothetical seller, each being under no compulsion to buy or sell, with each being aware of the relevant facts. This valuation may reflect the value of the company as a whole, or may reflect the valuation of a majority or minority interest in the company, which may or may not be a pro-rata portion of the value of the company as a whole, depending on the application of minority discounts or control premiums.

- **Negotiated Value.** This reflects the price for the company arrived at pursuant to negotiations between two unrelated parties; i.e., between a buyer presumably interested in paying the lowest price, and the seller, presumably interested in receiving the highest price.

- **Buyer-Specific Valuation.** This is a valuation based on the expected business value in light of the buyer-specific needs. For example, if your business possesses certain synergistic elements which would complement the business of the buyer, then this valuation may reflect a premium as compared to the price which might apply to a purely financial buyer.

- **Market Outlook Valuation.** This is an estimated value typically provided by a transaction intermediary (such as a business broker, a mid-range intermediary, or an investment banker) with the objective of providing you an estimate of what your business would bring on its sale today, under current economic conditions based on the industry which you are in and the types and extent of buyers existing today in the marketplace.

Valuation Methods

There are a number of valuation methods which are used, either by themselves or in combination, in each of the above types of business valuations. In the end, a true valuation for a closely held business is that price which an informed, willing buyer pays to an informed, willing seller. The following valuation methods are essentially simply the means by which buyers and sellers choose to inform themselves to determine their willingness to pay a certain price.

When the stock of a publicly held company is being valued, the process is much more precise. This is because stock in publicly held companies is valued every day by thousands of buyers and sellers who consider hundreds or thousands of relevant facts in reaching a determination as to what they will buy and sell the stock for. This, of course, depends on numerous factors which are internal and/or external to the company. Prevailing economic and financial sector conditions, as well as industry outlook, reflect some of the external factors. Internal factors include those various elements which reflect upon the profitability or cash flow of that particular company. The valuation which results is a true, as close to perfect as possible, valuation of that business at a particular moment, taking into account all of these external and internal factors. Even with this arguably near perfection in the public markets, there is room for better judgment, which reflects why some investment advisors will do better than others. In addition, there is room for immediate or rather rapid price changes in any given stock. A company that is worth $10 per share today might easily be "worth" $12 per share a week later, then be down to $8 per share a week after that.

The valuation methods used in valuing closely held companies reflect attempts by financial advisors to approximate the conditions of a public market, while reflecting the fact that the stock is not actually being traded on a public market. In the end, from a strictly financial and economic perspective, the value of a company today is the present value of the future stream of cash flow which that business enterprise will produce. This present value is a discounted future cash flow. In other words, it reflects the fact that a dollar today is worth more than a dollar received tomorrow or next year. A dollar received next year may, after application of the discount rate being reflected by the person doing the valuation, be worth only 75-95 cents today, in present value terms.

Some of the valuation methods used in valuing a closely held company include the following:

- **Book Value.** This may also be referred to as historical cost, adjusted book value, or depreciated book value. In essence, it represents the original cost (less depreciation where applicable) of all of a company's assets, offset by the total of the company's debts. This results in a net book value of the equity of the business. Depending on the type of business, this method of valuation might be highly relevant or it might be next to completely irrelevant. Rather than simply using straight book value, at times, it may be appropriate to use a multiple of book value. This may be true in particular, if there is evidence, for example, from the public marketplace, of companies trading hands at or within some range of book value multiples.

- **Recent Third Party Sales.** This method can reflect the valuation of a company when shares of stock in the company have been recently bought and sold between unrelated parties. This provides a reasonable indication of value to the extent that the amount of shares was significant, the two parties engaged in a meaningful negotiation which appropriately reflected valuation factors, and the transaction was relatively recent in time.

- **Price/Earnings Ratio.** This is also known as the PE ratio, which is a ratio of price to earnings. This is commonly used in reference to stocks traded on a public stock market. Often, stocks within a certain industry may trade within a certain PE ratio range at a given time during an economic cycle or under certain economic conditions. Stock traded on a public stock exchange is generally reflective of a minority share of stock in that company (and therefore, reflects a minority discount), but with no "lack of marketability" discount, because of the fact that the stock is generally easily marketable. Therefore, all other factors being considered equal for the sake of discussion, the PE ratio provides a useful reference to determine a company's valuation. In its essence, it reflects the rate of return that a buyer and seller would expect to see for the given risk level and future expectations of that company. For example, if a company was to be valued, if the marketplace for that type of company demanded a 10% rate of return, and the company was earning $8 per year, the price/value of that company should be $80. This is because 10% of $80 results in $8 of income. The PE ratio for the stock would be 10 ($80 divided by $8).

Once the appropriate PE ratio factor is known, it is necessary to determine what earnings will be used to determine the pricing. This will typically be some function of expected future earnings, which may be based on some average or weighted average of previous years as a reflection of expected future earnings.

- **Discounted Future Cash Flow.** Under this method, the present value of future expected dollars is literally discounted to today's net present value to determine the worth of the company. Typically, the expected future cash flow is estimated by management (based on historical results and reasoned future expectations) for the next 4-10 years, and a terminal valuation at the end of that 4-10 year period is also determined (i.e., as a reflection of cash flow after that timeframe). The sum of the net present value of these future cash streams reflects the valuation of the company.

- **EBITDA Multiple.** This is similar to a PE ratio; however, it reflects a valuation of the operations without a deduction for depreciation, amortization, or income taxes, and without reflecting the interest inherent in the debt structure of the company. EBITDA is Earnings Before Interest, Taxes, Depreciation and Amortization. The EBITDA to be used might be the most recent year or some simple or weighted average of the past few years, as a basis for estimating future expected years. For example, if the EBITDA for the company is $100,000, and the appropriate multiple is 5, then the business (before debt) is worth $500,000 for purposes of that valuation.

Premiums and Discounts

Once the valuation of the company as a whole is determined, the per-share true value is not necessarily a pro-rata portion of that total. This is because of the presence of premium and discount factors which influence the valuation of a share of stock.

The most common premiums and discounts fall into two main areas. The first area has to do with control or lack of control. If a share of stock is part of a controlling block of shares of stock in the company, then the per-share value, according to market influences, should be higher than the per-share value of a minority share of stock; i.e. of a share of stock which is not part of a controlling block of stock.

For example, if a company is worth $1 million as a whole, and there are 1,000 shares of stock, the implication is that each share of stock is worth $1,000. However, if you are the owner of only 100 of those shares of stock, it is less likely that a buyer would pay you a full pro-rata price, because the buyer would be purchasing a block of stock that does not have control over the business enterprise. In this case, a minority discount might be applied to the transaction.

These minority discounts can range significantly, but would commonly be in the range of a 20%-40% discount. Therefore, instead of your 10% share of the $1 million company being worth $100,000, it might only be worth $70,000 (assuming a 30% minority discount).

By contrast, the owner of 90% of the company might be entitled to a control premium. In other words, a buyer might be willing to pay more than $900,000 for that owner's 90% share of the company. In this case, if the control premium matched the minority discount, then the controlling owner might be entitled to a price of $930,000 for 90% of the corporation.

In practice, if the whole company is being sold, then it is likely that each seller would receive a pro-rata share of the overall price, based on percentage of ownership.

The second most common form of discount is a "lack of marketability" discount. This comes into play because a closely held company is not freely marketable on a stock exchange. A purchaser would typically be less than willing to pay a full pro-rata price for the company if the stock cannot be turned around and freely sold in the future. Since there is no public stock market for your stock, a lack of marketability discount could be applied in determining the value of your shares, whether these are minority shares or majority shares. The range of "lack of marketability" discounts is also broad, and depends on the circumstances, but might range from 10%-30%.

Valuation Facts
In order to value your company, it is necessary for the person doing the valuation to be provided with specific details regarding certain key facts affecting the company's financial and business outlook. Some of these facts can be gleaned from the following information:

- Credible financial statements (including income statement, balance sheet and cash flow statement) for the past five years.

- Company income tax returns for the past five years.

- Management forecasts of business operations for the next five years.

- Breakout of valuable intangible assets.

- Inspection of company facilities.

- Company status as leader in its particular market and product sectors.

- Industry and economic outlook.

- Status of litigation and other legal, business and competitive threats to the company.

- Depth of key management.

- Comparison of the company's financial results benchmarked with other similar companies in the same industry.

Relevance Of Rules Of Thumb

Certain rules of thumb are often mentioned with regard to valuation of a company. For example, you might be aware that another company in your industry recently sold for two times sales or 2.5 times book value.

By and large, these types of rules of thumb are not relevant to the value of your company. The factors that went into determining the price for that company may have had little to do with the multiple of sales or a multiple of book value, but instead dealt with the other types of facts and valuation methods discussed above. In the end, any price can be reflected as a multiple of sales or a multiple of book value, but that does not necessarily mean that that's a reflection of what your "basket" of tangible and intangible assets are going to be worth.

Other rules of thumb which are more reflective of the net comparable results of a company may be more relevant. For example, if companies in your industry are trading at four times EBITDA, this may be a reflection of the value of your company, since EBITDA often represents a true reflection of how well a given company is producing a net cash output.

Importance Of Cash Flows

To arrive at a valuation estimate (and to determine exit options and key employee retention alternatives), your exit advisors must have a good estimate of the expected annual cash flow your business can generate. Without this, a realistic Transition Growth Plan cannot be successfully developed.

Usefulness Of Preliminary Valuation

The above reflects simply some methods for arriving at some indicated valuations for your company. They do not represent a substitute for a good company business appraisal by a qualified business appraiser.

However, they do provide a way to develop a preliminary valuation, which is very useful in the Transition Growth and Exit Planning process. This is because the preliminary valuation can be arrived at fairly quickly which can help keep the Transition Growth and Exit Planning process moving forward without the need for an interim stoppage to obtain a full business appraisal.

Once the Transition Growth Plan is designed, depending on the Transition Growth and Exit Planning alternatives chosen and depending on the need for a more formal valuation, one of the Transition Growth Plan implementation steps can be to proceed with a full business appraisal, with the Transition Growth Plan then adjusted or accommodated to reflect the more certain indicated company valuation.

Valuing Your Particular Business

Various businesses will sell at particular valuation formulas due to the well-known nature, components, terms and conditions within your industry sector. These valuation methods are addressed in detail in the Transition Growth and Exit Planning process.

Building Block 3 - Protect My Family

Chapter 21

Update Regular Estate Plan

The Transition Growth and Exit Planning process also needs to address the financial plan which you want to leave behind for your family upon your death or permanent disability. Over the years, we have seen many business persons who brilliantly and very successfully operated their businesses during their lifetime, only to leave a mess or a disaster to be sifted through and sorted out by a surviving spouse or children upon their death or disability.

This is the type of final act which they generally did not intend to leave, but it was the direct result of their failure either to establish an Estate Plan or to establish an Estate Plan which was properly tailored to them as a business owner. Business owners have unique and more involved details which need to be addressed in a tailored Estate Plan suitable for business owners.

Had these business owners stopped to consider the likely outcome of their present course, they would have been able to detect those items which were missing, the presence of which would have provided a substantially better outcome for the legacy they undoubtedly wished they had left for their families.

This Chapter addresses the financial plan you want to leave – to prevent a mess that needs to be cleaned up by others and to have an Estate Plan which fits with your Transition Growth Plan.

Establishing Your Basic Estate Plan

As an initial starting point in the review of the health of your Estate Plan, you should consider whether you have in place the elements of a good Basic Estate Plan. These initial elements consist of the following basic documents, each with the following objectives:

- **Financial Power of Attorney.** If you were to become disabled to the point at which you are unable to handle your financial affairs, the laws in almost all states provide you and your family with two main alternatives for addressing your ongoing financial matters during the course of your disability. First, your family could file an application for the appointment of a conservator with the local probate court. Under this alternative, the family would typically need to hire an attorney to represent the family in court, during which time the family could recommend the appointment of a specific person by the judge to handle your financial affairs. This person has the legal title of a "conservator". Once appointed, the conservator is obligated to periodically report back to the court to summarize the financial matters which he or she handled on your behalf.

The other alternative is for you to execute a durable financial power of attorney before you are disabled. This is the preferred option, since it provides a step which you can take in advance to designate a person (and successors) to handle your financial affairs for you. Then, upon your disability, no court process is needed. Instead, the person you appointed is able to immediately step in to deal with financial matters as needed.

- **Health Care Power of Attorney.** The law provides you with two similar alternatives for dealing with your health care matters if you are disabled and unable to do so. First, your family can make an application to the local probate court to have someone appointed as your "guardian" to handle your medical affairs during your incapacity.

  The second alternative is for you to execute a durable health care power of attorney before you are disabled. Under this type of instrument, you can designate in advance the person (and successors) whom you would like to handle your medical affairs should you be unable to do so.

- **Health Care Directive (Living Will).** Most people understand this document as the "pull-the-plug" document. State law allows you to execute this type of advance directive which provides the legal authority to your physician and to the hospital to withhold or withdraw medical treatments which are considered to be extraordinary, i.e. those which present a disproportionate burden compared to the potential benefits. If this instrument is not executed in advance, then your family and health care providers are left to attempt to determine your wishes and may be in a position to be unable to legally implement them.

- **Pour-Over Will.** This is the type of Will which is typically used today for persons who wish to avoid the probate court process. As will be discussed next, this probate court process can best be avoided through the use of a Living Trust. The Pour-Over Will is used in conjunction with a Living Trust in order to transfer property into the trust upon your death, to the extent of property which you did not transfer into your Living Trust during your lifetime. The Pour-Over Will is also used by parents who have minor or disabled children, as a means to appoint a guardian and conservator for those children. The Pour-Over Will is also used to appoint your personal representative (executor) for your estate.

- **Estate Plan Letter.** This document is a detailed, practical instrument which enables you to specify certain wishes, and to detail certain information prior to your death, so that this information is available for your family. This specifically contains directions relating to your funeral and burial wishes, special gift of personal effects and mementos to your family and friends, a record of your key advisors and close friends, details specifying the location of your key financial and business records and instructions for raising your minor children.

The Living Trust

The anchor document to a good basic Estate Plan is the Living Trust. The Living Trust is the principal method in use today for avoiding probate court. Probate court is the process which our legal system utilizes for approving the transfer of title of assets out of the name of a deceased person into the names of that person's living heirs. This process typically requires that the family hire an attorney to open a probate court file upon your death, during which your last Will, and inventory of your assets, a listing of your creditors, and other information regarding your estate is required to be submitted to the court.

This process provides an opportunity for those who are interested to file an objection to challenge your Will or to challenge the liabilities which are reported as owing. The information filed with the court is typically open for public review. The process can typically take from nine months to two years. If challenges to the Will or other matters are filed by heirs or other interested persons, then the process can take longer.

The process can also be extended if liabilities are challenged, if the federal estate tax clearance process takes additional time due, for example, to an IRS audit, or if the estate is involved in a business dispute on account of a business issue that is pending or which arises on account of your death.

The laws in most states allow you to avoid the probate court process by executing, during your lifetime, a Living Trust. In essence, a Living Trust can be viewed as a bucket which you have created into which you have placed the instructions for how you would like your assets to be handled upon your death.

This set of instructions can include the provisions for distributing your estate to your spouse, provisions for holding your estate in trust for your children, and/or grandchildren for distribution upon certain terms or upon certain ages, and can include provisions detailing your charitable bequests. These instructions are completely revocable and completely amendable by you up until the date of your death.

Typically a separate Living Trust will be executed by the husband and by the wife (although for smaller estates a joint Living Trust can be utilized). The Living Trust will also typically contain the provisions which can be utilized to help attain the full lifetime federal estate tax exemption for both the husband and the wife.

You may have heard that Living Trusts can be referred to as a funded Living Trust or an unfunded Living Trust. Typically, in both situations, the Living Trust is the same. The difference is whether you have re-titled your assets into the name of your Living Trust.

This is essentially equivalent to an empty bucket (containing only your set of instructions) or a bucket into which you have placed your assets along with your set of instructions. If you placed ownership of your assets into your bucket during your lifetime, then upon your death, there is no need for the probate court process, because you have already handled the re-titling which the probate court would otherwise accomplish.

In essence, you have filled your bucket and, by naming appropriate persons (known as successor trustees) as part of your set of instructions, your bucket is automatically handed off by you to your successor trustee upon your death. Your Living Trust can also contain provisions which state that if you are disabled, then your Living Trust bucket is also handed off to your successor trustee during that period during which you are disabled.

Comparing The Difference A Living Trust Can Make

The Living Trust has become the tool of choice for parents across the country who want to maximize the Estate Planning opportunities and protections available for their families. The following chart compares the main features of the Living Trust.

During Your Life Your Living Trust Will:

- Allow you to manage and have total control over the assets of the Trust during your life.

- Allow you to amend or revoke your Trust any time for any reason.

- Allow you to add property to, or take property out of, your Trust at any time.

- Protect against conservatorship proceedings (or living probate) if you become legally incompetent or disabled.

After Your Death Your Living Trust Will:

- Distribute your assets to your spouse, children or other heirs as you've directed or continue to hold your assets in trust for certain beneficiaries (such as minors, young adults, grandchildren and spendthrifts) until an age or ages when they are financially responsible.

- Avoid or substantially reduce estate taxes, depending on the size of your estate, by obtaining the $3,500,000 (as of 2009) lifetime estate tax exemption for both spouses for married couples.

- Avoid probate for all assets and property transferred to the Trust during your life.

- Receive all assets probated after your death from your Will that were not transferred to the Trust during your life.

- Receive all life insurance and retirement plan proceeds where you've named the Trust as the beneficiary.

- Reduce the risk of a Will contest and court challenges to your Estate Plan.

Chapter 22

Pre-Fund Charitable and Education Goals

Accomplishing Charitable Objectives

Your transition from your company provides an opportunity to help meet your charitable objectives. Not only does it result in potential cash to meet charitable intentions, the use of certain charitable giving tools can reduce the tax cost of your exit, particularly if implemented **before** your exit.

Some of the charitable planned giving tools particularly useful in advance of your exit include the following:

- **Private Foundation.** The private foundation is a non-profit, tax-exempt corporation which can be established and controlled by you during your lifetime and by your family after you are gone. Stock in your company (within certain limits) transferred to a private foundation before the company is sold can avoid capital gain tax on that portion of your sale proceeds. In addition, the sale proceeds can remain in the foundation, earning income tax free, subject only to the requirement that at least five percent of the foundation assets be distributed each year for charitable purposes.

- **Charitable Remainder Trust.** Capital gain tax can also be avoided when a portion of your stock is transferred into a charitable remainder trust prior to execution of a stock sale agreement. In a charitable remainder trust, you can retain the right to distributions from the trust for your life or for a term of years (for you and your spouse), with the remainder to be distributed to charity at the end of such term or your deaths. Certain limitations apply, which are beyond the scope of this book, but which can be explained by your exit advisors.

- **"Intentionally Defective" Grantor Trust.** This charitable planning technique provides an opportunity, especially when funded with life insurance, to accomplish charitable and family obligations in a way that is very tax efficient (for income, gift and estate tax purposes).

Funding An Education Plan Upon Your Exit

As Harvard University professor Derek Bok has stated "If you think education is expensive, try ignorance."

Your exit from your company also provides you with the opportunity to help fund education needs for your children and grandchildren, assuming that your exit will result in cash proceeds from a sale. When this occurs before you exit, certain capital gain tax savings can result to the family, by shifting some of the capital gain to children and grandchildren in lower tax brackets.

The details of the various education funding alternatives are beyond the scope of this book. Some of the education funding tools include children education trusts, grandchildren education trusts, family limited partnership, limited liability company, Section 529 Plans, outright lifetime gifts, and specific bequests in a Living Trust.

Strategic Personal Philanthropy

Rather than simply designating a charity for a portion of your estate (for gifts today and in the future), the Transition Growth and Exit Planning process utilizes a "Strategic Philanthropy" approach to help you address the particular passions that you, your family, and in some cases, your employees, wish to influence. These passions might relate to community, charitable, scientific, education, health care or other areas of particular need or interest to the legacy you would like to help create.

This approach also enables you to determine the optimum type of charitable giving, whether this be through direct lifetime gifts or gifts after death, and the use of donor advised funds or private foundations.

Chapter 23

Protect Your Personal Assets

In the litigious society in which we live, it is generally prudent to protect your hard-earned assets through certain asset protection tools. These types of tools can protect your investment and other assets against unwarranted and unexpected, but potential, creditor claims, which may arise, for example, from business operations, personal accidents, personal injury, or other casualties and contingencies. The following are some examples of pre-exit personal asset protection planning tools which you should consider:

- **Observance of Corporate Formalities.** It is common knowledge that if you operate your business within a limited liability type of entity (such as a corporation or a limited liability company), then you are generally protected, as an owner, from liabilities incurred by the business operations. However, a significant exception to this rule is the legal principle known as "pierce the corporate veil". Under this principle, if you have not observed the corporate formalities of operating as a separate corporation or limited liability company, then, if challenged, a court has the authority to "pierce the corporate veil" by ignoring the presence of the corporation or limited liability company. Typically this occurs when two principal facts exist. First, when you have not provided reasonable operating funds within the business entity. Second, when you have ignored the usual formalities of treating that corporate entity as a separate legal entity (e.g. because you have not maintained separate bank accounts and corporate business records).

- **Removal of Personal Guarantees.** During the course of the life of your business, you may have been required, in order to obtain bank financing, to sign a personal guarantee on business debts. As your business becomes able to financially stand on its own, the removal of your personal guarantees should be negotiated when your business loans are being refinanced or replaced. This extends not only to your personal liability, but also to your pledge of personal assets as collateral for business obligations.

- **Operating in Limited Liability Entities.** Often we find that business operations are being conducted by business owners without the protection of a limited liability entity (i.e. a corporation or limited liability company). For example, if your business is held in your name as a sole proprietorship, or is held in a general partnership or a limited partnership, you run the risk, as the business owner, of being liable for all of the business debts.

- **Irrevocable Trust.** When investment assets are transferred out of your name as a gift to a family member, then those assets are not subject to your personal risk. Gifted assets would typically, however, be subject to the personal liability risk of the individuals who received your gift. By transferring investment and/or life insurance assets into an irrevocable trust for the benefit of your children or grandchildren, you can remove the assets from your personal exposure. By placing spendthrift provisions in the trust, you can also protect these assets from the personal liability exposures of your children and grandchildren.

- **Multiple Business Entities.** If you operate certain businesses which are more risky than others, then you can consider placing the businesses into separate business entities, so that a given business risk does not expose all of your business assets to those liabilities.

- **Asset Balance Between Spouses.** Both spouses typically have a certain amount of potential liability exposure (e.g. due to personal accidents). However, typically, the spouse who is active in business has a greater level of potential creditor claims. By balancing your assets between the two spouses, you can minimize the risk of a more substantial loss of assets than if your net worth is entirely in the name of the spouse who is most subject to liability exposure.

- **Investment Protection Entities.** Just as you can place a business operation into a corporate entity to shield yourself from those business risks, you can also place your investment assets into certain types of limited partnerships, limited liability companies, and asset protection trusts, in order to shield those assets from your business and personal risks. Under these types of entities, a litigation judgment against you can typically not be collected against the assets of the asset protection partnership or trust. Asset protection partnerships, LLCs or trusts established in the United States may provide a certain degree of protection. Due to more favorable laws enacted by some countries, a foreign asset protection trust may provide a higher degree of protection, although it also costs a significant amount more to implement and its effectiveness has been challenged in recent years.

- **Proper Insurance Coverage Mix.** The proper mix of business and personal casualty insurance protection, along with business and personal umbrella insurance should be implemented and periodically reviewed, depending on changing business operations and personal situation.

Chapter 24

Meet Business Owner Estate Needs

While the estate planning needs of a business owner include the same issues as non-business owners, your business ownership brings into play a series of additional estate planning issues and options to be addressed.

Case Study – The Widow

Sam and Sally were married in college and started a real estate development company shortly after graduation. Sam worked full-time in the business, while Sally helped to manage the office part-time, spending the balance of her time raising their children. They were very successful and ended up branching out into a number of retail operations. When Sam was 55, he was in a fatal car crash at the prime of their business life. Unfortunately, while Sam and Sally got along well, they did not get along well with some of their children. They also were an example of a couple who was too busy working in their business to work on their business. At the time of Sam's death, his only estate plan document consisted of a Will, which left a portion of the property to Sally and, to Sally's surprise, contained provisions which left approximately half of the estate directly to their children. The Will had been drafted prior to the 1981 change to the federal estate tax laws which allowed for a full 100% marital deduction rather than a deduction limited to 50% of the estate. Unfortunately, Sam and Sally had never gotten around to updating their Estate Plan before Sam's death.

In addition to not updating their estate plan, Sam and Sally had not developed an transition growth plan. They had never focused on developing a successor to Sam in operating their various businesses, and at the point of Sam's death, Sally was in no position to step in to try to run the companies. As a result, a number of their operations had to be liquidated, while at the same time some of the children decided to challenge their mother in court, claiming a full 50% of the estate. Uncle Sam also wanted his part, since the pre-1981 Will failed to utilize the full post-1981 marital deduction, resulting in an estate tax of approximately $2 million.

While we were able to negotiate a settlement with the children to drop their claim, this case illustrates the importance of addressing the Transition Growth process features in order to be prepared both for a planned and unexpected exit from your business.

Business Owner Estate Plan Provisions

As the owner of a business, you will often have estate planning needs which extend beyond the typical Estate Plan. This may be due to certain financial or business needs of the business or because of particular family issues which are already present or may arise upon your death or disability. In order to help address these types of specific estate planning issues, you may want to consider the use of the following tools.

- **Specific Bequest to Business-Active Children.** If you have one or more children who are active in the business and one or more children who are not, you need to consider whether you want to make a specific bequest of your business ownership interest to the active children, so that they have ownership control as well as the valuation benefit on account of their decision to be active in your business.

- **Non-Active Children Equalization.** When the business ownership has been specifically allocated in your estate to one or more children active in the business, an equalizing share can be allocated to non-active children through a specific bequest of other financial assets. If your estate does not have sufficient other financial assets to fully equalize the shares, then at least two other options exist. This can include a split off of non-operating business assets into a separate leasing or licensing entity which can be allocated to the non-active children. This would still leave the business operating assets intact in the business entity to be owned by the active children. As an alternative, life insurance can be obtained which would help fund the equalization to the non-active children.

- **Family Business Representative.** Typically an estate plan will appoint a personal representative (executor) and a successor trustee to handle financial and business decisions for your estate. In those situations where that representative or trustee is not well-equipped to make business decisions impacting your ongoing business, a family business representative can be appointed in your Estate Plan to make business decisions relating to management of the business. You have at least two ways this can be done. First, this representative can be given authority in your Estate Plan to override your regular trustee's authority. Second, the representative can be viewed as essentially an advisor, whose decisions are subject to the overriding decision-making authority of your regular successor trustee.

- **Business Sale Instructions.** As part of your Transition Growth Plan, if you have not completed your exit from your business at the time of your death or disability, but believe that the best alternative for the family is that the business be sold, then your Transition Growth Plan should contain sufficient details to provide instructions on how and to whom your business can best be sold or transferred should you die or become disabled before you complete your exit.

- **Successor CEO.** Your Transition Growth Plan can also designate your recommended successor CEO for the business. This is particularly important if at least two children may each claim that you intended to appoint them to run the company.

- **Contingency Plan Notifications.** Your Transition Growth Plan should also contain contingency plan notifications to your family and to your Board of Directors which detail the immediate steps to be taken upon your death or disability.

- **"Sweat" Equity Allocation.** You may decide that your estate is not to be divided exactly equally between your children due to a difference between the role which your children have played in the success or operation of your business. Your Estate Plan can include an allocation with regard to your business assets which recognizes the "sweat equity" contribution of those children who have been active in the business but who have been under-compensated based on their contribution to the success of the business.

- **Dispute Resolution.** If you have more than one child, it is possible your estate will encounter a dispute once you are no longer present. Your Estate Plan can include a dispute resolution provision which prevents a dissatisfied child from disrupting business operations. A dispute resolution provision can range from the appointment of a mediator to help resolve disputes, to instead including a provision which disinherits a child who challenges your Estate Plan.

- **Financial Resource Reserve.** If your business needs your ongoing financial support in order to thrive, then your Estate Plan can designate that a reserve portion of your estate be held as a financial resource to help support the business and/or its credit needs.

- **Family Council.** Your Estate Plan can designate a Family Council to be established to enable your spouse and adult children to be apprised of ongoing business operations and to discuss resolution of business matters impacting the family. Depending on the make up of your family and your use of a board of directors, in lieu of a Family Council, you can consider having your children serve on your Board of Directors as either voting or non-voting board members, as an additional way to keep the family members apprised of the ongoing challenges associated with the business.

- **Business Continuity Agreement.** While a Business Continuity Agreement can be utilized to help prevent disputes among co-owners during your lifetime, it can also be implemented following your death to help avoid ongoing or new disputes amongst family members. A Business Continuity Agreement can include provisions such as a family employment policy, a family compensation setting program (utilizing an outside compensation professional), a dividend payout policy, a stock redemption policy and voting agreement provisions.

Many of the above provisions can be included in your Living Trust or in alternative business documents executed prior to your death or disability pursuant to your Transition Growth Plan.

Chapter 25

Pre-Fund Personal Financial Gap Needs

Upon your (or your spouse's) death or disability you and your family will obviously face a different financial landscape than that which you would be facing without this adversity. The scope and extent of this is best addressed through a detailed Financial Needs Analysis performed by a financial advisor.

For example, if you and your family rely on your salary to cover living expenses and personal debts, the failure to have sufficient life insurance or disability insurance payable on your death or disability will either result in a financial shortfall to your family or could put a bind on your business if the business needs to both replace you and continue to pay your salary.

In addition to covering living expenses, your death could result in estate taxes, which may also put a bind on your family or your business if your ownership needs to quickly be turned into cash.

The Transition Growth and Exit Planning process will estimate your present ability to meet these needs and recommend changes to improve your shortfalls.

The following provides a way to estimate your personal ability to cover the following contingencies (based on your estimated needs and on expected cash and insurance funds you estimate you would have available):

Pre-Funding Financial Gap Due To Your And Your Spouse's Death or Disability

A. Cash Needed	Due To			
	My Death	My Disability	Spouse Death	Spouse Disability
• Living Expenses	$_____	$_____	$_____	$_____
• Support Spouse	_____	_____	_____	_____
• Support Children	_____	_____	_____	_____
• Child Education	_____	_____	_____	_____
• Grandchild Education	_____	_____	_____	_____
• Leave Inheritance	_____	_____	_____	_____
• Charity	_____	_____	_____	_____
• Other: _____	_____	_____	_____	_____
• Other: _____	_____	_____	_____	_____
• Other: _____	_____	_____	_____	_____
• Other: _____	_____	_____	_____	_____
Total $ Needed	$_____	$_____	$_____	$_____
B. Cash Available				
• "Cash-In-Pocket" Today	$_____	$_____	$_____	$_____
• Business Sale $	_____	_____	_____	_____
• Existing Insurance	_____	_____	_____	_____
Total $ Available	$_____	$_____	$_____	$_____
C. Shortfall A-B=C	$_____	$_____	$_____	$_____

These are the questions you should address:
• If you show a Shortfall, do you want to address this?
• How much of the Shortfall do you want to close?
• Do you want to obtain an insurance proposal detailing the type of insurance coverages which are optimum for your situation?
• Do you have an insurance advisor who can provide this?

Chapter 26

Adopt A Salary Continuation Plan

If you are still actively employed in your company, you are presumably still drawing a salary on which you, your spouse and perhaps your children are fully or largely dependent.

Assuming that you have been one of the principal driving forces for your company for some time, the odds are that you have taken an approach to your past compensation, not unlike that of many closely held business owners throughout the country - - you have probably drawn a salary less than the full fair market value compensation which you could have earned, because you have chosen instead to keep those funds working within the company.

This undercompensation can form the basis for an understanding amongst co-owners that upon your death or disability, the company will continue to provide a salary to you (if you are disabled) or to your beneficiary (spouse or children) upon your death or disability. This is known as a Salary Continuation Plan or Agreement.

Case Study – Salary Continuation Agreement

Larry and Suzy were introduced by mutual friends in college and married shortly after graduation. Larry soon became a respected inventor and developed a manufacturing business providing components to the developing personal computer industry. While Suzy stayed home to raise 6 children, Larry worked hard to develop and maintain the business through a series of successes and setbacks, eventually establishing a consistently predictable cash flow generating business at the time of his death after a long illness at age 60.

We visited with Larry about his Transition Growth Planning about 10 years before his death. He expressed the desire to transition the ownership of the business to his children, but also to make sure that there would be no dispute about a continuation of his salary to Suzy if something should happen to him. He was in good health at the time, so we implemented a salary continuation agreement with the company, backed up by a $2 million life insurance policy to make it easier for the corporation to fund the salary continuation payments to Suzy upon Larry's death.

This case illustrates a business owner who took the time to make sure that the number one person in his life would not have to worry about a continuing income upon his death, while at the same time he provided a continuing means of income and livelihood for his children into the next generation.

This can be structured for your company to provide all or some set portion of your most recent salary levels, to be paid on a periodic basis, for either a fixed number of years or until the death of your spouse.

Since the event arises due to your death or disability, it can be funded (assuming you are insurable) with an investment by the company in life insurance and disability insurance. Such an agreement should be established in advance of your death or disability and should be approved by the company's Board of Directors.

My Existing Salary Continuation Plan

Upon my death or disability, my salary to support my spouse and family will typically stop (or not be affordable by the company) unless prior arrangements have been made. This could be changed through a funded Salary Continuation Plan or Agreement.

I have the following in place:

☐ I have no Salary Continuation Plan or Agreement.
☐ I have a Salary Continuation Plan or Agreement which provides my spouse/family with a continued salary equal to ☐ $_____/year or ☐ _____% of my regular salary/year - - for _____ years.
    ☐ This plan is not funded
    ☐ This plan is funded with:
        ☐ $_____ Life Insurance
        ☐ $_____ Lump Sum or $_____ Monthly Disability Insurance.

Building Block 4 - Protect My Business

Chapter 27

Structure Business Entities For Asset Protection

One of the first keys to protecting your business is to operate under the best corporate structure. Businesses operate under a variety of corporate and affiliate legal structures. Often the entire business operation, along with all of its assets, is simply held in one entity, which is typically a corporation or a limited liability company.

There are a number of reasons for operating the business within a legal entity, rather than simply in the name of the business owner as a sole proprietor. These include the ability to limit an owner's personal liability from the debts or liabilities of the business and to provide an entity which is the legal owner of the basket of assets and revenues of the business operation as well as continuity of the venture upon the death or disability of the owner.

Depending on the size, scope and nature of the business operations, more than one legal entity is often used. For example, it is common to have a parent-subsidiary corporate structure or to have a parent corporation which owns more than one subsidiary in a parent-brother-sister operation.

Reasons for this structure may include a desire to shield potential liabilities of one business operation from the assets and revenues of another business operation. This structure may also provide a means to more easily have separate accounting and separate lines of responsibility for each business division or location.

When business owners start to contemplate their exit, (which ought to occur from day one of the business operation, but which often does not), they need to consider whether their corporate structure (entity, asset and debt structure) is in line with their exit objectives.

Case Study – Business Entity Restructuring

When approached about 20 years ago to help plan for potential exit alternatives by the founder and owner of JoCo, a manufacturing company, we wanted to accomplish a number of personal, financial and exit objectives, which could only be accomplished if the business entity structure was revised. The company was comprised of 2 principal divisions, each of which manufactured a separate product line in different product industries. As it turned out, one product line was more profitable than the other and also would more likely be the division to be sold to a third party should that opportunity be pursued in the future. As one business operation, however, the lesser profitable division resulted in an average net earnings which dragged down the financial appearance of the better division. In addition, the business owner had two capable family members and wanted each of them to preside over a specific division.

In this case, we suggested that the company should be split up into two separate corporations (which can be accomplished in a tax free reorganization) following which both corporations elected to become "S" corporations for exit tax planning purposes. This provided two separate corporations, each of which could establish its own financial statement track record for possible future sale to an outside third party.

The business owner also owned certain real estate and equipment used in one of the business operations, which we transferred into a newly formed limited liability company to help protect him against future potential liabilities with regard to property and to also provide a flow-through entity for income tax planning purposes. This also had the advantage, by keeping the property separate, of enabling the owner to retain the real estate and equipment and simply continue the lease of this property to the corporation in the event of a future sale of the business operations.

A Transition Growth Plan should contain a review of the business owner's objectives in light of its present business operating structure to determine whether any revisions to that structure are needed for Transition Growth and Exit Planning purposes.

Chapter 28

Plan For Pre-Exit Potential Dispute Avoidance

What do you expect will happen to your company if you were no longer around to act as the "traffic cop" to avoid collisions or as the "mediator" to resolve disputes? What already existing disputes will boil over? What latent potential disputes will surface?

This relates not only to those "constituencies" within your company but also to those outside your company which interact with you and other company personnel.

Case Study - Avoiding Disputes In Nebraska

This one isn't really a case study, but it's a good story. A big city lawyer went pheasant hunting in rural Nebraska where he shot and dropped a bird which fell into a farmer's field. The field was surrounded by a fence and as the lawyer was climbing over the fence to retrieve this bird that he had shot, an elderly farmer rode up on his tractor and demanded to know what the lawyer was doing. The lawyer responded "Well, I just shot a pheasant and it fell into this field, and now I am going to retrieve it". The old farmer replied, "This is my property you hot shot city slicker and you're not coming over that fence". Well, this unfortunately really punched the lawyer's buttons who indignantly sputtered "You old hayseed, you ignorant country bumpkin, I'll have you know I am one of the most successful trial attorneys in the United States and if you won't let me get my bird, I'll sue and take your tractor, your farm and everything you own." The old farmer smiled and scratched his chin and said "Apparently you don't know how we settle disputes here in Nebraska. We settle small disagreements like this one here with the Nebraska three kick rule." "What on earth," asked the attorney, "is the Nebraska three kick rule?" "Well," the farmer replied, "since the dispute occurred on my land, I first kick you three times, and then you kick me three times and so on and back and forth until someone gives up." The cocky lawyer quickly thought about the proposed contest and decided he could easily take this old codger so he agreed to abide by the local custom. The old farmer slowly climbed down from his tractor and calmly walked up to the attorney. His first kick planted the toe of his heavy steel toed work boot into the lawyer's groin and dropped him to his knees. His second kick, this one to the midriff, sent the lawyer on all fours. The old farmer circled around behind him and delivered his third kick to the lawyer's rear end, sending him face first into a fence post. The lawyer, groaning with pain and humiliation, summoned every ounce of willpower he had left and slowly staggered to his feet. Wiping off his face with the sleeve of his expensive Eddie Bauer hunting jacket, he choked out "Okay, you little coot, you will rue the day you ever challenged me to a contest by the Nebraska three kick rule. Now its my turn." The old farmer smiled, climbed back up onto his tractor, revved the engine and stuck it into gear and drawled "Awe, I give up young feller, you can have the pheasant."

How do you resolve disputes? Your exit is likely to cause some. We are a dispute-oriented society. If any of your exit constituencies believe they have a claim, they can generally find a lawyer or some activist to help them take it on. U.S. lawsuits cost more than $200 billion per year, the equivalent of about 2% of gross domestic product. Over a five year period, at least one in every four small businesses will be sued or threatened with a lawsuit.

It's important to think through ahead of time how to avoid potential disputes and to understand the means for resolving them. This question is important to a potential buyer, who doesn't want to walk into a minefield. It's also important to your key employees and family, so they don't inherit the minefield upon your death or disability or other exit.

The Transition Growth Plan process can identify where the "landmines" are located and help you address the right measures to "diffuse" them before they are stepped on by you or your successors.

Utilizing A Corporate Board of Directors

The proper use of a corporate Board of Directors in the governance of your company can be crucial to the short and long term success of the company, as well as to the avoidance and resolution of disputes. While this is detailed further in the Next Move Program module of this Building Block, such a functioning Board (if properly composed and utilized) can help guide the company business strategic planning, officer selection and compensation, dispute avoidance, dispute resolution and overall corporate management and well-being matters.

Chapter 29

Protect Transferable Intangible Assets

You cannot successfully transition from your business under the financial terms you might wish if you have not sufficiently protected your business along the way. Too many businesses – both large and small – fail to survive due to reasons that are often self-inflicted and avoidable.

This chapter is intended to help you and your advisors focus on those areas which often cause companies financial distress or destruction and which may need some "shaping up" for your company. This will help protect your business while you own it <u>and</u> will also provide a much more saleable business to a buyer.

Protecting Key Assets

What is it that adds value to your company – not merely while you own it, but also from the perspective of a potential buyer who is evaluating the price to pay for your company. In its simplest terms, the value of your business to a potential buyer can be measured based on the expected future cash flow which your business will produce, either by itself or as part of a larger organization.

The price which the buyer is willing to pay for this future cash flow depends on the predictability, sustainability and growth of that future cash flow. These elements of value depend on the continued presence of the key tangible and intangible assets which you have developed, assembled and implemented within your company. To the extent that these tangible and intangible assets work in sync to efficiently produce a product or service (and a process for developing new products and services) which a suitable marketplace of buyers needs or wants, then you have created a business for which you can negotiate some type of measurable price.

Identifying And Protecting Your Intangibles

The discussion of intangible assets is extremely important in the context of a business owner preparing to exit his or her business. These intangible assets are the life blood to most business operations. In Building Block 2 we identified the types of key intangible assets commonly utilized in business operations and which are valuable to a potential buyer.

Without these intangibles, the physical plant and equipment associated with your business take on only a liquidation value. A Transition Growth and Exit Planning review should help you to uncover those areas of your business in which you have not adequately protected your intangible assets. Some of the tools in this area include trademark/service mark and trade name registrations, patents for unique products and processes, trade secret confidentiality agreements, defensible covenants not-to-compete agreements, non-solicitation agreements and employment agreements.

Case Study – Protection of Intangible Assets

Craig had a sales organization which he had built but had just recently suffered a serious setback when he came to us to talk about his Transition Growth Planning. He had helped develop three key employees whom he felt were primed and ready to eventually take over and purchase the business from him. Unfortunately, he had not yet communicated his vision for these employees to the employees themselves. Shortly before he met with us, these three key employees decided that their best future would be to develop a new business on their own. So they left Craig and took their book of business with them. Much of this business had been initially developed by Craig, who had been transitioning his contacts over to these three individuals.

One of the first steps which we implemented with Craig was to establish an intangible asset protection program in which his remaining key employees were required to execute certain no-compete and non-solicitation agreements which prohibited or significantly limited their ability to take existing customers and staff with them should they decide to leave and develop a separate business on their own. The next step in the development of Craig's transition growth plan was to develop a key employee incentive which started to bring his new group of key employees into a minority ownership position with the company, with the prospects of eventually purchasing the balance of Craig's business in the future.

Protecting The "No Contingent Liabilities" Intangible

Each day every business in this country is faced with the risk of being hit with an unexpected event arising on account of any of several occurrences. We have seen the destructive force of these types of events arise within various industries and businesses throughout the country over the past couple of decades. This may be due to business cycle occurrences, unexpectedly swift changes in the economic cycle, new exactions within the regulatory environment, technological gains and financial market rollercoasters.

These types of sweeping changes to the business environment can present disasters for some, as well as tremendous opportunities for others. For example, the financial bankruptcies which prompted the government's reaction to its regulation of the savings and loan industry a couple of decades ago, presented new opportunities for product growth and location expansions in the financial institution sector. The government's reaction to stock market declines and ill-advised business transactions lead to knew services and techniques for accounting firms and law firms. Swift advances in software and related technology companies resulted in an equally swift demise of various businesses and the swift growth in opportunities capitalized on by other businesses.

These potentially destructive forces, and the potentially tremendous opportunities which the world of business has encountered at an accelerating pace, can only be expected to continue into the future.

To a large extent, this rapid change has been fueling certain aspects of the merger and acquisition marketplace. This has prompted many business owners to sell at valuations which only a few years earlier would have been unheard of. Likewise, it has prompted other business owners to sell their business while they can, rather than continue the every day fight to stay in the game.

Unfortunately, many of the business-destroying events which have afflicted business owners have been self-inflicted due to their own negligence by failing to put adequate protective measures into place.

None of us can predict when or if our home might be struck by lightning, a tornado, a fire, a flood, or a vandal. Most of us protect this asset through a variety of techniques available to each of us. This obviously includes a range of products and services starting with homeowner's insurance and umbrella insurance, to basic door and window locks, a fence and possibly an electronic security system.

We also tend to be equally protective of our cash. For example, most of us will not exceed the FDIC limits on a savings account and would opt for opening a second account at another financial institution rather than going over the dollar limit at the first financial institution.

In the context of planning your eventual exit from your business, it's important to preserve the value of your assets by minimizing the potential contingent liability exposures which you are subject to. Not only do these types of claims take money from your pocket, but they also reduce the potential selling price for your business if they are pending at the time of your sale. These kinds of claims might arise in a number of forms, including product liability claims, employment termination claims, pending tax audits, environmental accidents, worksite employee accident claims, employment discrimination claims, customer accident claims, contract disputes, manufacturer claims, and other pending litigation.

The nature and scope of these types of claims changes over time. This is why it is important to have in place a system for periodically reviewing your exposure. A good casualty insurance firm will help you to identify the risks most pertinent to your type of business operation. This type of annual review has the benefit of optimizing your premium dollars while making sure you provided yourself with appropriate amounts of casualty and business interruption insurance.

A legal audit or other due diligence review can help to address other exposures and help to protect both your tangible and intangible assets.

Chapter 30

Develop Contingency Instructions

Adverse Events

Most of a Transition Growth Plan is focused on helping to provide a better outcome for **your planned** exit. This Building Block 4 is concerned with taking prudent advance measures to help make sure that the business continues, even if you or another co-owner don't. This Building Block 4 is intended to help protect your business when the unexpected event occurs. These events include the 5 "Ds" which can impact any business:

- **Death**. The death of you or a co-owner.

- **Disability**. The disability of you or a co-owner.

- **Dispute**. An irreconcilable dispute between you and one or more of your co-owners.

- **Departure**. The departure (through unexpected retirement or other employment termination) of you or a co-owner.

- **Divorce**. Divorce by you or a co-owner.

Adverse Impact

The 5 D's can adversely impact the company's:

- **Financial resources**

- **Management talent**

- **Ownership continuity**

Whether you are the controlling shareholder or one of one or more noncontrolling shareholders, as an owner you want to achieve certain financial objectives for you, your family and your business should the unexpected happen. Business life typically doesn't award a "Mulligan" or a "do-over" just because you are unprepared for the unexpected event. Instead, these situations are best handled if you have laid the proper foundation for dealing with them ahead of time (and where applicable you have put the proper insurance coverages in place ahead of time).

This chapter is aimed at helping you assess how well you and your company are already prepared for these types of contingencies. Your Transition Growth Planning Advisor team wants to understand what you have and what is missing, the presence of which could make a substantial difference in providing a better outcome in the event of your unexpected death or disability. This assessment helps in the design of the right tools and components for your particular situation.

In particular, this Building Block 4 (along with Building Block 5) will help to assess and address your readiness in the following areas:

1. Ability of your spouse or family to receive cash for the full value of your stock upon your death or disability.

2. Ability of the company to resolve continuing ownership by one or more partners pursuant to a pre-determined method upon an irreconcilable dispute.

3. Ability of the company to control retention of ownership amongst the key owners upon a divorce.

4. Ability of the company to continue to obtain bank or other third party financing upon the loss of you as a financial resource, guarantor or lender.

5. Ability of the company to retain key employees, customers, suppliers and franchisor relationships upon your death or disability.

6. Existence of a definitive process for appointing an interim successor and permanent successor upon your death or disability.

7. The degree to which your death or disability will result in a family dispute that would be detrimental to the business.

8. Whether the company's financial structure relies on your continuing financial support.

9. Whether your company is financially prepared to deal with loss of a key employee.

10. Whether your company is financially prepared to deal with the loss of your key services.

Contingency Plan Notifications

As a starting point, you should consider taking the relatively easy first step of developing some contingency notifications and instructions. Upon your death or disability, the continuing financial success (or in some cases survival) of your company may be dependent upon the ongoing comfort level of those with whom you have been doing business. Notification of these persons, immediately upon your death or disability, that you have a Transition Growth Plan that addresses this, can go a long ways to establishing this comfort level to help assure business continuity or, alternatively, to provide for a controlled sale or controlled liquidation.

The following are examples you should consider:

*   Contingency Notification Letter to Customers/Patients.
*   Contingency Notification Letter to Lenders.
*   Contingency Notification Letter to Suppliers.
*   Contingency Notification Letter to Franchisor.
*   Contingency Notification Letter to Employees.
*   Contingency Press Release.

Contingency Plan Resolutions And Instructions

Upon your death or disability, the continuing financial success of your company may also be dependent on having left your management and family with clear instructions.

The following are examples of these to consider:

*   **Transition Growth Plan Letter to Family** – Written instructions to your spouse and family for handling business matters upon your death or disability.

*   **Contingency Shareholder Resolutions** – Written resolutions by the shareholder(s) for directing Board of Director actions upon your death or disability.

- **Contingency Board of Director Resolutions** - Written resolutions by your Board of Directors for handling business matters upon your death or disability.

- **Contingency Board of Directors Instructions** - Pre-existing board resolution for process for selecting an interim and permanent successor (or confirming your pre-designated successor) and/or taking contingency options to manage the company.

- **Contingency Reorganization Plan Instructions** - Pre-written directive as to how the company is to be divided into more than one entity to be owned/managed by one or more key employees/family members.

- **Contingency Sale Plan Instructions** - Pre-written guidelines for assisting your spouse, family and advisors in selling the company to a third party or insiders.

- **Contingency Advisor Instructions** - Pre-written designation to your spouse, family and/or board of directors naming principal Transition Growth Plan advisor(s) to assist in advising family and board on the transition of business matters upon your death or disability.

Chapter 31

Pre-Fund Financial Gaps Due To Loss Of Key Person

Regardless of the best laid plans, the loss of a key owner or key employee from your business can still cause a financial harm to the company. The potential for financial loss due to the death or disability of a key employee (both owner and non-owner key employees) can to a significant extent be lessened with the advance investment in key person life insurance and key person disability insurance.

Your exit advisors can help you to develop an appropriate key person valuation, which will help you estimate the financial loss and the amount of insurable financial recovery which you can establish today.

Key Person Financial Replacement Program

The loss of an active key owner or other key employee due to death or disability can cause a substantial financial hit to a company. What do you have in place on key owners or employees for your company:

Name:_____   Name:_____

Position: _____   Position: _____

☐   Key Owner Valuation $_____   ☐   Key Owner Valuation $_____
☐   Life Insurance $_____   ☐   Life Insurance $_____
☐   Disability Insurance $_____   ☐   Disability Insurance $_____
☐   _____   ☐   _____
☐   _____   ☐   _____

Name: _____   Name: _____

Position: _____   Position: _____

☐   Key Owner Valuation $_____   ☐   Key Owner Valuation $_____
☐   Life Insurance $_____   ☐   Life Insurance $_____
☐   Disability Insurance $_____   ☐   Disability Insurance $_____
☐   _____   ☐   _____
☐   _____   ☐   _____

Name: _____   Name: _____

Position: _____   Position: _____

☐   Key Owner Valuation $_____   ☐   Key Owner Valuation $_____
☐   Life Insurance $_____   ☐   Life Insurance $_____
☐   Disability Insurance $_____   ☐   Disability Insurance $_____
☐   _____   ☐   _____
☐   _____   ☐   _____

In order to fully protect your company, a number of potential financial gaps due to the loss of a key person must be addressed. The Transition Growth and Exit Planning process provides ways to address your company's ability to cover these financial gap contingencies (based on your estimated needs and on expected cash and insurance funds you estimate you would have available).

Pre-Funding Financial Gap Due to Death Or Disability of Name: _____ - You - _____

		Due To
	Death	Disability
A. Cash Needed		
Buy Stock	$_____	$_____
Stay Bonuses	$_____	$_____
Key Person Loss	$_____	$_____
Salary Continuation	$_____	$_____
Debt Payoff	$_____	$_____
Other: _____	$_____	$_____
Other: _____	$_____	$_____
Total $ Needed	$_____	$_____
B. Cash Available		
Company Reserves	$_____	$_____
Existing Insurance	$_____	$_____
Total $ Available	$_____	$_____
C. Shortfall A-B=C	$_____	$_____

Pre-Funding Financial Gap Due to Death Or Disability of Name: - Your Partner or Key Employee -		
		Due To
A. Cash Needed	Death	Disability
Buy Stock	$_____	$_____
Stay Bonuses	$_____	$_____
Key Person Loss	$_____	$_____
Salary Continuation	$_____	$_____
Debt Payoff	$_____	$_____
Other: _____	$_____	$_____
Other: _____	$_____	$_____
Total $ Needed	$_____	$_____
B. Cash Available		
Company Reserves	$_____	$_____
Existing Insurance	$_____	$_____
Total $ Available	$_____	$_____
C. Shortfall A-B=C	$_____	$_____

These are the questions you should address:

• If you show a Shortfall, do you want to address this?

• How much of the Shortfall do you want to close?

• Do you want to obtain an insurance proposal detailing the type of insurance coverage which are optimum for your situation?

• Do you have an insurance advisor who can provide this?

Chapter 32

Utilize A Stay Bonus Plan

Stay Bonus Plan

If you are viewed by your company personnel as the one person who's presence is necessary in order to keep the company afloat, how many of your key personnel would jump ship promptly upon your death or disability? They each need to think about their own continuing financial conditions and need to be in a position to look for the best employment opportunity which arises.

What does this do to the value of your business? If you don't have someone on your depth chart who can immediately step in and assume your position and do so with the confidence of your employment staff, you may find that the value of your company will dissipate quickly. Not only will key personnel depart, but key customers will also likely move on if they feel your business is jeopardized.

What does this do to the value that you have spent your life or many years of your life developing? Presumably your spouse and children may be dependent on a continuing income from the corporation. If not, you might in any case have been hoping that you could leave them with a company that was ongoing and had value.

What if you had a system in place for financially encouraging your key personnel to stay on board until the rough waters have smoothed out? This would provide your family and your advisors with the opportunity to hire a capable successor who could either keep the ship moving forward indefinitely or who could at least step in to oversee a carefully managed completion of pending projects and an orderly liquidation (rather than a fire sale at fire sale prices).

One of the best tools for accomplishing this is to establish a Stay Bonus Plan. Under this type of plan, you will have put into place an arrangement to promptly inform key personnel that they will receive a compensation bonus for staying on board during the rough waters. This would be a substantial bonus equivalent to 3-12 months of compensation.

Since this type of bonus would kick in only upon your death or disability, it is capable of being financed through the advance investment in a life insurance and lump sum disability insurance contract (assuming that you are insurable). The plan should also be documented and approved in advance by the company's Board of Directors.

My Existing Stay Bonus Plan

Upon a key or sole owner's death or disability, key personnel may decide it's time to quickly depart the company if they believe it's a "sinking ship" without me. Often, all that's needed in an understanding that you have a plan and that you're willing to pay something extra to key personnel to stay while your family transitions the business or while an orderly sale or liquidation can occur. A Stay Bonus Plan is a way to accomplish this.

I have the following:

☐ My Company doesn't have a Stay Bonus Plan.
☐ My Company has a Stay Bonus Plan which provides the following Stay Bonus upon the death or disability of:
  ☐ Myself.
  ☐ My partner.
  ☐ Other: _____.
Name or Group _____ Bonus: ☐ $_____ or ☐ _____% of Annual Salary.
Name or Group _____ Bonus: ☐ $_____ or ☐ _____% of Annual Salary.
Name or Group _____ Bonus: ☐ $_____ or ☐ _____% of Annual Salary.

This Stay Bonus is:
☐ Unfunded.
☐ Funded with $_____ Life Insurance and $_____ Lump Sum Disability Insurance.

Building Block 5 -
Protect My Ownership

Chapter 33

Establish A Business Continuity Agreement

Businesses, regardless of age and size, are often damaged or torn apart due to lack of a well-conceived system for avoiding and/or resolving disputes. These disputes can arise between co-owners, the spouses of co-owners and/or co-owner families.

The potential for disputes can become even more acute upon the death or disability of a key owner. The role of a spouse or other family member may take on a new significance when the other co-owners attempt to work out issues with the spouse or family member who may not be familiar with some of the innerworkings and understandings of long-term business partners. This issue can be just as problematic for a one-owner business which now finds itself being owned by a surviving spouse or surviving children.

In addition to issues regarding regular company operations, disputes can arise as to how family salaries are to be set, how dividend distributions are to be determined and paid and who is to run the business as your successor. The risk involves not only adverse financial impact to the company, but also can pose a threat to the harmony within a family. Various matters which functioned well when you were around as the "traffic cop" to avoid or resolve disputes might no longer function nearly as well. This can occur despite the best intentions and simply be caused by a difference of opinions.

In order to help minimize, avoid and resolve possible disputes amongst co-owners and family members, a well-conceived and thorough Business Continuity Agreement should generally be implemented. This type of agreement should operate in addition to a well-conceived Buy-Sell Agreement (discussed in the next chapter). The Business Continuity Agreement should address issues other than buy-sell obligations. The following are some of the features which we recommend be included.

- **Board Approval Actions.** The agreement should spell out those actions which require Board of Director approval. The typical Articles of Incorporation and Bylaws for corporations do not specify this type of detail. Bylaws will typically provide that the Board of Directors is to elect the officers and will specify general duties of the officers. In some instances, the applicable state business corporation act will contain further types of actions which require Board approval. Beyond that, the boundaries of the officers and directors authority may be largely blurred and subject to dispute. This portion of the agreement can set forth the approval requirements for a sale of company assets, loan transactions, change in accounting principles, acquisition of other businesses, issuance of additional stock, redemption of existing stock and the payment of bonus compensation.

- **Right to Engage In Competing Businesses.** Depending on the circumstances, the parties may agree that co-owners should not be restricted from investing in other types of business which may compete with the company. On the other hand, you may have reasons for restricting the ability of your co-owners to invest in competing businesses. This is best resolved by a clear understanding of this between co-owners ahead of time.

- **Confidentiality Provisions.** As a business owner, you typically receive and are entitled to receive detailed confidential information regarding your business operations. Typically, the disclosure of that type of information to outsiders or competitors would be detrimental to your business. The agreement should specify a requirement to maintain proprietary information in confidence.

- **Required Resignation.** The agreement can specify that if a co-owner sells his or her stock in the company, this results in an automatic resignation of status as an officer and director of the company, unless the parties later agree otherwise.

- **Financial Statement Requirements.** The agreement can specify the nature of the financial statements which the co-owners expect. This may include audited, reviewed or compiled financial statements on an annual basis along with the details for monthly and quarterly interim statements.

- **Subchapter "S" Protection.** Whether or not your company is a subchapter "S" corporation today, the agreement should include provisions that require the protection of that status as it exists today and as it may exist upon election in the future. When the owners intend to have "S" status maintained, this agreement can help avoid an inadvertent termination of the election.

- **Tax Payment Dividends.** If the company is a flow-through business, such as an "S" corporation or a limited liability company, then its income is taxed to the shareholders rather than to the company. Since the shareholders are taxed on this, there should be an agreement in place under which the company and the co-owners have agreed that sufficient dividends will be paid quarterly to the owners to enable them to make the tax payments on the company income.

- **Stock Redemption Provisions.** The shareholders may wish to have the opportunity to have some or all of their stock redeemed periodically. While this might result in full ordinary income taxation for "C" corporation owners, this type of periodic redemption can be tax efficient for an "S" corporation or limited liability company. Under programs that we have established, the company's board of directors can determine a redemption pool each year and allow shareholders to opt in periodically for a pro rata redemption from the funds available in the pool.

- **Annual Dividend Payments.** This provision can establish a policy which the company will follow for determining annual dividend payouts. This is intended to help reflect a balance between those owners who are full time employees of the company (receiving compensation) and those owners who are not employed by the company (and who would expect to see some return through dividend payments).

- **Non-Solicitation of Customers.** These provisions can detail the limitations which the co-owners expect to have in place to prevent other owners from soliciting the company's customers for other businesses owned by a co-owner.

- **Non-Solicitation of Employees.** These provisions can specify that co-owners are prohibited from soliciting employees of the company to work in another business operation of the co-owner without meeting agreed approval procedures.

- **Board of Director Composition.** These provisions can specify that each principal co-owner (and his or her family) is permitted to elect a certain number of the members of the Board of Directors.

- **Job Retention Guidelines.** These provisions can specify when and under what conditions it is expected that a co-owner would agree to retirement.

- **Family Employment Policy.** Some closely held companies have a restriction on hiring any family members while others have no restrictions at all. In order to maintain company harmony and to provide some performance motivation for a family member, we have found it helpful to include a family employment policy which specifies the pre-requisites before a family member can be hired.

- **Advisory Board.** An advisory board is being utilized more and more by companies of all sizes as a means to help provide company management with additional perspectives and experience which they might otherwise not encounter. This board can include lower level management members as well as outside business persons or advisors. The terms for this can be specified in the Business Continuity Agreement. This also provides an ongoing means of expertise and guidance upon the loss of a key-owner.

- **Corporate Formalities.** The agreement can also specify that the corporation will maintain standard corporate formalities and recordkeeping requirements. This would include holding regular shareholder and Board of Director meetings and documenting them with regular corporate minutes.

- **Conflict of Interest Policy.** In order to enable and require directors and officers to avoid conflicts of interest, the agreement can also contain the details of a conflict of interest policy.

This type of agreement is not intended to diminish the control of the controlling shareholders. Therefore, it would typically be amendable or could be terminated upon the determination of a controlling interest of the corporation, rather than all parties to the agreement. In addition, the agreement can provide that its provisions can be waived upon the determination of a controlling interest of the corporation. The objective of the agreement is to establish company guidelines, especially as they relate to business continuity issues. This agreement, in effect, lets all of the players know what the rules are, but it retains the ability of the controlling owner to change those rules as determined from time to time.

Case Study – Business Continuity

Betty and her husband had founded Betty Co several years before they visited with us about their Transition Growth Planning. One of their concerns was that of their six children, two of them had management positions in the company, along with two of their sons-in-law, who also had management positions in the company. The other two children received no salary income from the company for their families.

Betty was concerned that while she and her husband were around, their decisions on establishing salary to family members and dividend distribution amounts would be respected without dispute, however, upon their demise, they didn't want the children in the business to be disputing with the children not in the business as to what the proper salary levels would be as well as the proper dividend levels. They also recognized that the children and in-laws employed in the business were in different positions and had different capabilities. Therefore, they had been paying them different amounts and they recognized that this difference in capabilities and efforts needed to continue to be compensated accordingly – without dispute – when Mom and Dad were gone.

We incorporated two specific provisions into their business continuity agreement (which complemented the Buy-Sell Agreement which we had also put in place for them). Specifically, we included a family compensation setting policy and a dividend policy in the Agreement. Under the compensation setting policy, the company engaged an outside salary consultant who would annually review the performance of the company and industry salary and bonus data for similar companies to help establish specific recommended compensation levels for the corporate positions held by the family members. In addition, under the dividend policy, dividends were to be paid when specific financial targets for the company were met. These targets could be overridden by the Board of Directors to allow for a lesser or greater dividend amount depending on unanticipated circumstances.

Since Betty and her husband had gifted some of their shares in the company to the children and their respective families over the years, Betty also wanted to provide a way for some of the families to cash out of some or all of their stock should they choose in the future to rely financially more on their own separate investments rather than to be completely dependent on the family company. Therefore, we included in the business continuity agreement a redemption policy which allowed for the Board of Directors to annually establish a redemption pool amount, for which family members could choose to opt in to redeem part or all of their shares.

Chapter 34

Establish A Buy-Sell Agreement

A Buy-Sell Agreement is a contractually binding agreement amongst the co-owners of a business which addresses the times and the terms for the future purchase or sale of stock of a company. In a sense, this type of agreement is your own private stock market.

Unlike a public stock exchange, under this private stock market, you and other co-owners are not necessarily free to buy and sell stock to whomever you may please. However, this type of private stock market does create the ability to have some circumstances in which your stock can be purchased or in which you can cause the purchase of another co-owner's stock.

In addition, this type of agreement provides the ability to restrict co-owners from selling their shares to an outside party which the core owners do not want to share company ownership with. In this sense, it also acts as a very solid protective measure for the business operations.

A Buy-Sell Agreement is most commonly used when the company is owned by unrelated co-owners. However, it is also very frequently used when the company is owned by family members. This enables the family members to have a pre-agreed understanding amongst themselves as to how, when and under what terms stock will be purchased and sold upon future events and conditions.

The Buy-Sell Agreement has historically been less frequently used when there is only one present owner of the company. However, this does not mean that the agreement should not be used under that circumstance. Upon the death of the sole owner, that owner's stock would typically be distributed according to the terms of the owner's Estate Plan. The executor or trustee charged with handling the estate or living trust of the owner does not necessarily have the authority to add stock restriction or Buy-Sell agreement provisions before distributing the stock to family members pursuant to an Estate Plan – if those ownership restrictions were not already in place at the owner's death.

In the absence of such an agreement, after the owner's death, the stock could be owned by multiple family members, some of whom might find themselves in disagreement as to the company operations or stock ownership going forward.

Therefore, it's prudent for even the sole business owner to enter into an agreement before death. Since it takes two parties in order to have a binding agreement, this agreement would be between the sole owner and the company and would be binding on successors to the stock ownership pursuant to an Estate Plan distribution.

Case Study – Resolving Disputes

Sam and Louie had been in business for about ten years, operating a couple of retail clothing stores. They were 50/50 owners in a corporation which operated 4 separate retail outlets. When Sam approached us he had already been working for about 9 months to try to come up with a proposal which Louie would accept for dividing up their operations.

While they had gotten along well in the early years, Louie's substance abuse had gotten the best of him. He wouldn't consider any type of reasonable purchase by Sam or a sale by Sam to Louie. Sam and Louie had never entered into any type of a Buy-Sell Agreement, based on the belief that they would always be able to work things out. Here, no type of mediation was successful. Louie was simply unreachable regarding any type of purchase and the two were deadlocked and unable to reach agreement on any operational issues that needed to be dealt with.

The corporate statutes allow a shareholder to file an action in District Court for a dissolution of the company and a division of assets in this type of deadlock situation. However, it's a messy and costly litigation vetted in a public forum. A Buy-Sell Agreement, in particular one with a Texas shoot-out provision, would have enabled the parties to part company according to a predetermined process that would have enabled one of the parties to receive a reasonable, fair value for his stock and for the other party to continue to own and operate the business.

Buy-Sell Agreements are prepared based on the needs and objectives of the co-owners. Included below are the various types of provisions which should generally be included, or considered for inclusion in a Buy-Sell Agreement.

- **Stock Transfer Restrictions.** Shareholders of a closely held company should not be without limitation on their ability to transfer their shares to outsiders. Co-owners have some right to expect that they can choose their fellow co-owners in a closely held company. However, corporate law typically does not permit an absolute restriction on the right of a shareholder to transfer his or her stock. Therefore, the most common type of transfer restriction utilized in a Buy-Sell Agreement is the right of first refusal. Under this provision, if a shareholder wishes to transfer his or her stock to a third party, that shareholder must first offer the stock either to the company and/or to the other shareholders for sale on the same terms and conditions that would be offered to the outside third party. This provides the company and the other shareholders with the option to purchase the stock, thereby retaining ownership of the company within the closely held group of owners. Typically some exceptions would be made to this right of first refusal to enable shareholders to transfer stock to their spouse and family members, as well as a living trust for estate planning purposes.

- **Purchase Upon Death.** This type of provision operates in one of two ways. First, this can provide the company (and the other shareholders) with an option to purchase the stock of a shareholder who has died. Alternatively, this provision can give the estate of the deceased shareholder the option to sell (i.e. to "put") the estate's stock to the company (or the other shareholders). This gives the company and the other closely held shareholder group the option to control share ownership without letting it become disbursed throughout a fellow shareholder's family, in particular when that shareholder is no longer around to provide some control over potential disputes within the family. The alterative approach also provides some liquidity to that shareholder's estate by providing a limited market for the stock in exchange for cash at some pre-agreed value method.

- **Purchase Upon Total Disability.** This provision can also be established in one of two principal ways. The company (and other shareholders) can have an option to purchase the stock of a shareholder who has become totally disabled. Alternatively, the disabled shareholder can have an option to "put" the stock to the company (and/or other shareholders). This again provides the company and the closely held shareholder group with the ability to pull in stock from a shareholder who is no longer active, whereas the alternative provision provides an ability for a disabled shareholder to have a limited market for the sale of his or her stock in exchange for cash.

- **Termination of Employment.** A termination of employment provision in a Buy-Sell Agreement will give the company (and/or the other shareholders) the option to purchase a shareholder's stock upon termination of employment. Alternatively, the provision may give the terminated shareholder an option to "put" his or her stock to the company (and/or the other shareholders). This provides the company with the option to call in the stock, depending on the circumstances of the termination, whereas the alternative provision gives a terminated shareholder a limited market for his or her stock upon termination. When the shareholder receives the stock as a stock bonus, then it is possible that the stock pricing upon termination of employment might be less than fair market value. In addition, it is possible that the shareholder/employee would not yet be fully vested in all of the shares he or she owns. These terms could be set forth in the Buy-Sell Agreement, or in a separate Agreement relating to the stock bonus program.

- **Purchase Upon Bankruptcy.** It is common to include a provision that enables the company to call in the stock if a shareholder was to declare bankruptcy. This helps to provide the company with the option to disentangle itself from the individual financial problems of a shareholder.

- **Purchase Upon Divorce.** Typically, if a shareholder is involved in a divorce from his or her spouse, and as a result of the divorce proceedings is not awarded the stock in the company, then, to prevent disputes and business disruptions which might be caused by the marital separation, the shareholder member of the couple who was initially issued the stock would typically have an option to purchase this stock from his or her spouse, with a secondary option to the company (and/or the other shareholders) if the first option is not exercised.

- **Texas Shootout.** In a Texas Shootout, the shareholders are given the ability to each go their separate ways. This type of provision would more frequently be included in an agreement where you have roughly equal shareholders. If a shareholder wishes to separate, then he or she can make an offer to sell all of his or her stock to the other shareholder upon stated pricing, terms and conditions. The other shareholder either must accept the offer, or refuse the offer, in which case, the initial offering shareholder must purchase the stock of the other shareholder.

- **Drag-Along Option.** This type of provision typically exists when a majority shareholder or group of shareholders wish to sell the stock of the company to an outside third party. Since an outside third-party would most likely want to be able to purchase 100% of the stock, this provision gives the majority owners the right to require the minority shareholders to sell their stock on the same terms and conditions which the majority stockholder is receiving.

- **Tag-Along Option.** Under this provision, a minority shareholder would have the option to require that a majority shareholder include the minority in a transaction for the sale of the stock of the company. This would occur, for example, when the majority shareholder did not exercise a drag-along option, but the minority shareholder, nevertheless wanted to be included in the sale.

Case Study – The Buy-Sell Agreement Taking Effect

Jeff, Bob, Jim and Tom were 4 brothers who had inherited a poultry production business from their parents. Over the fifteen years since the death of their father, they had expanded the business to new levels by always being on the front end of new production and agricultural developments. Each of the four brothers had their special niche within the company. One handled the financial matters, the other oversaw the day-to-day production, another managed the research and development division, while the fourth acted as president of the company. They were the model second-generation corporation, with all four brothers and their spouses getting along great and maintaining a high level of interest and success in their efforts to continue to grow and develop what had now become a business worth about $15 million.

Nevertheless, they were realists. They recognized the possibility that sometime down the road they could have a falling out. Therefore, we put into effect a Buy-Sell Agreement which provided an option to the company, with a secondary option to the other brothers, to purchase the stock of any of the brothers who decided to terminate his employment.

The pricing in the Buy-Sell Agreement for this option was established at a discount to the full fair market value of the company, on the basis that each felt that should any of them decide to leave the venture ahead of the others, he should be expected to take a haircut in the price, since the remaining brothers would be opting to continue the family venture.

About 10 years after the Buy-Sell Agreement was executed, Tom had a falling out with the other three brothers. He gave his notice to terminate his employment. When the other three brothers caused the corporation to exercise the purchase option, Tom objected to the haircut in the price and ended up pursuing a claim in District Court to have the Buy-Sell Agreement overturned. The Court found the Agreement enforceable and required Tom to sell the stock at the agreed discounted price.

This case is an illustration of the reason for entering into a Buy-Sell Agreement even in the best of circumstances. Here, the four brothers specifically agreed to the result they each wanted to see should any one of them decide to leave before normal retirement. Had the Agreement not been in force or had it not contained the proper trigger and pricing provisions, the unhappy brother could have ended up causing significant damage to the company's operations and the ongoing business value.

Building Block 6 - Grow My Investments

Chapter 35 -   Develop A Comprehensive
                     Wealth Plan

Develop A Comprehensive Wealth Plan

A business owner's personal wealth planning is critical to successful transition and exit planning. The failure to address your personal wealth planning can delay or diminish the odds of meeting your key business transition and exit objectives.

Wealth Plan – Investment Plan

A properly prepared Comprehensive Wealth Plan will review and evaluate your personal investment growth plan. This involves a review of your present personal investment plan and will address step-by-step guidance for achieving the personal investment goals you have set.

Establish Your Personal Investment Goals

Before developing any type of Comprehensive Wealth Plan, it is critical to first determine your principal investment goals. Obviously, the underlying goal of any investment or wealth management program is to make money, rather than to lose money.

However, when implementing an investment or wealth growth plan, it is key that both you and your financial advisor have a deeper understanding of your particular situation and objectives.

This is particularly true when you are the owner of a business. Often, for business owners, a very high percentage of your net wealth is still invested in your business. Often, the principal wealth invested outside the business may be in the qualified retirement plan established through the company. In addition, you may have some separate savings and investment accounts. Generally speaking, the strategy and asset allocation for these accounts will largely depend on how near in time you are to completing your transition from your business.

In order to properly assist a business owner with developing a Comprehensive Wealth Plan, a financial advisor needs to have an in depth understanding of you, your family, your objectives, and your financial situation.

This should begin with the following review of your personal investment goals and objectives.

Your Personal Investment Goals and Objectives

Achieving your financial goals and objectives normally requires a consistent, well-conceived plan, implemented and managed over a period of time. In order to assist your financial advisor, you should express your intentions as to the following personal financial goals and objectives:

- To achieve a comfortable retirement, which I hope to begin by age ____ or year 20____.
- To accumulate sufficient investment assets to maintain our standard of living for my spouse and children, even if I should die or become disabled prior to retirement.
- To be able to purchase a second residence in the State of _____ as a part-time retirement or vacation home. I estimate that the cost of this will be $_____.
- To establish sufficient funds so that in addition to our normal living expenses, I can afford to take ____ trips per year, at an estimated travel cost of $_____ per trip.
- To be able to assist my children and grandchildren with their education costs. Estimated funding for this as of 20___ would be $_____.
- To be able to assist my children with purchasing their homes. Estimated funding for this as of 20___ would be $_____.
- To be able to have a fund to be designed for my charitable giving. The estimated funding for this as of 20___ would be $_____.
- To be able to set aside $_____ of funds per year, starting 20___ to invest towards my retirement funds.
- To create a diversified portfolio of investments in order to reach an optimal risk/reward result. Subject to further review with my financial advisor, I presently believe that I should be investing my personal investment and retirement funds on the basis of _____% equities, _____% bonds, _____% alternative investments and _____% cash.
- I would like to have my investment assets rebalanced periodically to meet my desired asset allocation and to have this reviewed at least annually/quarterly/monthly with my financial advisor.

Achieve Comprehensive Wealth Planning

There are a variety of ways in which Comprehensive Wealth Planning is approached today by various financial advisors. While I have included below some of the more common areas which are covered by financial advisors during the course of developing a Comprehensive Wealth Plan, this list of items I have included should not be considered as exclusive or as necessarily required by every financial advisor.

- **Cash Flow Liquidity.** One of the elements of many Comprehensive Wealth Plans is a cash flow analysis, which will take into account your current and expected income sources and expenses. This begins with a discussion and understanding of your current and future cash flow sources and cash need objectives. This includes not simply a review of needs, but also a review of your particular desires. This may include early retirement, education funding for your family, the purchase of a second residence and charitable/philanthropic objectives.

The next step after this initial review is to determine whether your current wealth and income is consistent with your cash need objectives. This entails a review of your current assets and liabilities, your current and projected business and employment situation, as well as the timing of your expected retirement.

After these first two steps are completed, your financial resources can be compared against the projected net, after tax expected economic results from your current investment plan, as well as that which can be expected after developing a new Comprehensive Wealth Plan.

- **Wealth Growth and Enhancement.** The key, of course, to growing and enhancing your investment wealth is to have the right mix of assets as a part of your investment portfolio. This includes not simply your particular choices amongst various stocks, bonds and other financial investment alternatives, but also the proper or optimal asset allocation amongst various investment classes. A financial advisor will typically review your asset allocation, and will recommend revisions based on your particular liquidity needs, your risk tolerance, and your time horizon.

This review will identify your overall investment portfolio objectives to identify your needs with regard to income, growth and balanced investment alternatives.

- **Asset Protection.** Asset protection in the context of a Comprehensive Wealth Plan refers to utilizing the various types of tools available today for protecting your investments from overzealous or unexpected claims of creditors. This is not simply with regard to your situation, but can also rise with regard to the steps you take to protect the gifts and inheritance to your children and grandchildren from their potential creditors or their potential mismanagement. This is covered at Building Block 3 – Protect My Family.

- **Tax Minimization.** Wealth planning opportunities today for minimizing income taxes generally consist of the following choices:

  - Minimizing the applicable federal income tax rates which apply to different types of income.

    Example: Long term capital gain rather than short term capital gain.

  - Minimizing the applicable <u>state</u> income tax rates which apply to various types of income.

    Example: Long term capital gain rather than short term capital gain.

  - Deferring income taxes until funds are withdrawn at retirement or some other date.

    Example: 401K Plan and other qualified retirement plans.

  - Permanent deferral and tax "forgiveness" upon death.

    Example: Whole life, variable life and universal life insurance policies.

  - Full tax exemption due to the nature of the income.

    Example: Municipal Bonds

- **Retirement Planning.** Retirement planning entails a thorough review of your current and projected resources, your expected timeline for retirement, and your expected plans upon retirement.

In order to help incent savings for retirement, the Federal government has instituted a number of qualified, tax deferred retirement planning vehicles in the form of various retirement plans. These include, for example, 401K Plans, Profit-Sharing Plans, ESOPs and IRAs. Each financial advisor firm with which you work will have detailed information about the suitability and pros/cons of each of these tools.

- **Wealth Plan Insurance**. Your Comprehensive Wealth Plan will also review and recommend a program of life, disability and casualty insurance to assess and address your personal contingency risks for unexpected death, disability and casualty.

- **The Link Between Business Debt and Personal Debt**. Any plan for debt payoff pursuant to a contingency plan should be consistent with your overall Wealth Plan.

As a business owner, you know that you have a number of constant issues which either keep you awake at night or occupy a lot of your thoughts during the day. Depending on where you are at in the life of your business, this may include concerns about making payroll, landing the next major contract, resolving employee disputes, dealing with a government or tax investigation, or making debt service payments. Each of these issues would likely become even more intense upon your death or disability or the death or disability of a co-owner.

Your company's debt level can be of particular concern because your unplanned absence due to death or disability may result in a call for repayment or the inability to refinance the debt in the future, particularly if the bank has looked to your presence or financial backing in its lending program to your company.

Since death and disability are insurable, they provide at least some ability to offset the detriment occurring on account of them. If your death or disability, or the death or disability of a co-owner, will intensify the ability of your company to make its debt service payments (the default on which could sink your company), then you should consider targeting an insurance program to specifically meet the debt service obligation and at least eliminate that problem from posing a threat to the ongoing success of your company.

- **Legacy Planning**. While you have worked hard to create and to save wealth, both in your business and in your personal investments, this wealth can often be dissipated or misused by a second or third generation. While we are all familiar with many of the "rags to riches" scenarios which exist throughout the country, there are just as many "riches to rags" scenarios in which the second or third generation has (through mismanagement, lack of drive, or lack of appreciation for what they have received) promptly proceeded to lose or dissipate much of what the first generation has worked hard to create and save.

As you consider your Comprehensive Wealth Plan, in addition to addressing the "financial wealth" (i.e. the hard, investment assets), you should also consider the extent to which you need to develop your family's "human wealth". This includes your relationships with and amongst your family members as well as the degree to which you have instilled in them the family, personal, financial and business acumen and responsibility which you would like them to have in order to carry on the legacy which you have created.

This can be accomplished through a variety of means, including the actions which you take to personally instill these traits into your family members, as well as introducing and helping them to pursue proper social relationships and financial training.

In addition, by utilizing the steps included in Building Block 3 – Protect My Family, you can help assure that your financial and personal legacy will be maintained through your succeeding generations.

Your Personal Legacy

In order to help ensure that your children and grandchildren are careful to maintain the personal and financial legacy you have developed, you should consider doing the following as part of your Comprehensive Wealth Plan:

• Establish a Family Council to discuss financial matters. This Council should meet a selected number of times per year and may include children, their spouses and adult grandchildren.

• Have your Financial Advisor provide you with a selection of financial planning advisors which your children can use and financial planning education programs which your children can attend.

• Plan to provide a gift of a paid Estate Plan and Financial Plan for each of your adult children as a birthday or other holiday gift when they reach a certain age or ages.

• Include the appropriate long term Living Trust or Generation-Skipping Trust within your personal Estate Plan.

Protect Your Most Valuable Assets

A Comprehensive Wealth Plan, regardless of a consistent and persistent sold investment return, is not completely successful if you have not taken care of your most valuable assets, which are you and your family. Every business owner should take a few minutes to make an honest assessment of your and your family's health and wellbeing with the intention of taking those actions that are necessary to help provide reasonable assurance that you and your family can live long lives to enjoy the "fruits of your labor".

Engaging A Financial Advisor

The first step towards creating your Comprehensive Wealth Plan is to select a Financial Advisor who can capably help you achieve your financial objectives for your non-business family wealth. This may, of course, be a Financial Advisor whom you have already established a solid relationship with, or it may be someone entirely new.

In order to help evaluate which Financial Advisor you should use, it is necessary to understand your Financial Advisor's investment philosophy, style and practices.

Understanding Your Financial Advisor's Approach

In selecting and working with a Financial Advisor, it is important to understand that advisor's overall investment approach and philosophy. Some of the principal factors to consider include the following:

- Whether the Financial Advisor's advice is independent or whether the advisor relies on proprietary investment products.

- Whether the Financial Advisor is supported by a solid investment research and analysis team with a proven, positive track record.

- Whether the Financial Advisor relies on in-house investment committee guidance for its investment portfolio or relies on third party investment guidance.

- Whether the Financial Advisor's platform utilizes both passive investment tools (e.g. index funds), active investment tools (e.g. open or close-ended mutual funds, private money managers, etc.) or both.

- With regard to its active, managed portfolios, whether the Financial Advisor utilizes a solid strategic asset allocation modeling approach.

- Whether your Financial Advisor actively takes into account your risk tolerance and your tax-efficient objectives.

- Whether the Financial Advisor provides a clear transparency with regard to fees which are charged to your account and whether these are explained up front and in detail.

- Whether your Financial Advisor provides you with detailed reporting on a monthly or quarterly basis.

- Whether your Financial Advisor provides an active monitoring of your portfolio to help assure that your results are consistent with your goals.

- Whether your Financial Advisor provides you with the ability to easily access the results of your account online so that you can monitor daily activity and progress.

Building Block 7 - Grow My Business

Chapter 36

Adopt A Continuous Business Model Innovation Program

There is a lot of misunderstanding as to what exactly is a business model. A company's business model represents the business logic, at the strategic level, by which a company operates to make a profit. It is a representation of how a company makes (or would intend to make) money.

In order to visualize this conceptually, the informal descriptions of business models can be formalized into building blocks relationships. Many different conceptualizations have been developed in the business literature. An example is the business research study by Dr. Alexander Osterwalder: The Business Model Ontology – A Proposition In A Design Science Approach (2004).

By comparing the similarities in this range of models, attempts have been made to synthesize these models into a single reference model. The following (based on that of Dr. Osterwalder) provides a business model design template that can be used for our purposes to describe a company's present business model and to plan for improvements.

The business model choices you make in operating your business will cause the success or failure of your enterprise. The 2006 and 2008 IBM Global CEO Studies demonstrate that CEOs believe that business model innovation is becoming the new strategic differentiator. These studies found that companies which focus on business model innovation outperform companies which focus on operations in terms of operating margin growth.

The objective after you have described your business model is to continuously improve it. This can occur at each layer of the company. This can be at the overall company level, the business line level or for a particular product or service.

BUSINESS MODEL COMPONENTS

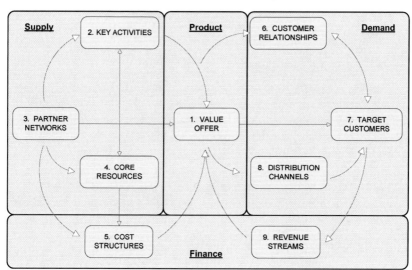

Business Model Components

These business model components can be described as follows:

1. **Value Offer**. The overall view of the bundle of products and services I offer.

2. **Key Activities**. The arrangement of the activities and resources I use to make and provide my products and services.

3. **Partner Networks**. The outside partners and alliances that help me make or sell my products or services.

4. **Core Resources**. The principal or unique repeatable capabilities I have for creating value for my customers.

5. **Cost Structures**. The sum of the monetary approaches and cost methods I use to run my business model.

6. **Customer Relationships**. How I keep what I make in sync with what my target customers want or need.

7. **Target Customers**. The customers I want to offer value to.

8. **Distribution Channels**. The means by which I deliver products and services to customers (including marketing & distribution strategies).

9. **Revenue Streams**. The various ways I price what my customers must pay for what I sell.

Business Model Examples

Any given company may excel or be distinctive in one (or more) of these Business Models components (and may just be average in other components). Some examples of well known companies which illustrate the specific business model components that they emphasize or are known for include the following:

1. **Value Offer**. The Wall Street Journal – which is well known for its offering of excellent business and financial analysis and its editorial independence.

2. **Key Activities**. Cisco – which became famous for its capacity to configure activities into new and innovative supply chains.

3. **Partner Networks**. Intel – which excels in its ability to get partners to build on its computer processing platform.

4. **Core Resources**. Apple – which has resurged due to its core capabilities of bringing design to computers and electronic gadgets.

5. **Cost Structures**. Walmart – which is well-known for its actions to drive down product and supply costs to be able to offer low price products to its customers.

6. **Customer Relationships**. Gillette – which maintains its customer relationships through its razor handle and disposable blade systems. They have extended this with the adjacent markets of shaving cream and deodorants to help achieve significant profit margins.

7. **Target Customers**. EasyJet – which became an industry leader by targeting the low-cost, frequent flyer, short-haul flight customer market throughout Europe.

8. **Distribution Channels**. Dell – which combined the features of the Internet with its build-to-order value proposition. This also results in

a very lean and agile activity configuration, which favored a low cost structure due to lower inventory and working capital needs.

9. **Revenue Streams**. Google – which, by understanding the increasing revenue returns to scale of its advertising hub, has become the leading example in the revenue model component.

Types Of Business Model Innovations

There are two principal types of business model innovations: supply driven business model innovation and demand driven business model innovation.

- **Supply-driven innovation**. This occurs by doing things in a new way or by applying new technologies to an existing business model. Dell provides an illustration of both. It innovated the computer hardware business model by selling directly to customers, and it also applied a new technology, the Web, as a distribution channel to reach the new customers.

- **Demand-driven innovation**. This is customer driven, based on new or changing customer needs, tastes, and preferences. An example is where the music industry was pressured to develop a more innovative business model in response to the development of the Napster and Kazaa file sharing platforms which allowed people to download music for free.

Ways To Innovate A Business Model

There are three ways to innovate a business model.

- **Change the business model**. By doing similar things differently. This means offering similar value propositions in an entirely new fashion. Skype is an example. It offers a value proposition that is very similar to phone companies: phone calls. However, its business model allows it to use the Internet as a free telecom infrastructure/network. This has extremely low variable costs and enables it to reach customers worldwide. Its business model offers the same ting, but differently because it uses different resources, needs different competencies and uses different distribution channels.

- **Extend the business model**. This means building on the current business model building blocks by adding new ones. An example is where competing telecom and cable industries aim at offering mobile and fixed communication, Internet broadband and TV all in one package.

- **Create a new business model.** This occurs when an entirely new business model is created when new markets emerge. Downloading ring-tones for mobile phones is an example. This illustrates what can happen when entrepreneurs find ways of exploiting new technologies and trends.

How To Describe, Assess and Improve Your Business Model

Below is a three step process that I use to improve and strengthen a Company's business model.

This process helps business owners achieve better discussions regarding their business models. This leads to a more focused way of business model innovation.

This process begins with drawing a clear picture of the Company's existing business models (using the 9-building blocks described above). This is followed by an assessment of the strengths, weaknesses, opportunities and threats of the present business model. This analysis provides the basis to design an improved business model.

Describe	Assess	Improve/Innovate
• Set-up a team with diverse views on the Company's business model. • Apply a clear definition of what your business model is. • Have the team draw a clear picture of how your current business model looks, using the 9 building blocks whiteboard.	• Drill down and analyze every described business model building block. • Note strengths and opportunities for each building block. • Note weaknesses and threats for each building block. • Come to an overall conclusion on your business model.	• Build on your assessment by considering, with your advisor's assistance, the various potential designs being utilized by others both inside and outside your industry. • Brainstorm on how the building blocks of your business model could be improved. • Synthesize these ideas into feasible developments and sketch an improved or even new business model.

Continuous Business Model Improvements

Fortune Magazine recently reported (October 2, 2006) that "business models are living much shorter lives these days."

By continuously looking to evaluate and improve your business model components, you can significantly improve your chances of continuous profitability and success.

Below is a Business Model Whiteboard which I use to start to identify improvements to a Company's present business model components.

Business Model Whiteboard

Partner Networks	Key Activities	Value Offer	Customer Relationships	Target Customers
	Core Resources		Distribution Channels	
Cost Structures			Revenue Streams	

Chapter 37

Document A Transition Period Growth Strategy

Why would anyone want to buy your company? More specifically, why would anyone want to buy your company at the price you are asking?

Value Drivers

The answer tends to consistently be very straightforward. Most buyers are interested in acquiring a company if they have a relatively high degree of certainty that the company will produce steady, fairly predictable, growing net cash flow. The "present value" of future cash flow is typically the best way to develop a price for a business. Essentially, a buyer's willingness to pay your price depends on your ability to deliver to the buyer a basket of tangible and intangible assets which function together like a well-oiled piece of machinery to produce this steady, predictable and growing cash flow.

What's more, this basket needs to produce the cash flow **without you**. Often, a buyer may insist as part of the transaction, that the principal guiding hand for the company stay on for a period of time after the sale, either continuing as CEO/President or in a consulting role. In any event, presumably your objective is to receive a reasonable asking price, along with the ability to retire or to move on. So, one of the most important items to have in the "basket" is a key management team capable of not only assuming the job of being the conductor of your train, but also having a sufficient management team capable of keeping the train on the track and operating up to its potential.

Different buyers will have different objectives and requirements. Since Transition Growth and Exit Planning needs to typically begin before an actual buyer is identified, it is generally necessary to plan for a variety of potential buyer types, whether these be specific strategic buyers or financial buyers. Overall, these buyers will seek some set of established "value drivers" to help assure a predictable, steady, growing cash flow.

The following are 18 of the over 50 value drivers which I use when counseling business owners on how to improve and grow their business:

Partial List of Value Drivers for Growing Your Business and Establishing Reasons A Business Would Be Attractive To An Inside Or Third Party Buyer.

- Loyal, diversified customer/client base.
- Efficient production/manufacturing facilities.
- Loyal key management group.
- Leading edge products and/or services.
- Effective supplier network.
- Efficient distribution system/network.
- Intellectual property rights (such as patents, trademarks, trade name and other good will).
- Steady, predictable solid profits and cash flow.
- Proven growth record.
- Effective workforce in place.
- Transferable franchise or license.
- Key location or territory.
- Barriers to entry for a startup.
- Research and product development team.
- Company name.
- Exclusive territory.
- Above industry average financial ratios.
- Systematized business processes (in writing) so continuing success is not dependent on any particular person (including owner) continuing in business.
- Credibly addressing the impact of the "Porter Forces" on your business.
- Capably evaluating and enhancing your "Economic Moats".

These are areas of your business which you should normally work to develop and maximize in order to demonstrate the potential for steady, predictable growth in the future.

Industry-Specific Business Benchmarks

You cannot exit your business if the price your company would realistically bring is insufficient to meet your retirement or other financial objectives. This strategy is intended to help you and your advisors focus on those areas of your business which could be improved to help achieve better business value and cash flow (and a better price).

Knowing and understanding how your competitors are deploying their resources, and how efficient they are in utilizing them, can tell you a lot about their strategies and how this compares to yours. This is important not only to you, but is of critical importance to a potential buyer of your business. If your business operations deploy financial and human capital less efficiently than others in your industry, you can expect this will negatively affect price. On the other hand, if you are more efficient than others in your industry, you can utilize this fact to negotiate better pricing. A benchmarking process can also assist companies in anticipating critical issues, rather than just reacting after the fact.

In order to provide some insight into how well your business systems are operating (and to help demonstrate value in the event of a sale of the business), we often utilize a benchmark process as part of the Transition Growth Plan to measure your business operations against comparable companies in your industry.

Business Benchmark Review

This analysis is intended to help you compare the operation of your business against similar businesses within your industry. Your type of business has specific benchmarks against which you can measure and manage your business based on the operations of successful operations in your industry. This ratio analysis may point out areas of your business that are the strengths of the business and areas in which your business is below the industry norm. You can build on the strengths of your business to maximize the value you receive for your business.

More importantly, this analysis will point out what aspects of your business should concern you now and which could concern a purchaser (and adversely impact selling price). This knowledge will help you improve those aspects of your business before a potential sale. It will also help point to potential problems that might need attention to help keep your "ship afloat" so you have a business to exit from.

We can draw an analogy between this ratio analysis and visiting a physician. When you visit a physician for a checkup, the physician will do a blood test to see if there is anything wrong with you physically (by comparing your results to patient norms). This ratio analysis acts like a blood test for your business – it diagnoses if your financial results are in line with industry norms. If not, and if steps are not taken to improve results, your business may be in poor financial health and either may not survive until you are ready to retire or will be worth far less at that time than it could be worth.

While ratio analysis is not the only way to analyze the value of a particular company, most potential purchasers of your business will conduct a ratio analysis of their own. Purchasers will adjust what they are willing to pay for your business based on these or similar ratios. Thus, it is in your best interest to be cognizant of how your business ratios compare to those of other firms within your industry and to try to improve those ratios which may not measure up.

Transition Period Strategic Growth Plan

Another way to demonstrate your financial fitness to a buyer is to have a well constructed strategic plan for achieving profitable growth into the future (and for achieving it without you). Like a good business plan, a strategic plan for future growth should demonstrate your place in your industry and your industry's place in the overall economic momentum. In essence, you need to demonstrate that you can grow.

Every business either grows or dies. Even a business with flat sales growth or flat net income is composed of elements of growth. This is because no business is static. Employees change. Employees age. Employee objectives change. Customers change. A customer's personal or business situation changes. Equipment breaks. Equipment wears out. Buildings need maintenance. Products need enhancements. New products need to be developed. Customers leave. New customers enter. Employees leave. New employees enter. Pricing structure changes. Cost structure changes. Good locations become bad locations. New locations become good locations. Competition becomes more intense. Competition may become less intense. Technology advances and the opportunities or necessities for technological change in your business operations become basic requirements going forward.

The company which has mastered the ability to deal with these ever-changing situations and to capture a net growth is the company which is going to demonstrate the steady, consistent growing cash flow which a buyer wants to see. Larry Bossidy and Ram Charan in their best selling "Confronting Reality – Doing What Matters To Get Things Right" have described this in terms of achieving lasting growth through continually differentiating your products in the marketplace.

IBM CEO Samuel J. Palmisano put it bluntly: "Either you innovate or you're in commodity hell. If you plan to avoid commodity hell, you will have to be exceptionally alert to changes in your business environment and able to move swiftly to exploit them."

Your strategic plan should objectively quantify your value drivers. For example:

- Quantify your customer retention and repeat business rate.

- Quantify your employee retention/turnover rate.

- Document and map your business processes and systems.

- Benchmark your business results compared to industry norms.

All companies reflect certain organizational behaviors and certain individual human behaviors, each of which impact your value drivers. To help attain and maintain your Company value through and beyond your exit, I work with a number of management advisory firms which can quickly assess and address those organizational and people deficiencies which may, if not dealt with, hinder a company's growth and your successful exit.

To the extent that you have developed a well-stated, well-constructed business model and strategic plan to demonstrate exactly how you intend to sustain the vitality and growth of your Company, your ability to sell your business, your ability to attract a quality buyer, and your ability to achieve your asking price are all enhanced.

Building Block 8 - Prepare My Management

Chapter 38

Build Your Leadership Team Depth Chart

In his groundbreaking study and the follow-ups, best selling book "Good To Great: Why Some Companies Make the Leap and Others Don't", Jim Collins stressed the importance of getting the right people "on the bus", getting the wrong people "off the bus", and the right people in the right seats on the bus. This is a key to not just profitably operating and growing a successful business, but also key as you address your transition/exit plans and contingencies.

The expected retirement of a key owner or other key employee, or the unexpected loss of a key owner or other key employee due to death or disability, can pose a significant financial hit to any company. Pre-planning to be prepared for this can reduce the adverse impact.

So, what should you do now? The immediate answer is not unlike that encountered every day by professional and college sports teams. They have a depth chart. In an ideal situation, there is always a back up player for whichever specialty position needs refilling due to the loss of a player, whether by death, injury or retirement. In the context of a business operation, the first line of defense is to have a company depth chart. Those next on the list are ideally always close to ready to step in as needed.

Robert Galvin of Motorola Corporation summarized the issue as follows:

"One responsibility [we] considered paramount is seeing to the continuity of capable senior leadership. We have always striven to have proven backup candidates available, employed transition training programs to best prepare the prime candidates, and been very open about [succession planning] …. We believe that continuity is immensely valuable."

Active Board of Directors

A Company's management team begins with its Board of Directors. Many companies do not take advantage of the strength and guidance provided by an active Board of Directors.

Most companies should be utilizing an active Board of Directors which consists of certain key insiders and at least one outsider who can provide insight to your industry and business. This Board also helps provide management continuity and immediate oversight in the event of your unexpected death or disability.

Advisory Board

Depending on the nature of your business, you should consider establishing an Advisory Board. The members do not have management responsibility, which enables you to focus specifically on enlisting the assistance of capable persons in your industry who do not want the responsibility or potential liability of being on the Board of Directors. An Advisory Board can be tailored to help you address one or more of such business needs as executive performance, production efficiency, strategic planning, strategic sourcing, business acquisitions, cost containment, distribution network, customer engagement, employee engagement, brand management and product/service development.

Management Recruiter Firms

Absent your own depth chart for the company, you should be prepared to quickly access the depth chart which exists throughout your industry. If you have strong talent in your company today, you would be naive to believe that they have not been in contact with, or been contacted by, executive or management recruitment firms to fill the gaps in management talent encountered by other companies throughout your industry. Whether your key employees have told you about these calls doesn't mean the calls are not occurring. Many strong management personnel have themselves developed a management recruiter contact to keep them informed of opportunities which come up through the industry to provide them with better opportunities if they aren't available with your company. This is one of the reasons for the key employee retention tools discussed elsewhere in this book.

You as a business owner should be no less aggressive and strategic in planning for the possible loss of any given key employee. If your inside depth chart is insufficient, you should have developed your own ongoing relationship with a management recruiting firm, particularly one which is familiar with your industry. To the extent that you incur an adverse financial impact from the loss of any key employee, this can be lessened by the speed with which you are able to replace that individual.

An ongoing relationship with a management recruiting firm which is already familiar with your business will help this to occur.

Develop A Specific Successor And Back-Up Successor

An Owner/Executive's transition from a business is generally not immediate, but instead is often accomplished through a transition of both ownership and management responsibilities over a period of time. According to a study by the Raymond Family Business Institute (2003), about half of CEOs over age 60 who plan to retire within five years have chosen a successor. A Management Responsibility Transition Plan represents your intent for transitioning your management responsibilities over the period of time you have chosen. This issue, like your Transition Growth Plan, is subject to the principle that: "All plans are firm until changed." However, it is a process which should be undertaken and revised each year until you have ended your "Active Duty".

Jack Welch, former CEO of General Electric, speaking about succession planning in 1991 – nine years before his anticipated retirement, had the following to say:

"From now on, [choosing my successor] is the most important decision I'll make. It occupies a considerable amount of thought almost every day."

How do you select a successor who can keep the train on the tracks in today's environment. Larry Bossidy and Ram Charan in "Confronting Reality – Doing What Matters to Get Things Right" have stressed the fact that businesses which want to last today need to raise the bar with regard to leadership. In addition to the leadership qualities which have always existed, they have pointed out that two leadership qualities that are indispensable today are business acumen and a constant need to know about what is new and different.

Not every key employee is suited to become the next leader of your company. I work with a number of advisors who help us to evaluate key employee potential and to help further develop leadership skills and, to address other potential leadership issues. This can be evaluated in the context of a Transition Growth Plan.

Case Study – Broaching The Leadership Topic

Charles presented a particularly sensitive, but not uncommon, issue regarding his succession. His son Tim had the knowledge and skill to operate the company, but he had an untreated chemical dependency problem which posed a number of obvious problems (amongst the family and employees). Charles wanted his son to succeed him, but was unwilling to trust the company to his leadership. He hadn't felt comfortable confronting his son about the problem, yet we couldn't move on with decision's regarding Charles' Transition Growth Plan options until we knew whether his son was willing to seek and abide by a treatment plan.

Part of our role as exit advisors is to help assess the likelihood that a plan will work and to help explain the prerequisites to a potential successor. We addressed this through three steps. First was to activate the company's Board of Directors, to be composed of both inside and outside members. This provided a mechanism with authority (both while Charles was around as well as after his death) to monitor whether Tim was acting responsibly and to take action to remove him if necessary. Second, we sat down with Tim and Charles to review the standards which I felt, as an exit advisor, were necessary for Charles' successor, starting with a commitment to a health physical, followed by a chemical dependency treatment plan and such other treatment as determined by the health care professionals. This put Tim in a position to agree to address the problems as a condition to succeeding his father or to tell us he would not do it, which would enable us to pursue our next Transition Growth Plan option. Our third step, once Tim was in agreement, was to enroll Tim in a leadership training program to help groom him for his new responsibilities.

Are You A Family Business With A Nonfamily CEO

If your company is a family business in which the CEO is a nonfamily member (or where you are a family member CEO who is considering a nonfamily CEO to succeed you), you will typically face unique challenges and the potential for disruptive disputes. To be successful, an effective nonfamily CEO needs to possess strong business skills, while at the same time be adept at navigating the variety of family dynamics and personal relationships that exist in a family business. The presence of a sound corporate Board of Directors as well as a Family Council can be crucial to a successful nonfamily CEO's efforts to sustain and grow the company.

Leadership Team Development Program – Sample Components

- Key Employee Retreats, pursuant to the Key Employee Retreat Agenda.
- Company Culture Survey to gain a better understanding of your Company culture and work environment.
- Leadership Team Training Program.
- Management Succession Planning Worksheet to transition management duties to one or more key employees.
- Leadership Team Depth Chart.
- Leadership Team Assessment to assess whether your management team members have the entrepreneur and management talent and skills and leadership capabilities needed as part of your business growth and transition plans.
- Activate or revise your Board of Directors.
- Create or revise your Advisory Board. The Advisory Board could help you address executive performance, strategic sourcing, distribution network, brand management, production efficiency, business acquisitions, customer engagement, product/service development, strategic planning, cost containment and employee engagement.
- Management Recruiter Engagement to become familiar with your Company and to be in a position to assist quickly as the need arises.

Chapter 39

Create A Transition Flexible Key Employee Retention Incentive

This step in the Transition Growth and Exit Planning process is intended to help you and your advisors focus on building and retaining a successful key employee management group. Having the right team in place builds company value and enhances a sale to a third party. An inside key employee or key employee group could also become a purchaser of your business in a sale to insiders.

Strong key employees will either make your company more profitable and valuable (or they will make your competitor's company more profitable and valuable if that is the better opportunity for them).

Key Employee Incentives Now

It is generally in your best interest to provide your key employees with an incentive package that motivates them to continue to excel and to remain with you. Your immediate task is to identify these key employees, determine the right incentive package and implement it. A key employee ownership incentive agreement is intended to maintain your exit flexibility.

Such an agreement will address the employee's desired and expected development, as well as provide the type of cash and equity (real or synthetic) which will best achieve these objectives.

Key Employee Incentives At Time Of Sale

While it's important to address key employee retention incentives years ahead of your exit, it is also often necessary to address this at the time of your actual exit. One typical example is the "stay bonus", which can be used not only in the event of your unexpected exit, but can also be used to help retain key personnel for at least a given period after your planned sale. This can help provide comfort to a buyer of a successful ownership transition by helping to keep your team on the new owner's "bus".

Case Study - Retention Incentive

Bob and his partner had operated a successful chain of convenience food marts for the past 20 years. They had 18 store operations throughout the Midwest. Bob and Bill were looking to exit from active duty within five years and exit from ownership within five to ten years. They had developed a fairly effective management team, with a store manager in each separate location. They wanted to explore the possibility of selling to an outside third party, however, they believed the best fit both for themselves and for their loyal managers was a sale to their management group.

About half of the store managers were approximately the same age as Bob and Bill (with similar active duty retirement objectives), while the other half of the store managers were in their 30's and 40's and were intent on continuing to grow the operations of the business. Again, this company was referred in to us through one of our banker relationships on account of their interest in seeing that this long-term bank customer was successful in their exit and overall business transition.

In order to achieve the objectives of both the older managers and the younger managers, as well as Bob and Bill, the plan was developed to divide the company into two separate entities, one of which would hold the business operations and the other of which would hold the real estate for each of the store operations, which it would then lease across to the business operating entity for a fixed rental. While there were a number of tax issues which needed to be worked out in order to make this feasible, this approach allowed Bob and Bill to effectuate a part sale, part incentive bonus over a period of years to both their younger and older store managers.

Overall, the younger store managers opted to own the business operating entity, while the older store managers opted to hold the real estate leasing entity. This provided upside growth potential long term to the younger managers, while providing a steady fixed income to the older managers as they approached and implemented their own personal retirement.

The variety of alternatives for designing an effective retention incentive are addressed in the Transition Growth and Exit Planning process.

Existing Key Employee Incentive Plan

In order to help build and retain an effective management team, I currently utilize the following:

☐ Equity based incentive program.
  ☐ Stock bonus.
  ☐ Stock option.
  ☐ Stock purchase.
  ☐ ESOP.

☐ Cash based incentive.
  ☐ Cash bonus.
  ☐ Deferred compensation.
  ☐ Phantom stock bonus.
  ☐ Stock Appreciation Right.
☐ Supplemental Employee Retirement Plan.
☐ Executive Coaching Program.
☐ Other _____

Awards under this plan are based on:
☐ Individual key employee performance.
☐ Key employee group performance.
☐ Company net income growth.
☐ Company sales growth.
☐ Other _____
☐ Vesting Formula: _____
  _____

☐ Forfeiture Events: _____
  _____

Key Employee Incentive Agreement

In order to help incent key employee performance and retention and to help determine whether our key employees will be suitable and willing owners, and to begin to implement my exit through an insider transfer, the following transfers to key employees would be structured:

☐ Transfer up to _____% of outstanding shares now over _____ years (a) as part of a key employee incentive plan and/or (b) as the beginning steps of a full transfer to key employee(s) and/or family.

☐ These shares will be in the form of:
    ☐ Actual ownership shares.   ☐ Stock Appreciation
    ☐ Phantom Stock.   Rights.

☐ The share purchase price would be:
    ☐ Full appraised value.   ☐ Book value.
    ☐ Full formula value using the   ☐ _____% of above.
        following formula: _____   ☐ Bonus.
    ☐ Full agreed value of $_____   ☐ Other _____.
        per share.

☐ Implement a ☐ one time _____ year vesting or ☐ rolling vesting plan with a _____ year vesting formula.

☐ Require a sale-back of all shares upon:
    ☐ voluntary termination of   ☐ at a price equal to ☐
        employment   then fair value; or
    ☐ involuntary termination of   ☐ a percentage of
        employment.   value or as follows: __
                                     _____.

☐ Employee share ownership would be subject to:
    ☐ Transfer restrictions.
    ☐ Voting restrictions.
    ☐ Must sell requirements if company is sold.
    ☐ Buy-back on voluntary termination at _____% of _____.
    ☐ Buy-back on involuntary termination at _____% of _____.
    ☐ Buy-back on retirement at _____% of _____.
    ☐ Buy-back on death at _____% of _____.
    ☐ Buy-back on disability at _____% of _____.

☐ I would maintain control shares till my final exit.

☐ Key employee group would have:
    ☐ Right of first refusal to purchase my control shares.
    ☐ Option to purchase my control shares at time to be designated by me.

☐ I would retain the right to re-acquire the shares if I decide to sell the business to a Third Party.

☐ The employees to be included will be:
☐ Name: _____ at _____%
☐ Name: _____ at _____%
☐ Name: _____ at _____%
☐ Name: _____ at _____%
☐ Name: _____ at _____%
☐ Name: _____ at _____%
☐ This Share Purchase would be documented with a separate Key Employee Incentive Agreement.
☐ The shares would become subject to the Buy-Sell Agreement.
☐ The key employee shareholders would be subject to the Business Continuity Agreement.

Building Block 9 - Prepare My Company

Chapter 40

Structure Business Entities For Your Transition

Depending on the make up of your Company's businesses and assets, and your objective for what components you wish to ultimately sell or keep, it may be necessary to restructure your business entities. For example, you may wish to retain a particular operating division, either due to personal preference or because you don't believe it will be an attractive or feasible part of the business mix that your anticipated buyer will want to acquire.

You might also wish to retain the real estate which your company uses and lease this to the buyer.

Another type of asset class which can in the right circumstances be retained is specifically identifiable intellectual property that your business utilizes. This may be a particular process, technique, know how, trademark, etc. which you wish to keep and license to the buyer.

Business entity restructuring may also be necessary due to the change in management you anticipate upon your exit. For example, if you have two distinct divisions which require different management talents that you could handle but your successor doesn't have, it may be necessary to divide the company into more than one entity to suit the management talent you have available to you. A corporate restructuring may also be desirable where you have more than one child who is capable of managing the Company and you wish to place each in the leadership of a particular Company division.

You may also find that due to your tax savings plans it becomes necessary to revise your company corporate structure. This may, for example, be due to "S" vs. "C" status under your Federal Income Tax Plan or to better address your nexus factors under your State Income Tax Plan. Or you may restructure to meet your Estate Tax Plan.

Present Structure

New Structure

OWNERS
You

OWNERS
You
Family

OWNERS
You
Family
Key Emp.

Main Entity No. 1

Entity Name: AB, Inc.
Tax Status: "S"
Type of Entity: Corp
Main Activity: Mfg.
Main Assets:
Inventory, Equipment,
Workforce
Other Facts: Son can
Manage

New Entity No. 2

Entity Name: CD, Inc.
Tax Status: "C"
Type of Entity: Corp
Main Activity: Distrib.
Main Assets:
Distribution Channels
Other Facts: Key
Employee can
manage

Main Entity No. 1

Entity Name: ABCD, Inc.
Tax Status: "C"
Type of Entity: Corp.
Main Activity: Mfg.& Dist.
Main Assets: Inventory,
Equipment, Workforce,
Other Facts: Both
divisions profitable

Other Existing Entities:

Real Estate
Limited Partnership

Reasons for These Changes:

1. To enable son to become president of AB, Inc. and other employee president of CD, Inc.

2. To enable AB, Inc. to become "S" tax status, but keep "C" for CD, Inc.

3. To provide ownership to key employee only in the distribution business.

4. To keep CD, Inc.'s multiple state nexus from reaching AB, Inc.'s income.

Other Existing Entity Changes:
• Convert Real Estate Limited Partnership to a Limited Liability Company to enhance limited liability protection.

Chapter 41

Secure Pre-Exit Outside Consents

Various outside third parties with which you regularly transact business may have a strong interest in having some control over who owns your company as a condition for that person to continue to do business with you. For this reason, various types of agreements and business relationships will have provisions buried within them which prohibit the sale or control of your business - or which prohibit the sale of substantially all of the assets of your business – without first obtaining their written consent.

Therefore, as you look ahead toward your future exit, these types of agreements and business relationships need to be reviewed to determine if they present potential roadblocks to proceeding as you may otherwise wish to proceed.

One of the objectives of this book is to suggest to business owners the fact that they should always operate their business with a view towards their future exit. It makes sense, therefore, to negotiate flexible future exit alternatives into agreements and business relationships if and when an outside third party seeks to impose constraints during the course of your business operations.

This is not always possible and, in fact, might be adverse to the business if a certain element of control would provide a favorable comfort level that would enhance a relationship with an important third party. Nevertheless, these types of provisions should not be freely granted when negotiating an agreement, but should instead be looked upon with the continuing view towards your expected or unexpected exit.

Typical Consents Needed

One of the most frequent contracts in which you will find "change of control" provisions is in a loan agreement with a third party bank or other financial institution. This is especially the case when the bank is lending largely on the basis of the strength of the current owner or owners.

While less common, it's also possible to find "change of control" provisions in certain customer and supplier agreements, as well as within the body of certain government granted licenses or permits.

Franchisor's Consent

Of particular interest to franchisees is the "change of control" provision in a franchisor/franchisee agreement. Here, the franchisor will often want to maintain control, or at least have the option to veto a change in control, so as to have the opportunity to evaluate whether a new business owner will be satisfactory for the franchisor's standards of operation.

Franchisors are typically going to want to know the following about a potential buyer of your franchise:

- That the buyer is suitable and financially strong.

- That the buyer will implement the franchise operating systems.

- That the buyer will contribute to the health of the franchise network.

- That the buyer meets the current franchisee criteria.

- That the buyer will be a good fit.

- That the buyer won't overpay and be unable to be successful.

The franchisor's elements of control and direction will usually be found in your franchise agreement and the franchisor's uniform franchise offering circular. Franchisors generally cannot (and should not want to) unreasonably withhold consent but instead should operate with a sense of good faith and fair dealing.

Franchisees should expect a franchise transfer process will exist. This would typically include the following elements:

- An established transfer policy.

- A franchisor "transfer package".

- A need to sign a general release.

- A need to submit 2 years tax returns and financial statements to be checked for under-reporting.

- That the buyer must sign the franchise agreement.

- A need to submit the purchase/sale agreement for review.

- A need to submit the buyer's financial statement and background.

- A requirement that the buyer should go through full franchise training.

Chapter 42

Create Pre-Exit Accounting System Credibility

No matter what you think your business may be worth, and no matter what you believe your earnings have been, none of this matters unless the buyer believes it. A buyer will believe it only if your accounting system is credible, and only if you utilize methods of accounting which provide a sufficient reflection of the true net income, net cash flow, and net worth of your business. This holds true whether the buyer is an outside third party or whether the buyer is a capable inside key employee.

A credible accounting system and a proper regime of accounting methods is also important to most business owners as continuing owners of a business. This is really the only way that an owner can have an accurate idea of exactly how well or how poorly his or her company may be performing. A frequent reason companies end up in bankruptcy is because they failed, due to bad accounting, to realize the actual financial condition of their company.

The presence or absence of a credible accounting system and proper accounting methods is not necessarily dependent on the size or age of a business. While it can normally be expected that a younger, smaller company is more likely to be deficient, we have seen good accounting systems in small young companies, and poor accounting systems in larger older companies. Accounting systems have gained a lot of national attention in recent years, due to some of the high profile companies utilizing improper accounting practices, which, at a minimum, were aimed at deceiving investors and, which in a number of instances, have resulted in the downfall of the business.

It is outside of the scope of this book to go into detail on how to establish and to test your accounting system and methods with respect to your particular business or industry. When we determine during the Transition Growth and Exit Planning process that a company's accounting system is deficient, we work with CPAs to assist the business owner in making the changes necessary. What is within the scope of this book, however, is to touch on a few of the particular aspects of accounting which impact the viability of a business owner's exit.

If you originally bought your business, or if your company has been actively engaged in acquiring other businesses as part of your growth strategy, then these concepts should be readily apparent.

The most effective way to answer the question as to whether your accounting system is credible, and whether your accounting methods accurately reflect the performance of your business, is to take off your seller's hat and put on your buyer's hat. Would you buy your company based on the reliability of your accounting system?

Outside Account's Report

First of all, knowing what you know about your business, answer the question of whether you would find a high degree of comfort in believing your own financial statements if they were placed in front of you by a third party. There are several reasons for the role of an outside independent accountant during the life of a business. The accountant performs an attest accountability function, based upon an outside look, as to the reliability of a set of financial statements. The accountant lends this accountability, typically in one of three possible levels of comfort.

The Compilation

The first is that of a compilation, which provides the least amount of comfort to a third party. The compiled financial statements by an accountant simply represent a means to provide a fairly uniform approach for reporting financial results in a commonly-accepted format. The compiled financial statements provide very little comfort to a potential buyer. A compilation is limited to presenting in the form of financial statements and supplementary schedules information that is the representation of management. The CPA has not audited or reviewed the financial statements and supplementary schedules and does not express an opinion or any other form of assurance on them.

In addition, typically, management elects to omit substantially all of the disclosures required by generally accepted accounting principles.

The Review

Second is the reviewed financial statements. Here, the accountant will provide a limited amount of review of a company's accounting systems and will sign off on the reviewed financial statements only if the accountant's limited tests have been met. A review consists principally of inquiries of company personnel and analytical procedures applied to financial data. It is substantially less in scope than an audit in accordance with generally accepted auditing standards.

The review is made for the purpose of expressing limited assurance that there are no material modifications that should be made to the financial statements in order for them to be in conformity with generally accepted accounting principles.

The reviewed financial statements provide a better level of comfort to a buyer, which some buyers will accept.

The Audit

The third and highest level of independent comfort which can be provided to a buyer by an outside accounting firm is the audited financial statement. Here, the accountant, utilizing generally accepted auditing standards, has analyzed the company's accounting methods and tested the company's adherence to those methods, to the extent necessary to render its opinion that the financial statements fairly represent the financial results of the company.

Even the audited financial statements present a limited review, because the accountant does not guarantee that the statements are necessarily completely accurate. An audit includes examining, on a test basis, evidence supporting the amounts and disclosures in the financial statements. An audit also includes assessing the accounting principles used and significant estimates made by management, as well as evaluating the overall financial statement presentation.

The CPA will, if approved, render an opinion that the financial statements present fairly, in all material respects, the financial position of the company and the results of its operations and its cash flows for the years then ended in conformity with accounting principles generally accepted in the United States of America.

The audited financial statement provides a high degree of reliability on which a potential buyer can rely.

If these accounting attest functions came to the business without a price tag, then, of course, every business would engage an accountant for an annual audit. However, each level of review comes with an increasing annual cost for the business. Often, a business owner will decide that he or she is comfortable with their own internal accounting systems and methods and either will not engage an outside accounting firm or will engage a firm for only a low level of review. This is primarily a matter for the company's owners to determine the extent to which they wish to place reliance on the level of report which they are obtaining.

If the company relies on a material amount of outside lending to support its operations, then the lender may require as a condition for the loan that your financial statements be audited, or at least reviewed.

Pre-Exit Prep

Regardless of how you have chosen to use an outside accounting firm in the past, as you approach your exit, you need to focus on obtaining at least a reviewed or audited financial statement, for at least three to five years prior to your exit. Many financial buyers and strategic buyers will require reviewed or audited financial statements for this period of time at a minimum. If your potential buyer is itself a publicly held company, and if the acquisition of your business is material, then the publicly held company will probably not be in a position to even consider buying your business unless you have at least three years of audited financial statements.

The bottom line is that whether or not you believe your accounting system is credible, it will typically be viewed as credible by a third party only to the extent of the independent outside attestation rendered by a certified public accountant. The higher degree provided, the more likely that a buyer will be interested in your business, and if interested, the less likely that the buyer would attempt to discount the price based on accounting statement uncertainties.

Accounting Methods

While there are a number of accounting methods that impact various parts of a company's financial statements, the biggest difference in methods are the cash method of accounting versus the accrual method of accounting. The basic difference, while more complicated than this, is essentially that in the cash method of accounting, income is reported as cash is received, and expenses are reported as they are paid.

By contrast, with the accrual method of accounting, income is reported as it is earned, and expenses are accrued as they are incurred. By and large, the accrual method of accounting provides a much more accurate reflection of the actual performance of a business for a given accounting period. Buyers will frequently not even consider purchasing a company unless the company utilizes the accrual method of accounting for its financial statements.

For many types of businesses, the accrual method of accounting is required for income tax purposes, which is often the reason in the first place why a company has started using the accrual method of accounting for its financial statements. In any event, as you approach your exit, if you have been operating under the cash method of accounting, you need to seriously consider having your outside accountant establish your business on the accrual method of accounting.

Accounting Detail

Credible financial statements utilizing the proper methods of accounting still do not complete the picture for the potential buyer. The sophisticated buyer is going to compare your company's performance against that of other companies in your industry, and then attempt to measure that in reference to the investment and cash flow objectives of that buyer. Part of the review which we can perform through our Transition Growth Planning teams is to assess the financial detail provided by a company's financial statements in comparison to that which will be expected by a buyer.

The best way to demonstrate to a buyer that steady growth will exist is to have at least three to five years of consistent, steady cash flow growth, which can be demonstrated through credible financial statements and a credible accounting system.

Financial Stability

Do your financial statements demonstrate financial stability? Do they demonstrate strong financial ratios? Do your financial metrics score well under an Altman Z financial predictor analysis? The future purchaser of your company will be looking for this.

Chapter 43

Assure Pre-Exit Inside Control To Sell Company

In order to have your business in an ongoing position to be sold to a third party, whether based on present plans to sell the business in the near future or based on a decision to always be in a position to sell should the right offer come along unexpectedly (or if you should die or become disabled), certain steps should generally be taken well in advance of a sale.

One of these steps is to assure that you have the necessary control to be able to sell your entire company – whether this is through a sale of the stock or assets of your company. You don't want to be in a position where a minority shareholder can unreasonably hold up the sale of the company.

You can typically authorize the sale of all or substantially all of the assets of your company, followed by a liquidation distribution, (under most state business corporation laws) if you own at least two-thirds of the voting control of your company.

However, if your sale will be of the company's stock, buyers will often want to be able to purchase 100% of the stock. By negotiating a "must come along" or "drag along" provision into your Buy-Sell Agreement in advance of your exit, you'll know you have the option to deliver 100% of the stock in your company in the event of a sale.

Under such a "drag along" provision in a Buy-Sell Agreement, the terms will typically provide that the majority owner can require that the minority owners must also sell their stock to the buyer. This will typically mean that the terms for the minority owner would be the same as that of the majority owner.

Absent such control, and absent the ability to purchase the stock of non-consenting minority shareholders under a Buy-Sell Agreement, it may be necessary to utilize a reverse merger (also known as a squeeze out merger) to cash out the non-consenting shareholders. This can present delays and disruptions if it needs to be done at the time you are trying to sell the Company.

Sample "Drag Along" Provision in Buy-Sell Agreement

"**Drag-Along Upon Sale of Company (At Option of Majority Owner).** In connection with any Transfer, other than a Permitted Transfer, in an arms length transaction for value to any person or persons who are not a party to this Agreement by one or more Owners who Transfer fifty percent (50%) or more of the voting interest or value of the Company ("Selling Owners"), the Selling Owners shall have the right to require each non-selling Owner ("Minority Owner") to Transfer, and each Minority Owner shall be required to Transfer, that portion of its Shares that represents the same percentage of the total Shares held by such Minority Owner as the Shares being disposed of by the Selling Owners represents of the total Shares held by the Selling Owners, such Shares to be Transferred free and clear of all Liens. All Shares Transferred by Minority Owners pursuant to this section shall be sold at the same price and otherwise treated identically with the Shares being sold by the Selling Owners in all respects, provided, however, that the Minority Owners shall not be required to make any representations or warranties in connection with such Transfer other than representations and warranties as to (i) such Minority Owners' ownership of his, her or its Shares to be Transferred free and clear of all Liens, (ii) such Minority Owners' power and authority to effect such Transfer, and (iii) such matters pertaining to compliance with securities laws as the transferee may reasonably require. The following additional terms shall apply [Not provided in sample]."

Chapter 44

Initiate Pre-Exit House-In-Order Check-Off

Every buyer will expect to "kick the tires" before purchasing your business. This is typically referred to as a "due diligence" review and will entail the review by the buyer and its legal counsel of various documents and other information pertinent to your business.

The objective is to learn the details about your business which the buyer wants to know before completing a purchase and to determine the scope and extent of potential liabilities and surprises.

Never Underestimate The Other Side

If you are not prepared for this at the time of your exit, or if such a review uncovers significant issues, then your sale can be delayed or indefinitely sidetracked or a particular selling opportunity can be lost. While both parties to a business sale typically hope to be cooperative and constructive in negotiating and implementing a business transfer, never forget that the buyer is still an opponent during this process who is attempting to negotiate price and terms which might not be in your best interests. Be prepared and don't underestimate the scope of the effort the buyer will bring to bear.

You should always have your "house-in-order" and ready to sell. By reviewing and preparing for a "due diligence" review ahead of your exit, you can be prepared to handle a buyer's questions, objectives and negotiating tactics to help achieve a more successful exit when the time comes.

What follows is a sample "due diligence buyer checklist" typically used in a business purchase.

Due Diligence Buyer Checklist

1.   **Corporate Records**. Full and complete copies of the corporate minute books and related records for the company. This information should include, but not be limited to, charter documents, by-laws, shareholders minutes, directors minutes, stock registers, etc.

2. **Countries**. A list of all domestic and foreign jurisdictions where the company is qualified to do business.

3. **States**. A list of states where the company transacts business and a description of the activities in each state.

4. **Tax Jurisdictions**. A list of all jurisdictions where the company files tax returns and a description of all federal, state and local taxes paid.

5. **Tax Reporting**. Copies of all federal, state and local tax returns relating to the company for the past five years and for any other open years.

6. **Management**. A list of current officers and directors of the company.

7. **Royalties**. A list of any royalty or similar payments (e.g. technical assistance payments) being made to any foreign party.

8. **Debts**. A description of all of the company's presently outstanding indebtedness, including original and current amounts outstanding, due dates, and interest rates, and copies of all documents relating to such indebtedness, including, without limitation, mortgages, indentures, loan agreements and promissory notes.

9. **Financial Commitments**. A description of all guarantees, commitments, indemnification agreements and other arrangements that the company is a party to and copies of all such documents relating to such arrangements.

10. **Depreciation**. A copy of the company's tax depreciation schedule and financial depreciation schedule.

11. **Financial Statements**. Financial statements for the company for the past three years.

12. **Real Estate**. A list and complete legal description of all real estate owned by the company, together with evidence of title,

deeds, title insurance, surveys, title opinions, mortgages, deeds of trust, etc.

13. **Leases**. A list of all leased real estate, together with copies of all such leases, as amended.

14. **Contracts**. A list of all material agreements and contracts that the company is a party to. Copies of all such contracts will usually be requested, together with a summary description of any oral agreements to which the company is a party.

15. **Employment Contracts**. A list and copies of all employment and consulting agreements, labor or union contracts, executive compensation plans, bonus plans, deferred compensation plans, pension and profit sharing plans, retirement plans, group life insurance, health and welfare plans, severance plans and other employee plans whether written or oral, providing for benefits for employees of the company together with IRS determination letters and most recent Form 5500's and funding contracts.

16. **Intellectual Property**. A list of all trademarks, trade names, copyrights, patents or registrations or licenses which are presently utilized by the company for the conduct of its business.

17. **Employees**. A list of all employees of the company indicating years of service and compensation.

18. **Licenses**. Copies of all material licenses, permits, decrees and orders of all governmental bodies or agencies or courts, owned, or held by, or applicable to the company.

19. **Litigation**. A description of all pending or threatened litigation, administrative proceedings, arbitration or governmental investigations (whether domestic or foreign) relating to the company. This list should also include a summary of all material litigation or investigations which have occurred during the past three years and copies of lawyer's replies to audit letters insofar as they relate to the company and copies of consent decrees, injunctions, etc., relating to the company.

20. **Investigations**. Copies of all investigations, inspections or citations under any federal, state or local laws or regulations.

21. **Banking**. The name of each bank and financial institution in which the company has an account or safety deposit box, together with the account numbers and the persons authorized to draw thereon or procure credit therefrom.

22. **Related Party Transactions**. A list and description of all transactions between the company and its directors or officers.

23. **Stock Agreements**. A list and copies of any agreements relating to shares of stock (e.g. options, warrants, stockholders' agreements, etc.) issued or to be issued by the company.

24. **Environmental**. Environmental information pursuant to an Environmental Questionnaire and Disclosure Statement.

Business Pre-Flight Check-Up

While the Transition Growth and Exit Planning process should begin 5 – 15 years ahead of your planned exit date, when you are within 2 years of your planned sale to a third party, we want to review and implement our 25 point "Pre-Flight Check-Up" to help assure you are ready to go to market.

The Business Sale Process

In a separate Chapter I discuss the business sale process. By understanding that process today and by keeping your house in order through an up-to-date Due Diligence Buyer Checklist and the "Pre-Flight Check-Up", you will be better ready for sale, whether your sale or exit occurs on your timeframe or pursuant to an unexpected offer.

Building Block 10 – Prepare My Tax Savings Plans

Chapter 45

Reduce Your Estate Taxes

Should You Be Concerned With Estate Tax?

Under the Federal Estate Tax law, you are subject to this tax if you die with an estate worth more than the sum of your marital deduction (if applicable) and your lifetime exemption. The estate tax lifetime exemptions phase-in over 2002-2009. For those persons with taxable estates who die before 2010, the tax rates range from top rates of 50% in 2002 to 45% in 2009. The estate tax is repealed for only year 2010. After 2010 the estate tax is reinstated at the old tax rates (up to 55%) with only a $1 million exemption (subject to expected Congressional change).

Do You Have A Taxable Estate?

You have a taxable estate if the value of your Estate (less your marital deduction) exceeds the following exemption amounts:

Year of Death	Exemption Amount	Year of Death	Exemption Amount
2001	$ 675,000	2007	$2,000,000
2002	$1,000,000	2008	$2,000,000
2003	$1,000,000	2009	$3,500,000
2004	$1,500,000	2010	N/A (Tax Repealed)
2005	$1,500,000	2011+	$1,000,000 (Tax
2006	$2,000,000		Reinstated)

As of the date of publication, the Congress is expected to enact legislation in 2009 that would set the exemption and retain the estate tax.

Do States Impose Death Taxes?

Depending on the State, either or both a State Estate Tax and Inheritance Tax can apply.

What Tools Exist For Reducing Or Eliminating Federal Estate Taxes Through Proper Estate Planning?

The following are some of the tools which presently exist for reducing or eliminating your Federal Estate Taxes. These are based on specific provisions which have been established in the law to enable taxpayers to plan their affairs in a legal manner for reducing the estate taxes which would otherwise be due by their estates.

- **Annual exemption gifts.** The present estate tax laws permit you to make gifts of up to $13,000 to as many persons as you would like free of federal gift tax. This is an annual exemption which is available to both spouses. It is typically used for annual exemption gifting to children, grandchildren, and/or children's spouses. These gifts can include shares in your business or other investment assets. A gifting program should never be started until you've determined the coverage of your and your spouse's lifetime needs.

- **Gifting Vehicle.** Often, a parent or grandparent would prefer not to make their gifts directly to their children or grandchildren in the form of cash. A common technique to address this objective is to create a family limited partnership or a family limited liability company. These types of techniques can also be viewed as creating a bucket, into which you place a certain amount of cash or other investment assets. Then, just like giving shares of stock in a corporation, you can gift shares of ownership interest in the bucket to your children, grandchildren, and/or children's spouses. Under this arrangement, you would typically retain some portion of the ownership, which would represent a controlling ownership (even if it represented less than 50% of the total value of the "bucket").

  Other gifting vehicles to be reviewed with an exit advisor include grantor retained interest trust (known as a GRAT, GRUT or QPRT), an "intentionally defective" grantor trust, a generation shipping trust, a private annuity, and a self-canceling installment note. Details of these techniques are beyond the scope of this book and are addressed further in the Transition Growth System.

- **Lifetime Exemption Gifting.** You can during your lifetime utilize up to $1 million of your lifetime exemption to avoid payment of the gift tax, should you wish to gift more than the $13,000 annual exemption amounts. This can be done, for example, if you wish to have a means to move future growth out of your estate. For example, if you owned an asset which today is worth $1 million, but which on the date of your death had grown to $3.5 million, then you would need your full lifetime exemption (presently $3.5 million) to avoid paying estate taxes on that portion of your estate. If instead, you gifted that asset today, using $1 million of your $3.5 million lifetime amount, then the asset (and the future growth) has been removed from your estate using only $1 million of your $3.5 million lifetime exemption amount. This would leave the balance of your $3.5 million lifetime exemption amount (i.e. $2.5 million) to avoid estate taxes on another $2.5 million remaining in your estate. The family limited partnership or the family limited liability company can be utilized for this type of lifetime exemption gifting as well.

- **Life Insurance Trust.** If your combined estates (husband and wife) are presently valued at over $7 million (including the value of your life insurance), then a commonly used estate tax reduction technique is the life insurance trust. This is a powerful estate tax planning technique for the following reason. Let's assume, for example, that you and your spouse have estates consisting of $7 million in investment and business assets, along with $1.5 million in life insurance. This life insurance would be valued at the full face amount of $1.5 million upon your death. However, during your lifetime, it's valuation is relatively small (basically equal to the unearned portion of your last premium payment and any cash value).

Typically, this life insurance is in place in order to provide funds for a surviving spouse and for surviving minor or young adult children. Unlike an investment account or a business, it's not something that you otherwise need or use during your lifetime. Therefore, for that reason, it is an ideal asset to gift to your children, since they will be the ultimate recipients of the proceeds anyway. It is particularly ideal because its present gift tax value is, as previously stated, extremely low in comparison to its future estate tax value, because the estate tax value literally blossoms into existence upon your death. Therefore, it is an asset which you can easily gift, typically, using your annual exemptions (and/or part of your lifetime exemption).

Since, however, you may not wish to have the life insurance proceeds immediately available to your children upon your death, a trust can be used to hold the proceeds until that point in their lives at which you would like the proceeds to be distributed. A trustee can be appointed to make distributions as needed for their living, education, and health-related expenses. In addition, provisions can be included which provide that the funds can be used for your surviving spouse as needed for your surviving spouse's support (without pulling the life insurance proceeds into your surviving spouse's estate). Since this technique constitutes a gift of an asset out of your estate, the estate rules for "completed gifts" need to be met. For this reason, your gifting of life insurance into a trust typically needs to be an "irrevocable trust" which provides that you cannot revoke the gift at a later date.

- **Disability Gifting**. If you have established the above type of gifting program, then you would typically not want this to be disrupted if you became disabled. The law allows you to establish a Gifting Power of Attorney in which you have appointed someone to continue your gifting program should you become disabled.

- **Payment of Estate Taxes**. If you anticipate an estate tax liability despite the above gifting tools, and you anticipate that your estate will not have enough readily available liquid assets to pay the estate taxes, then the estate taxes can be pre-funded through the purchase of life insurance. Since estate taxes become due only upon the death of the second spouse, a second-to-die life insurance policy provides a more economical way to fund life insurance, since the life insurance risk is based on two lives rather than simply one, resulting typically in a lower annual premium investment.

Case Study – Estate Tax Reduction

Charlie came in to meet with us about 12 years ago regarding his future exit. He anticipated operating Charlie Co for another ten years, and then wanted to retire from active duty, with the possibility of either retaining his stock ownership within the family and living on company dividend distributions or selling should the right buyer come along. Charlie had five married children, 10 grandchildren, and his wife was still alive. He estimated the value of Charlie Co at approximately $9 million. Based on a further valuation analysis, the full estimated fair market value of Charlie Co in a sale to an outside strategic buyer was estimated at $10 million. Charlie's estate plan consisted of a Will which left everything to his wife if she survived him, followed by equal distributions to each of their children following both of their deaths.

We estimated that if Charlie and his wife had died then, they would have received only one of the available two federal estate tax lifetime exemptions of $600,000 (as it existed at the time). Their deaths would have resulted in federal and state death taxes

---

of approximately $4 million. Since Charlie's net estate consisted mainly of the corporation, he and his wife did not have sufficient cash assets in their estate to pay this estate tax. Further, the estate tax would have strapped the corporation for cash if it had to come up with this to fund the estate tax obligations. The entire stock of Charlie Co was in Charlie's name, with none in his wife's name.

There were a number of steps which we took to begin reducing the potential death taxes. First, we revoked Charlie and his wife's Wills and replaced them with Living Trusts which utilized the proper formulas to obtain the then $600,000 federal estate tax exemption for each spouse, for a total of $1.2 million of federal estate tax exemption (which today would be a total of $4.0 million exemption). Second, using the Gift Tax marital deduction, we split Charlie's stock ownership with his wife, so that she would have a portion of the estate in her name in order to fully utilize her estate tax exemption should she pre-decease Charlie. These two steps meant that their net taxable estate had now been reduced from $9.4 million to $8.8 million, a federal estate tax savings so far of approximately $300,000 (a savings today of about $1.0 million).

Third, we obtained a full business appraisal for Charlie Co in order to determine and document the extent of minority and non-marketability discounts available for reducing the federal estate and gift tax impacts. This appraisal indicated a combined valuation discount of 30%.

Next, we implemented a gifting program to Charlie and his wife's children, their spouses and the grandchildren. The then-existing annual gift tax exemption (per donee) was $10,000. Between the five children, their spouses and the grandchildren, this presented the opportunity for 20 annual exemptions, totaling $200,000 per year for Charlie as well as for his wife. This provided the opportunity to remove $400,000 per year from their estate. In light of the 30% minority and non-marketability discounts, this enabled us to transfer approximately $600,000 of face value stock to them each year.

Over time, this could result in Charlie and his wife transferring over 50% of the company stock to their family members. Charlie did not want to risk a loss of control of the corporation.

Therefore, we substituted his existing single class of voting common stock through a recapitalization of the corporation which resulted in the issuance of voting and non-voting stock to Charlie and his wife in place of their single class of voting stock. This enabled Charlie and his wife to use non-voting stock for the gifting to their children, in-laws and grandchildren.

We also wanted to provide for the continuation of the gifting program if Charlie or his wife were to become disabled and unable to make gifts on their own. Therefore, we executed gifting powers of attorney for each spouse.

Lastly, in order to provide for future control over the stock ownership in the event of a family dispute or child divorce, a Buy Sell Agreement was executed, to which the gifted stock would be subject.

Charlie and his wife's 10 grandchildren were not evenly divided amongst the five children. In order, however, to use the full gift tax annual exclusions, while at the same time wanting to maintain equality amongst the five children's families, the full annual exemption gifts were made to each grandchild and additional shares were transferred to the children who had less children of their own. In order to do this without current gift tax, Charlie and his wife elected to use part of their $600,000 lifetime exemption to offset the additional gifted amount.

In addition, in order to provide cash liquidity funding for the balance of the estate tax, we suggested that Charlie and his wife invest in a second-to-die life insurance policy to be placed in a separate life insurance trust. Under this arrangement, life insurance proceeds would be paid upon the death of the last of Charlie and his wife to die (which also would be the time when the estate taxes would be due). Further, by placing the life insurance into a life insurance trust, the life insurance proceeds themselves would not incur additional estate taxes for their estates.

Chapter 46

Take Pre-Exit Tax Reduction Steps

A Transition Growth Plan provides the opportunity to significantly reduce both the seller's taxes and the buyer's taxes upon the sale and purchase of a business.

Most business owners are familiar with the fact that a sale of their business will typically result in federal and state income tax obligations which will be created and due upon the sale of a business. Depending on the (a) business structure, (b) terms of the sale, (c) the location of the seller, and (d) pre-exit tax planning by the seller, these federal and state income taxes will either be maximized or minimized. In addition, depending on the state within which the business operates, there is the potential for sales/use taxes, franchise taxes or other transfer taxes, particularly if the transaction is an asset sale which is not covered by an exemption.

What is less frequently known or understood is the fact that a buyer also needs to pay federal and state income taxes upon the purchase of a business. This is because in order for a buyer to pay the purchase price, the buyer needs cash. In order for a buyer to possess cash, the buyer needs to earn cash. Those earnings, like other earnings, will be subject to federal and state income taxes.

For example, if the buyer needs to pay the purchase price of $1,000,000, the buyer needs to earn pre-tax cash of approximately $1,700,000. Assuming normal income tax rates (combined federal and state of approximately 40%), then $700,000 of this pre-tax cash would be paid in federal and state income taxes, leaving a balance of $1,000,000 to pay the purchase price.

The reason for this is that the buyer can typically not deduct the price paid for the business (although when assets are purchased, some portion of the price may be deducted over time as depreciation). If the million dollar price was fully deductible currently against income taxes, then there in effect would be no tax on the buyer. This is because the buyer would need pre-tax cash earnings of only $1,000,000 to pay for the business, because the deductible purchase price (if that were possible) would offset the million dollar pre-tax cash earnings to result in no income taxes on those earnings.

Below are some of the pre-exit tax reduction election and other tax steps which can be taken to help minimize the potential income taxes to both the seller and the buyer. For purposes of these illustrations, the following assumptions are made. First, the stated value/sales price for the full ownership of the business is $1,000,000. Next, the tax basis of the stock, as well as the tax basis of the assets are each $200,000. The corporate and personal ordinary income tax combined rate is 40% (35% federal, 5% state). The personal capital gain combined tax rate is 20% (15% federal, 5% state).

The sale is structured as an asset sale, on the basis that the buyer has specified a preference to purchase the assets of the business rather than the stock ownership of the corporation. This would mean that in order for the business owners to receive cash upon the sale, the selling price would be paid to the corporation and then distributed to the stockholders in liquidation of the corporation.

"C" Corporation Asset Sale

Upon the sale of the business under the above assumptions, the following would be the seller's tax and buyer's tax for the transaction.

	"C" Corp Asset Sale
Price:	
Sale Price	$1,000,000
Basis	-200,000
Taxable Gain	800,000
Seller Tax:	
Corporate	320,000
Personal	100,000
	420,000
Buyer Tax:	700,000
Total Tax	1,120,000
Buyer $ Needed	1,700,000
Net $ to Seller	580,000

"S" Corporation Asset Sale

If instead the corporation had elected to be taxed as an "S" Corporation, then the above double seller's tax could be avoided. This is because the "S" Corporation would not have a tax obligation on the sale of the assets. In order for this to be fully effective, the "S" election (to convert a "C" corporation) must be made at least 10 years in advance of the owner's exit. Under such circumstances, the transaction can be compared to the "C" Asset Sale as follows:

	"C" Corp Asset Sale	vs.	"S" Corp Asset Sale
Price:			
Sale Price	$1,000,000		$1,000,000
Basis	-200,000		-200,000
Taxable Gain	800,000		800,000
Seller Tax:			
Corporate	320,000		-0-
Personal	100,000		160,000
	420,000		160,000
Buyer Tax:	700,000		700,000
Total Tax	1,120,000		860,000
Buyer $ Needed	1,700,000		1,700,000
Net $ to Seller	$580,000		$840,000

Case Study – Tax Elections

Frank met with us about 15 years ago to discuss his Transition Growth Planning for his wholly owned company which manufactured school supplies. He anticipated selling the business one day to an outside third party, although he also wanted to be in a position to sell the company to one or more inside key employees, depending on how his key employees developed over the next 10 to 12 years. Amongst other things, Frank was interested in minimizing his income taxes upon the sale of his business.

Frank wasn't sure if an outside buyer would purchase the stock or assets of his company. He was pretty sure that if he sold his company to an insider, they would purchase the stock of the company. Frank had started the company approximately 12 years earlier. He had very little tax "basis" in his stock, and his assets reflected his depreciated cost basis.

The immediate question was whether Frank could or should elect subchapter "S" status. He had been a "C" corporation since he had founded it 15 years earlier. We utilize a multi-factor analysis in advising our clients on making this election. Given that analysis, Frank elected to be an "S" corporation. This had the benefit to him of enabling him to sell the assets of the corporation without a double income tax. It also provided him with the ability to continually "step-up" the "tax basis" in his stock each year based on company earnings net of dividends, which also provided him the potential for a reduced single income tax should he end up selling the stock of his company, either to an outside third party or to his insiders. In order to receive the full benefit of obtaining a single tax on the sale of the assets of his company, Frank needed to make the "S" tax election at least 10 years prior to his actual exit.

Avoiding State Capital Gain Taxes

Those states which impose an income tax also typically impose the tax on the sale of a business. One of the most frequent pre-exit steps we advise business owners to take in advance of selling their businesses, if they are residents of a taxing state, is to first consider changing residency to another state which does not impose an income tax (e.g. Florida, Texas, Washington, Nevada, Wyoming, South Dakota).

To be effective, this needs to be done before entering into any type of a sales agreement. By establishing residency in a no-tax state, the state income tax (or capital gains tax) could be avoided completely.

The two main ways in which to avoid a state income tax upon the sale of a business are to either reside in a state which does not impose any income taxes or to reside in a state with (and to meet the specific requirements for) an exemption to such taxes upon the sale of business.

For example, in Nebraska, I and one of my partners had the opportunity in 1987 to explain to the Nebraska Governor and Legislature that Nebraska's tax on business owners who sell their companies was counterproductive. It was just causing our business owners to move out of Nebraska and so the State wasn't collecting the tax anyway. We convinced the State to enact a statutory exemption for the sale of stock by a business owner. This enabled Nebraskans to stay in Nebraska. The Nebraska exemption provision applies if there are at least five shareholders and at least 10% of the corporation is owned by shareholders who are not related to the other 90% (a provision also designed to encourage employee ownership).

The impact of avoiding state income tax in the above illustration can be shown as follows:

	"C" Corp Asset Sale	vs. "S" Corp Asset Sale	+ No State Tax
Price:			
Sale Price	$1,000,000	$1,000,000	$1,000,000
Basis	-200,000	-200,000	-200,000
Taxable Gain	800,000	800,000	800,000
Seller Tax:			
Corporate	320,000	-0-	-0-
Personal	100,000	160,000	120,000
	420,000	160,000	700,000
Buyer Tax:	700,000	700,000	700,000
Total Tax	1,120,000	860,000	820,000
Buyer $ Needed	1,700,000	1,700,000	1,700,000
Net $ to Seller	$580,000	$840,000	$880,000

Case Study – State Capital Gain Taxes

Hank came to us in 1985 wanting to sell Hank Co within the next couple of years. He estimated he should be able to sell the company for $12 million, which would result in a capital gain of approximately $10 million. He and his wife were longtime residents of the State of Nebraska. He asked about the steps he should take to try to reduce the capital gain tax which he expected to pay. Besides the federal capital gain tax, we estimated a Nebraska capital gain tax of approximately $600,000. Since this occurred before Nebraska enacted its capital gain exclusion, our first recommendation to Hank was to "leave Nebraska".

More specifically, Hank and his wife had indicated a desire to have a second home in another state, possibly Florida or Nevada, while maintaining a residence in Nebraska. We suggested that if he took the steps necessary to change his state of residency to a state other than Nebraska, in particular, to a state which did not impose a state capital gain tax, then the Nebraska capital gain tax could be entirely avoided. There are approximately a dozen factors which can impact what is considered to be your "tax home" for state tax purposes. It was necessary to implement these changes before the sale if this was to be effective. Fortunately, this plan was consistent with Hank's desire to establish a second home and to also start transitioning duties to a key employee, enabling Hank and his wife to begin to spend time outside of Nebraska. The estimated savings in state capital gain taxes more than paid for the cost of buying the second home.

Minimum Price With Deferred Compensation

As mentioned earlier, if the entire purchase price could be deducted by a buyer, then the overall buyer's tax can be reduced. While it may not be possible to deduct an entire purchase price, it is possible to establish the selling price at a lower amount by establishing a deferred compensation agreement with the business owners.

Provided that the federal income tax requirements for establishing deferred compensation are satisfied, this deferred compensation acts as a liability on the balance sheet payable to the business owners which must be satisfied once the buyer assumes ownership of the company. Therefore, it's possible to provide the sellers with a combination of consideration for their stock and past (perhaps under compensated) services, this being a combination of the selling price and deferred compensation.

While deferred compensation is taxable to the recipient as ordinary income (rather than capital gain), it is fully deductible by the payor (the buyer), which therefore has the result of decreasing the buyer's tax. Depending on the negotiations between the parties, this decrease in total seller/buyer taxes may be negotiated with some or all of the tax savings to go to the buyer or the seller.

The illustration below demonstrates one way to do this with all of the savings going to the seller, without adjusting the buyer's cash needed.

	"C" Corp vs	"S" Corp +	No State +	Min Price
	Asset Sale	Asset Sale	Tax	w/Def. Comp
Price:				
Sale Price	$1,000,000	$1,000,000	$1,000,000	$300,000
Basis	-200,000	-200,000	-200,000	-200,000
Taxable Gain	800,000	800,000	800,000	100,000
Deferred Comp				1,200,000
Seller Tax:				
Corporate	320,000	-0-	-0-	-0-
Personal	100,000	160,000	120,000	495,000
	420,000	160,000	120,000	495,000
Buyer Tax:	700,000	700,000	700,000	200,000
Total Tax	1,120,000	860,000	820,000	695,000
Buyer $ Needed	1,700,000	1,700,000	1,700,000	1,700,000
Net $ to Seller	$580,000	$840,000	$880,000	$1,005,000

Other Tax Planning Steps

It's beyond the scope of this book to detail all of the potential transaction designs and tax planning tools which can act to minimize the seller's and the buyer's taxes. Other considerations typically are reviewed in the course of the Transition Growth and Exit Planning process.

Chapter 47

Reduce State Taxes While Growing

Business Location Trends

Over the past two decades companies have become much more analytical in making their decisions on where to locate business activities. The motivation behind this is pretty simple, which is this. One of the principal keys to business success and profitability is to operate from the right location under the right economic conditions.

This increasing focus on proper business site selection has been due to a number of factors. These include changing demographics, competitive pressures, new strategic sourcing techniques, more sophisticated distribution methodologies, increased shareholder scrutiny, business expansion, merger/acquisition activity, changing technologies, and cost containment efforts.

Adding to this effort to find the right location under the right economic conditions is the fact that businesses today can be much more mobile than they were in the past. Vast improvements in the transportation industries and the voice and data communication industries have enabled many companies to operate from any of several different locations. Therefore, these companies have tended to more aggressively seek locations that have the most favorable business climates.

The Site Selection Consultant Industry

A review of any of a number of site selection publications or websites today is a bit like reviewing the advertisement inserts in the Sunday newspaper. These publications are filled with promotional advertisements by states and communities throughout the country touting their state and their community as having the best business climate within which to profitably operate a business. These same publications are also full of promotional advertisements from countless site selection consultants offering to assist companies in analyzing the maze of factors that impact company site selection decisions.

These consultants are quite competent and quite aggressive. Due to the depth, variety and intensity of business climate data available through the internet, it's no longer possible for any state or community with a mediocre business climate to go unnoticed.

Competing State Business Climates

As consumers of numerous products and services provided by the business community throughout the country, we are all taught to believe and understand that competition is a good thing. The result of competition is better products and better services at more competitive prices. In order for the business community to be able to accomplish this, business enterprises have needed to become more and more productive and efficient.

The business factors affecting business profitability and success which a State can positively or negatively control or directly impact are the factors which make up that State's business climate. These factors impact the competitiveness of that State amongst other States.

Site Selection Factors

Business site selection decisions are made based on a state-by-state comparison of several business, market, location, and cost factors. These factors include some or all of the following:

- State Business Incentives
- Proximity to Markets
- Proximity to Supplier Networks
- Transportation Options
- Communication Infrastructure
- Marginal Tax Rates
- Legal and Political Climate
- Air Transportation Capabilities
- Availability of Suitable Sites
- Work Force Availability, Diversity and Rates

- Demographics
- Utility Infrastructure
- Operating Costs
- Company Preferences
- Academic Institutions
- Quality of Life Factors
- State Tax Climate
- Proximity to Headquarters, Research/Development Facilities and affiliates

---

Utilizing State Business Incentives To Reduce Taxes

Every year, State and Local governments award billions of dollars in State Business Incentives to those businesses throughout the country who actively seek these benefits as part of their site location and expansion decisions. These incentives are used by State and Local officials as a way to help incent the addition or retention of jobs and investment in their community.

The availability of most incentives is normally dependent on the Company actually identifying, seeking and applying for the incentives before undertaking a project expansion or relocation. Often these incentives need to be negotiated with the State or Local communities as part of an overall site selection and incentive package. A typical incentive package will be based on the level of projected new jobs and/or new investment the Company will add to the community. Some incentives are being awarded for company restructurings or retoolings that do not require net job increases.

Nebraska's Approach to Tax Incentives

My home State of Nebraska provides a good example of the potential tax incentives available to growing companies in many States.

Nebraska provides many of the State Business Incentives in use today. Nebraska's incentive programs create a package that is substantial enough to impact a Company's location decision. At the same time, its incentives are performance-based, generally requiring the Company to meet and maintain certain designated new job and investment thresholds in order to earn the tax benefits.

Nebraska's program is of particular interest to me because I have been the principal designer and drafter of Nebraska's main economic development incentive programs, beginning with the 1987 Employment and Investment Growth Act (known as LB775) through its successor in 2005, the Nebraska Advantage Act (known as LB312), including several additional incentive programs enacted in between.

The Nebraska Advantage Act is now Nebraska's principal incentive package. It substantially reduces a Company's income, sales, withholding and personal property taxes for up to 15 years if certain new job and investment thresholds are met by qualifying types of businesses, as summarized below.

Performance Thresholds	Tax Benefits
Tier 1: $1 Million New Investment and 10 New Jobs	• 3% Investment Tax Credit. • 3, 4, 5 or 6% Sliding Scale Annual Job Credit. • Refund of ½ of Sales Tax on most capital purchases.
Tier 2: $3 Million New Investment and 30 New Jobs	• 10% Investment Tax Credit. • 3, 4, 5 or 6% Sliding Scale Annual Job Credit. • Refund of Sales Tax on most capital purchases.
Tier 3: $0 New Investment and 30 New Jobs	• 3, 4, 5 or 6% Sliding Scale Annual Job Credit.

Tier 4: $12 Million New Investment and 100 New Jobs	• Tier 2 Benefits Plus:
	• 10 Year Property Tax Exemption on:
	  - Turbine-powered Aircraft.
	  - Mainframe Computers and Peripherals.
	  - Agricultural Product Manufacturing Equipment.
	  - Distribution Equipment.

Tier 5: $36 Million New Investment and 0 New Jobs	• Refund of Sales Tax on most capital purchases.
Tier 6: $12 Million New Investment and 75 New Jobs or $122 New Investment and 50 New Jobs	• 15% Investment Tax Credit. • 10% Annual Job Credit. • Refund of Sales Tax on most capital purchases. • 10 Year Personal Property Tax Exemption.

Some of the features of these incentives are:

- Credits can generally be used against the Company's income tax, sales tax and new employee wage withholding tax. Under Tier 6, the credits can also be used against real property taxes.

- A Company has up to 7 years to attain the thresholds (up to 5 years for Tiers 1 and 3). After that it has 7 years to earn and use the benefits (5 – 7 years for Tiers 1 and 3). After that, unused credits can be carried over and used for 1 – 8 more years (0 – 3 years for Tiers 1 and 3), depending on the time it took to attain the thresholds.

- Failure to maintain the thresholds for the earn/use period (or to maintain the attainment year job levels for 10 years for Tier 5) results in pro rata recapture (repayment) of the incentives.

- Qualified business activities include:

  - Research and Development.
  - Data processing.
  - Telecommunications.
  - Insurance.
  - Financial Services.
  - Manufacturing & Processing.
  - Distribution.
  - Storage & Warehousing.
  - Transportation.
  - Internet portal.
  - Nonretail Sales.
  - Headquarters.
  - Targeted Export Services.
    -- Software development.
    -- Computer system design.
    -- Product testing.
    -- Guidance or surveillance systems design.
    -- Technology Licensing.
  - Export Sales.

- For Tier 1, the qualified business activities include only research and development, manufacturing and the targeted export services. For Tier 6, all types of business activities qualify except retail sales and restaurants.

Nebraska's Other Incentive Programs

Nebraska also offers a series of other tax incentives, as well as statewide job training grants, tax increment financing and other incentive options. These include the following:

- Nebraska Advantage Research and Development Act: A 3% refundable research and development credit.

- Nebraska Manufacturing Equipment Sales Tax Exemption.

- Nebraska's Job Training Fund.

- Capital gain exemption on an owner's sale of stock acquired while employed or on account of employment.

- 15 year tax increment financing in designated areas.

- Single factor sales corporate income tax formula (without throwback).

- Custom Grants/Loans from CDBG Program.

- Accelerated depreciation business equipment property tax.

- Inventory property tax exemption.

- Sales tax exemption on energy for manufacturing.

- Pollution control equipment sales tax refund.

The Importance of Incentives

The Directory of Incentives for Business Investment National Association of State Development Agencies states:

"State economic development has become a billion dollar industry and has shown remarkable survival stability in an era of tight budgets. Tax incentives continue to be the most widely offered and commonly used inducement to leverage investment by businesses."

Growing companies need to actively address the potentially available incentives for reducing the tax and other costs of growing their businesses. This provides you with the opportunity to further enhance your Company's growth and value during your ownership transition and exit.

Building Block 11 – Plan My Inside Route Exit

Chapter 48

Determine Inside Route Assessment

In an ideal world, when you are ready to sell your business, an overabundance of ready, willing and able outside buyers, with cash, would be knocking on your door. However, in today's world, this is often not the case. For this reason, as well as to meet personal preferences, many business owners would like to sell their business to management, to family members or to a partner ("insiders").

Determine Potential Inside Buyer Outlook

There are three principal directions to exit ownership of your business through a transfer to an insider or insiders. These consist of:

1.   Sale to co-owner (s) (either directly or as a stock redemption).

2.   Sale to key employee (s) (either directly or through an ESOP).

3.   Transfer to family (during life or at death).

Some combination of these is often utilized with a transfer to insiders.

According to a 2003 study by the Raymond Family Business Institute, almost nine of ten family-owned business leaders think their businesses will continue to be run by the same family or families in five years. One of the objectives of Building Block 11 is to help determine whether a sale to an insider (family or non-family) is even financially feasible. If so, this step will help manage and overcome the problems associated with a transfer to insiders. This step is intended to apply for either an immediate or possible eventual sale or transfer to insiders.

Many business owners we visit with have already considered various alternatives for transferring ownership to insiders. Many have also already gifted shares to family members, often for estate planning reasons or perhaps because one or more children have been active in the business.

The first decision in this step is to understand your most likely inside transferee and your expected timetable. If you are the sole owner and you are absolutely certain you intend to exit through the lifetime gifting or death inheritance of your stock to your family, then there is no need for a lot of further analysis under this step. Your transition planning becomes a matter of addressing the other Building Blocks, realizing however that you should consider having a backup plan to be prepared for an outside sale opportunity.

However, if you anticipate a sale to a partner, key employee (s), ESOP or family, then the purpose of Building Block 11 is to assess the desire and ability of such insiders to actually purchase your stock and to develop the best means to do so. With a sale to insiders, owners often face a common problem — the proposed buyer does not have enough cash to meet a fair price and the seller is required to assist in financing the transaction. A number of pre-transfer steps and actual transfer design tools can help address this.

Whether or not your proposed inside buyer has independent cash, every buyer will look to the future cash flow of the business to justify the price being paid to you – either to see whether the business will "cash flow" the debt service to you and/or to determine the potential for future profit on the purchase. To determine this, your Transition Growth advisors should perform an estimated future cash flow analysis. The results of this help determine the pricing as well as the terms of payment and security for payment.

Employee Stock Ownership Plan ("ESOP")

If you would like to sell to the company's employees rather than just to your key employee management team, you should consider establishing and selling to an ESOP. This enables you to reward and incent your employees while enabling them to buy you out with pre-tax dollars (because the price paid can be deducted by the company).

The ESOP was the creation several decades ago of attorney Louis Kelso (1913-1991). I had the opportunity to visit with Mr. Kelso at an ESOP conference before he passed away. He told me that the main reason he designed the ESOP was to expand our nation's economic prosperity by extending the ownership of productive assets to the company's workforce. Mr. Kelso convinced the then U.S. Senate Finance Committee Chair Russell Long to champion the program through Congress in the 1970's.

The ESOP enacted by Congress aims to achieve its economic objectives by allowing the company to deduct the purchase price paid to purchase your stock. It also provides you as the seller the ability to defer the tax on your gain if after the sale the ESOP owns at least 30% of the company and within fifteen months (starting three months before the sale) you invest the proceeds in qualified replacement securities (generally domestic company stocks and bonds).

According to the National Center for Employee Ownership, 20 million Americans own stock in their employer (through a 401(k) plan, ESOP, direct stock grant or similar plan). Another 10 million own stock options. There are over 9,000 ESOPs with a total of about 10 million participants. Surveys also show that companies with ESOPs experience annual growth of 2.4% more than in their pre-ESOP years. Due to a combination of equity market and present tax law considerations, I expect the growth in the number of ESOPs to expand considerably over the next several years.

The ESOP is not suitable for every company and certain technical requirements must be met. Before deciding to pursue this exit route, we will first evaluate whether a company (in light of the business owner's exit objectives) is a suitable candidate for an ESOP.

Chapter 49

Plan For A Tax Efficient, Bankable Sale To Insider

Exiting your company through a sale to one or more insiders is not easy and, as will be seen below, can involve terms and conditions which at first may appear counterintuitive to a business owner.

As a starting point, the business owner needs to first and foremost understand that the most likely way to be successful in a sale to one or more insiders is to accomplish this in at least two stages. In other words, you will likely be less successful if you believe that a sale to an insider or insiders should occur in one phase at or near the time of your actual ownership exit.

The Problems With A One-Phase Transfer To Insiders

Under the right circumstances, a one-step transfer of your ownership to insiders can work. This requires the simultaneous presence of capable inside purchasers coupled with your intention to exit now. This is because the type of ownership-interested, capable key insiders whom you would like to purchase your company may very well not be interested in hanging around without some commitment from you if you plan to exit several years in the future. In addition, even if your capable key insiders were interested in hanging around until you exit, a bank is unlikely to finance 100% of a key-employee stock purchase, leaving you in the position of providing seller-financing which could run several years after you have exited management of the company, resulting in a higher probability of default.

The Two-Phase Ownership Exit

Under a two-phase ownership exit, a portion of your stock would be transferred to your inside buyer or buyers now, while the balance would be transferred at a later date. There are at least eight possible scenarios for how the second phase of the transfer might occur. You don't necessarily need to decide phase two today in order to accomplish phase one. This two-phase approach has the following advantages:

1. Providing stock ownership to key employees today can provide an incentive for higher personal achievement in their job performance.

2. Providing stock ownership to key employees today can help reduce the risk that they will be attracted to a job offer from a competing company.

3. Providing stock ownership to key employees today improves the likelihood of a bank financing the balance of their purchase in the future upon your final exit.

4. Providing stock ownership to key employees today, particularly if they have been required to invest part of their personal funds in the purchase of some or all of that stock, gives them some "skin in the game," which serves as an additional motivation to help the company be successful.

5. Providing some stock ownership to key employees today, while you retain the balance of your ownership, enables you to continue as controlling owner, as well as becoming a mentor to your key employees to further develop their skills and management talent under your watchful eye.

What About Minority Shareholder Issues?

Business owners have reason to be concerned about transferring partial ownership to key employees, who would now constitute minority shareholders. If not properly planned, this could raise issues on how such stock is to be voted and whether you can receive the return of such stock if your key employee leaves the company. These types of issues can be dealt with through a Business Continuity Agreement and a Buy-Sell Agreement, discussed elsewhere in this book. For now in the discussion, let's make the assumption that minority shareholder issues can be dealt with to your satisfaction.

Evaluating Whether Your Key Employees Actually Want To Be Owners

It's important to determine, rather than assume, that your key employees in fact actually want to be owners. A key employee may have discussed a desire in the past to be an owner and may actually tend to think or act like an owner. However, if you don't have a high degree of comfort that you have one or more key employees who can actually become the company's leader, then you need to face the fact early on that an inside transfer might not be your best exit route, but instead should become a backup route, with a sale to a third party taking the place as your primary exit route.

Equally important with regard to whether a key employee could be a successful owner is whether your key employee or key employee group is of such an age that they may have little interest in spending a number of years acquiring stock ownership, only to then be faced with their own rather immediate need to attempt to sell the company, in particular before they have had enough time to realize full value. If your key employee group or a member of your key employee group is over the age of 50, then you need to seriously consider their ownership objectives and whether you should instead be providing simply some means of ownership incentive, such as phantom stock or a stock-appreciation right plan.

How Much Skin In The Game?

When considering the transfer of stock to a key employee or a key employee group, you need to determine how much risk you want them to bear in the first step of the purchase. Sometimes owners are willing to allow the key employees to pay for their stock solely out of future cash flow which they receive as dividends on the purchased stock. Often, though, owners want their key employee groups to have some skin in the game and to bear some risk of loss by putting in some of their own money, or pledging some of their own assets as security for the purchase of their stock. This becomes a balance between the financial capabilities of the key employees and the departing owner's desire to become less exposed to the risk of the business.

Selling High Or Selling Low

One of the counterintuitive realizations which an owner needs to come to in the course of selling his or her stock in the company is that the owner may be able to actually net higher overall exit proceeds if a lower overall valuation can be supported for the company (with the understanding that the owner will also receive other net benefit in the transaction, such as consideration in the form of a deferred compensation or salary continuation payments). This is because a combination of stock selling price along with a deductible deferred compensation payment can reduce the overall, combined seller and buyer taxes on the transaction.

Most business owners are aware of the fact that they will need to pay a tax on the sale of their business. However, most owners are not aware of the fact that a buyer also pays an income tax on the purchase of the business. This can be easily illustrated.

Assume that a buyer has agreed to purchase your stock for one million dollars. Where does the buyer get the money to pay your selling price? The buyer needs to earn the cash from somewhere in order to be able to pay for your stock. Typically, a buyer expects to earn this cash from the future operations of the business that he or she is buying from you. This is regardless of whether the buyer borrowed money from a bank in order to finance the purchase. The bank still needs to be paid off in the future.

If a buyer needs to pay you $1.0 million for your stock, then, considering normal income tax rates, the buyer needs to earn $1.7 million from the future business operations, on which the buyer will pay approximately $700,000 of income tax on those earnings, leaving the buyer a net $1.0 million available to pay for your stock. You would owe $200,000 in tax on the sale, netting $800,000. Total combined seller and buyer taxes would be $900,000 to transfer the $1.0 million business.

If instead, your stock was valued at $400,000 (e.g. based on applicable valuation factors and assumptions and the presence of a deferred compensation liability added to the books) and the buyer also agreed to provide you with a deferred compensation payment of $900,000, the buyer would now only need pre-tax earnings of $1.565 million, because the deferred compensation payment made to you would be tax deductible by the buyer. Of course, the deferred compensation payment to you would be fully taxable as ordinary income rather than at lower capital gain rates. This interplay between value and other consideration for your exit can be negotiated in a manner in which both the seller and the buyer benefit, resulting in an overall less combined seller/buyer tax on the transaction and a better deal for both the seller and buyer. In this example, the total exit proceeds paid to you of $1.3

million would net you $860,000 after taxes. Both parties would have benefited by a combined total of $155,000 (because combined taxes were reduced by this amount).

Case Study – The Partner Sale

When John and Katie met with me in 1992 to discuss their Transition Growth Planning, we soon came to the conclusion that John's most likely exit from his company would be a sale of his stock to his partner. He was a minority shareholder owning 45% of the company, while his partner owned the other 55%. They owned a business-to-business service operation with 24 locations throughout the Midwest. None of John's children were active in the business, while his partner's son was being groomed to become the next president. At the time, the company was worth about $8 million and operated as a "C" corporation.

A couple of things became clear fairly quickly. First, the corporation was the main asset owned by John and Katie. John and his partner had plowed most of the profits back into the company and did not have a lot of separate personal wealth. Second, this meant that upon John's death, his salary with the company would be discontinued, leaving Katie with little to live on and the difficulty of attempting to negotiate a sale of his stock for some type of price with John's partner. Third, upon the death of both John and Katie their estate would incur a significant estate tax and not have the cash with which to pay it. Fourth, John and his partner didn't get along all that well. His partner rebuffed our initial suggestions to establish a Buy-Sell Agreement and a salary continuation plan.

The partners did agree, however, to our suggestion that they re-capitalize the corporation to establish voting and non-voting stock (to enable both partners to begin gifting programs to their children to reduce estate taxes without diminishing voting control) and also to elect to be an "S" corporation. From John's perspective, this had the advantage of beginning to build "tax basis" in his stock so that upon his eventual sale of the company to his partner, his capital gain taxes would be significantly reduced.

John, Katie and their family continued their ownership of the company over the next 10 years. While it took us some unusual steps in order to be able to negotiate a full fair value for his stock in a transaction with his partner, this was eventually accomplished. The company value had grown during this time to $25 million, resulting in a cash buyout to John with substantially reduced capital gain taxes on account of the "S" election.

Free Cash Flow

In order for a key employee group to purchase your stock, assuming that some or all of the purchase price is to come from the key employee group's share of dividends on that stock, it's important that the company have a consistent "free cash flow." "Free cash flow" is the cash flow that's available for distribution to the stockholders. This is sometimes called "discretionary cash flow." This represents the cash generated by the business that is not required for either the operations of the business or for the debt service/capitalization of the business.

In order to properly plan for a sale of stock to insiders, it's necessary to have a solid estimate of the future free cash flow expectations. This can be easily illustrated. If the free cash flow of the company (after distributions to pay income taxes) is projected to be $800,000 each year, and the first step of the stock sale to the key employee group is 10% of the company, then the key employee group will have approximately $80,000 available to pay for the stock each year. If free cash flow is inadequate, and assuming the key employees do not have substantial cash of their own, then the key employee group is not going to be in a position to pay full value for the stock. If that's the case, then either the pricing needs to be reconsidered (with possibly a portion connected to deferred compensation) or you need to further consider whether your primary exit route should instead be a sale to an outside third party. In addition, you need to consider whether you can meet your exit objectives on the timing for your exit and instead need to work on developing a stronger cash flow for your business.

Subchapter "S" Or LLC Status

The sale of stock to insiders is generally best accommodated if your business entity is a "flow-through" entity for income tax purposes. A flow-through entity is either an "S" corporation or a limited liability company ("LLC"). Under either of these arrangements, the business entity itself does not pay income taxes, but instead the business entity's income is automatically taxed to the business owners. Typically, this type of business entity would distribute sufficient cash to the owners to pay for this tax liability.

The principal advantage of this flow-through entity structure is that dividends can be paid by the company to the owner's without additional tax. In other words, the dividends can be placed into the hands of the owners having incurred only one tax (i.e. a federal and state income tax only once).

By contrast, a regular "C" corporation must pay income tax on its earnings and the shareholders must pay a second tax when those after tax earnings are distributed in the form of dividends. Since dividends are not deductible to a "C" corporation, this results in a true double taxation on the same income.

When an "S" corporation or LLC is utilized, the key employee group can receive its share of company dividends free of additional taxation and use the dividend proceeds dollar-for-dollar to pay for their stock investment.

This means that when you enter into the process of planning your exit, it is time to consider whether you should make an election to become an "S" corporation. When you're not in exit mode, it may well have worked just fine to be taxed as a "C" corporation, in particular if you were only receiving deductible salary compensation and bonuses from the company and were not receiving any non-deductible dividends. It's important once you are in exit-mode planning that a Transition Growth Planning CPA or attorney review the specific considerations which go into switching from a "C" corporation to an "S" corporation.

No Loss Of Control

The transfer of stock to key employees does not mean that a business owner needs to give up control over that stock. Nor does it mean that the owner must give up the ability to recall the stock if the owner determines that future events or conditions warrant this.

What is meant by control and how does this impact the business owner? The following elements of control can typically be relevant:

- **Annual stockholder meetings.** The principal occasion for a shareholder to exercise his or her ownership rights as a shareholder would be at a shareholder's meeting, whether an annual meeting or a special meeting. Typically a pre-exit transfer of stock ownership to key employees will be less than a majority of the stock, e.g. typically 10%-25%, whether initially or over time. This amount of ownership by the key employees provides a better ability for the key employees to obtain bank financing for the purchase of your remaining stock when you complete your exit. However, this percentage of ownership does not give the key employees control of votes during shareholder meetings. As long as the company's Articles of Incorporation and Bylaws have been properly structured, the majority owner can maintain control over the voting which occurs at a shareholder meeting. In addition, voting control can be further established through a Business Continuity Agreement.

  Another alternative is to issue only non-voting stock to the key employees in the pre-exit phase. If your corporation is not presently set up to issue non-voting stock, this can be easily handled through an amendment to the corporation's Articles of Incorporation. This alternative exists even if the corporation is an "S" corporation. While the tax rules limit an "S" corporation to only one class of stock, non-voting stock is not considered a second class of stock for purposes of these rules.

- **Control as to selling the company.** Corporate laws generally require that certain major events, such as liquidating a corporation or selling all or substantially all of the assets of the corporation to a third party, require at least two-thirds approval by the shareholders. As long as you maintain this percentage of ownership, you have retained the ability to control the decision regarding such a sale. In addition, you can provide in a Business Continuity Agreement that your control for this type of decision is maintained.

- **Control over selling 100% of the stock to a third party.** Suppose that the best exit in the future becomes a transfer to an outside third party rather than a transfer of the balance of your stock to inside employees. Suppose further that an outside third party only wishes to buy your stock if it can acquire 100% of the stock (i.e. also acquire the stock held by your key employees). This objective can be accomplished through a Buy-Sell Agreement through such provisions as a "drag along" provision in the agreement which requires the key employees to sell on the same terms and conditions which you are able to negotiate for the sale of all the stock of the company.

- **Stock recall.** If your key employees turn out to be problematic, you may want to have the ability to recall, or re-acquire, the stock which had been previously transferred to them. This objective can be met through provisions in a Buy-Sell Agreement.

- **Helping assure key employee loyalty.** You have transferred stock to your key employees for three principal reasons. First, to provide an incentive to the key employees to perform and to remain with the company. Second, to provide you with the first step for accomplishing your overall exit. Third, to demonstrate your commitment to them, which you expect would be reciprocal. In addition to transferring stock to your key employees, a business owner also typically wants to begin to transfer management duties. While this has the advantage of starting to provide you with more free time, it can result in some shift of operating control (e.g. through customer relationships) to your key employees, which provides some risk that a key employee will leave and begin competing against your company. All business decisions have the potential for upside and the potential for downside. This is simply another occasion for managing, reducing, or eliminating the downside risk. In this instance, it can be done through the combination of non-compete terms, employee non-solicitation terms, customer non-solicitation terms, and confidentiality terms, all of which provisions can be included in a Business Continuity Agreement.

While the conventional expectation of most business owners is that non-compete terms are not binding, this is generally a risk if the employee is only an employee (and not an owner) and is generally a risk when the terms of the non-compete are too broad and overreaching. These issues can be substantially dealt with. In addition, an employee non-solicitation provision and a customer non-solicitation provision, as well as a confidentiality provision, are generally very enforceable and often target precisely the human capital, customer relationship capital and intellectual property capital which you are most interested in protecting in any event. To the extent you have protected this, you have also discouraged that key employee from believing that he or she can leave the company and take this along.

These types of provisions in a Business Continuity Agreement are important not only to you, but also to the other members of the key employee group, who likewise should want to see a high degree of loyalty to the enterprise, which benefits everyone provided they remain loyal to the company. Its extremely important to prevent a former key employee group member from harming your company. Therefore, attention needs to be paid to these details.

Tax Consequences Of, And Payment For, Stock Transfer To Key Employees

The transfer of stock to your key employees will typically occur in one of two ways. First, you might want to transfer some of your stock to them. Second, the corporation might want to issue new stock to them. Payment for this stock also will generally occur in one of two principal ways. First, the stock could be bonused to them or, second, the stock could be sold to them. If the stock is sold to them, then payment for the stock typically occurs in one of two ways. Either they will pay cash up front for the stock or they will sign a promissory note in which they pay for the stock over a period of time (with part of the note possibly forgiven each year the employee stays with the company).

The key employee funding for such payments would also typically occur in one of two ways. First, they would pay for the stock out of their own assets or, alternatively, their payment of the stock would be funded through dividend payments they receive pro-rata on their shares of stock.

Security for their payment of stock would also typically exist in either one of two ways. First, you would receive no security or collateral backing up their obligation or, alternatively, some assets would be pledged to secure the payment obligation against potential future default.

Lastly, the price paid for the stock is established in one of two ways. First, it could be a fair market value based on a pro-rata percentage ownership of the company or it could be a discounted value (e.g. reflecting minority discount, lack of marketability discount, or some bonus compensation element).

Your actual terms with your key employees might also be some combination of these alternatives.

Typically we would see the following choices. The stock sold would consist of shares which you own (rather than newly issued shares by the corporation), the stock would be sold at a price (bonused or some combination), the stock pricing would reflect minority and lack of marketability discounts, the repurchase price (if for some reason you decide to recall the stock) would be based on the same type of pricing as the initial purchase, the stock would be paid for in installments over time (rather than cash up front), the installment payments would be funded through dividends (though this might be partially from employee compensation and savings), the employee would provide collateral as security for the purchase (although this might be limited to simply pledging the stock purchased as collateral rather than pledging other employee assets as collateral).

One other set of alternatives for the transfer of stock to employees would be to transfer them stock with or without requiring the execution of a Business Continuity Agreement and Buy-Sell Agreement or to require this as a condition for the transfer. Typically these agreements should be required.

Rolling Vesting

If part of your combination of stock issuance to employees will be stock which is fully or partly a stock bonus, then you should consider issuing this stock on a rolling vesting approach. Under this approach, the stock bonus represents part of the overall compensation to the employee in the form of performance incentive and employment retention compensation.

Under this approach, the amount of stock to be bonused would be based on a performance incentive which applies either to each individual key employee or to the performance of the key employee group as a whole. The standards of performance can be tied to the business results that you wish to see. This might include, for example, revenue growth, net profits, cost control, or any of the most relevant business or financial ratios covered elsewhere in this book in the business benchmarking section.

Simply because stock is then issued under this type of stock bonus formula does not mean the stock can be retained should the key employee terminate his or her employment. Instead, the key employee should always have some risk of leaving some of his or her stock ownership on the table should the employee leave the company. Under a rolling vesting approach, the employee will vest in a given year's stock issuance over a period of subsequent years that the employee remains with the company.

For example, if the employee is issued 100 shares of stock in 2009, based on performance in 2008, under a rolling vesting format, the employee could vest in those 100 shares at the rate of 20% per year over five years. For example, if the employee leaves in one year, then the employee would only have earned ownership in 20% of the 2009 100 shares. If the employee leaves after two years, the employee would have ownership in 40% of the 2009 100 shares.

Likewise, if shares are issued in 2010, the employee would have a similar vesting schedule for those shares. This doesn't mean that the employee can retain ownership of those shares upon termination, but instead reflects the number of shares to be considered as owned, and therefore the shares for which the company would pay a price to recall those shares upon termination of employment.

Securities Law Considerations

Stock issued directly by the company to key employees is subject to securities law compliance, as is every other stock issuance by a company to shareholders or potential shareholders, in particular if the employee pays for the stock. A full discussion of this is beyond the scope of this book. Briefly, the securities law provides for certain exemptions from its registration requirement for non-public or otherwise limited stock issuances. Even when an exemption exists, it is important that an employee receive financial information regarding the company. This is particularly true if the employee is purchasing stock from the company with the employee's funds.

Tax Considerations

When stock is bonused by the company to an employee (or issued at a price less than its fair market value), the bonus component will typically constitute taxable compensation to the employee (and an offsetting deduction to the corporation). This taxation typically occurs when the stock is either transferable by the employee or no longer subject to what the tax law refers to as a "substantial risk of forfeiture".

Depending on the circumstances, the company can decide to "gross up" the employee for these tax consequences by paying a cash bonus to the employee as part of the overall stock bonus, so that the tax impact is covered by the company (which is receiving a tax deduction to offset this payment and stock bonus). Under certain circumstances, a transfer of stock by a controlling shareholder to an employee might be viewed as an indirect stock issuance by the company which is subject to these compensation rules.

Explaining Your Stock Transfer Proposal To Key Employee Group Members

Obviously the terms and conditions of a stock transfer or stock bonus to your key employees requires a series of discussions, explanations, and feedback. One of the expected primary concerns from the key employee group members will relate to their ability to pay for the stock which they are becoming obligated to purchase. It is important to have a demonstration of the company's cash flow and dividend payout expectations, which will typically be the primary means of funding their purchase. It is also important to consider designing some flexibility into the promissory note to help alleviate the risk to the key employee group of a default should the company face a downturn and be unable to pay the full dividends on time as expected.

Why Should Any Owner Do This?

It is a fair question as to why an owner should be interested in bonusing stock to key employees or selling stock to key employees which will simply be funded by company dividends to be paid on that stock. Wouldn't the owner be better off to simply retain the stock and therefore retain full ownership of the dividend proceeds.

For some business owners, this might be the better scenario. This really depends on a couple of factors. First, can you attract and retain the type of key employees which you need to profitably continue to grow and maintain the company without providing stock ownership to those key employees. If they in fact are good, they will want to be owners, and if you can't provide it, you should expect they will look elsewhere. In addition to the objective of having strong management to help you grow the company, if your eventual exit is a sale to a third party, the ability to sell, as well as the ability to sell at a full fair price, will depend on the strength of your management team in your absence. While this may vary depending on whether the outside buyer is a strategic buyer or a financial buyer, as a general principle, the value of your company will be worth more to the extent that it can operate successfully without you.

Second, if you anticipate that the balance of your stock will upon your exit be transferred to your key employees, this will be facilitated if they have already achieved a certain level of minority shareholder status. You might decide to provide seller financing for the sale of the balance of your stock.

However, if one of your objectives is to not retain that risk, by hoping that a bank will provide financing for the balance, then this is more likely to happen if your key employee group already has a significant minority ownership interest and a proven track record as representing key owners.

Addressing The Second Phase Of Your Exit – Keeping Your Options Open

We have discussed so far the concept of transferring a significant minority interest in the stock ownership of your company to your key employees over a period of time. This type of incremental stock sale approach tends to have less overall risk and tends to help achieve overall objectives better than simply expecting to be able to sell 100% of your stock to a key employee group upon your exit.

However, this phase one sale of a significant minority interest of your stock to your key employee group should not be viewed as limiting your flexibility for your final exit. Overall, the objective is that phase one has enhanced your feasible alternatives for your final exit. In phase one, you will have transferred a non-controlling portion of your stock to your key employee group. Once that phase is completed, you have a choice of at least eight possible approaches for addressing your exit. These include the following:

1. **Keep your remaining stock until death.** You might decide to keep the balance of your stock until your death and then pass on the stock to your family. This would enable you to continue to receive distributions on the stock until your death and for your family to continue to receive distributions after your death. Your family could decide down the road the final exit for the family from the company.

2. **Sell the balance of your stock to your key employee group in installments.** Under this alternative, you could sell the balance of your stock to your key employee group over time. This could be at a preset price or it could be at a price which fluctuates with the value as the company goes forward.

3. **Sell to new key employee group members.** You could use some or all of the balance of your stock to provide additional incentive for attracting and retaining additional key employee group members to your company or to recognize other employees who have risen within the ranks of your company to this status.

4. **You could sell the balance of your stock to an Employee Stock Ownership Plan (ESOP).** This type of sale has certain tax favored advantages, which are discussed elsewhere in this book.

5. **Sell to key employee group at your retirement for cash.** Under this alternative, the balance of your stock would be sold in one transaction upon your retirement to your key employee group. Anticipating that they would not have the cash to fund this, the expectation would be that your prior implementation of phase one has now put them in a position to secure bank financing which would be used to cash out your stock.

6. **Sell to key employee group at your retirement for a package.** Under this alternative, you would sell the balance of your stock at one time upon your retirement in exchange for a promissory note equal to the low end of the range of your stock's value. In order to receive the full financial benefit of your stock ownership and your years of service which may have been under-compensated, this package could also include a deferred compensation or salary continuation agreement. This approach provides a tax advantage to the key employee group buyers, because the company can deduct the deferred compensation and salary continuation payments. That portion of the payments would be subject to ordinary income taxation to you, which can, however, be minimized by a longer compensation payment and if this is spread over time and into potentially lower tax brackets.

7. **Sell to an outside third party.** You might decide that your best option at the time of your final exit is to sell the company to an outside third party. Your Buy-Sell Agreement should include provisions which anticipate this in two aspects. First, the Buy-Sell Agreement should include a "drag along" provision by which you can require your key employee group minority shareholders to sell their stock as part of this overall sale to the third party who likely will expect to be able to purchase 100% of the stock. It is possible that the third party might decide to leave the key employee group members as minority shareholders which can be negotiated at the time. Second, in order to receive the full incentive impact intended initially by your stock transfer to key employee group members, your Buy-Sell Agreement should also include, typically, a provision known as a "bring along" or "tag along" provision. Under this, your key employee shareholders would have the right, should they so elect, to require that you include them in the sale to a third party. The combination of

these provisions provide you with the control to cause a 100% sale of the stock to happen while at the same time provide the key employees with the incentive to help grow the company to reap the benefits of a potential favorable sale to an outside third party.

8.   **Re-purchase the stock from the key employee group.** You might decide upon your exit to move into a different direction than that originally anticipated during phase one. If that is the case, you want to have the ability to re-purchase the stock from the key employee group members or from a selected number of key employee group members. Again, to achieve the incentive elements intended by this stock transfer in the first place, this re-purchase should be based on some formula or method for determining that selling price so that the key employees have been able to share in the potential upside while they were owners.

Is Your Plan Bankable?

It's extremely important to be working today with a bank that understands Transition Growth and Exit Planning and which will pro-actively work with you to help develop a Transition Growth Plan that fits you, your company and your bank. As you develop a Transition Growth Plan, you want to structure it in a manner where a bank is willing to step in to provide the financing for the buyer's purchase when you exit from your ownership.

Chapter 50

Plan For A Tax Efficient Transfer To Family

Whether or not you plan to transfer your Company to an outside buyer, to your key employees, or to your family, you should consider the use of certain tax-advantaged ways to transfer all or part of your Company to family members during your lifetime or upon your death. These are summarized below.

Company Transfer Alternatives To Family At Your Death

The following alternative should be considered and determined for transferring all or a portion of your Company to family members at your death.

1. **Spouse Inheritance**. Transfer of the Company to your spouse on your death through the provisions of your Estate Plan, specifically your Living Trust. The key tax planning action is to be sure you have a Will or Living Trust which provides you with optimal Estate Tax marital deduction.

2. **Child Inheritance**. Transfer of the balance of your ownership in the Company to your children upon your death or upon the last to die of you and your spouse. The key tax planning action is to reduce your ownership of your Company to less than 50% before your death, so your Estate can claim a minority discount off of the taxable value.

3. **Grandchild Inheritance**. Transfer of the balance of your ownership in the Company to your grandchildren upon your death or upon the last to die of you and your spouse. The key tax planning action again is to reduce your ownership of your Company to less than 50% before your death, so your Estate can claim a minority discount off of the taxable value. In addition, proper use of your Generation Skipping tax exemption can help reduce overall family death transfer taxes.

Company Transfer Alternatives To Family During Your Lifetime

The following alternatives can be considered and determined for transferring all or a portion of your Company to family members during your lifetime.

1. **Annual Gifting Program**. Transfer of part ownership in your Company to your children, grandchildren, and/or children's spouses up to your annual Federal Gift Tax Exemption amount ($13,000 per recipient as of 2009). This can save up to about $6,000 per gift in future Estate Taxes as well as saving the tax on future appreciation.

2. **Lifetime Exemption Gifting**. Transfer of shares in your Company to your children, grandchildren, and/or children's spouses up to your Total Lifetime Gift Tax Exemption amount of $1,000,000 for you (and $1,000,000 for your spouse). This enables you to save future Estate Tax on the value appreciation of the gifted assets.

3. **Fair Market Value Cash Sale**. Transfer of your Company to designated family members at full fair market value for cash. If your Company value will grow faster than the invested cash, then the excess will escape future Estate Tax.

4. **Installment Sale**. Transfer of your Company to designated family members at a price equal to full fair market value with payments to be made over time pursuant to an installment promissory note. This enables you to help fund the purchase by your family, while moving excess appreciation Estate Tax free to the next generation.

5. **Stock Redemption**. Redemption of your stock by the Company at full fair market value for cash. This could apply when you intend to completely terminate your stock ownership and to fully retire from all positions with the Company. It would apply when family members already own the balance of the shares of the Company. Care must be taken to achieve capital gain rather than dividend treatment.

6. **Private Annuity**. Similar to an installment sale, however, this represents a sale of the Company to family members in exchange for a guaranteed retirement income represented by a series of periodic

payments for life. This enables the excess of Company growth in excess of the annuity rate to be transferred free of Estate Tax.

7. **Self-Canceling Installment Notes**. This is similar to an installment sale and a private annuity. In exchange for your transfer of the Company to designated family members, you would receive an installment note payable for a term of years. If you die before the end of the term, the note is cancelled. This can enable the remainder to be transferred free of Estate Tax.

8. **Grantor Retained Annuity Trust**. Your shares of the Company would be transferred to an Irrevocable Trust which in turn provides you with an annuity for a specified number of years. After the term elapses, the Company ownership would pass to the Trust beneficiaries, typically designated family members. This is similar to a part sale/part gift. The annuity payable would typically be stated in terms of a fixed dollar amount. The excess of Company growth over the GRAT interest rate would pass free of Estate Tax.

9. **Grantor Retained Unitrust**. Similar to a GRAT, however, the annuity payments are a fixed percentage of the fair market value of the trust, re-determined annually. This enables the excess of Company growth over the GRAT interest rate to pass free of Estate Tax.

10. **Intentionally Defective Grantor Trust**. This is a sale of your Company to a so-called "defective" grantor trust in return for a promissory note, with the intended result that the Company is not included in your estate, while the sale is disregarded for income tax purposes. Due to a lower required interest rate, this tax planning technique can enable a larger portion of future company growth to pass to your family free of Estate Tax.

11. **Charitable Remainder Trust**. This involves the transfer of your Company's shares to a charitable trust which is either a form of charitable remainder trust (in which the charity receives the Company after a period of years) or a charitable lead trust (where the charity receives the Company for a number of years, after which the Company is transferred to family members). This tax planning technique can generate both Income Tax and Estate Tax savings.

12. **Spin-Off Real Estate**. The real estate used in your Company can be spun off to you (e.g. by sale or dividend) and leased back to your Company (and separately sold or gifted to family).

13. **Spin-Off Intellectual Property**. The intellectual property used in your Company can be spun off to you (e.g. by sale or dividend) and licensed back to your Company.

Various business, financial, family and tax considerations apply to each of these alternatives which need to be carefully considered before final decisions are made and before any of these techniques are actually implemented.

Building Block 12 –
Plan My Outside Route
Exit

Chapter 51

Determine Outside Route Assessment

Building Block 12 in the Transition Growth and Exit Planning process is intended to answer some fundamental questions:

1.   Is there a market for the sale of your business to an outside third party?

2.   How do you pursue a sale to an outside third party?

3.   What kind of price and terms can you expect or require?

The results of this review will help you decide whether you should plan for a sale of your business to an outside third party as your primary or fallback plan.

There are four principal directions to exit ownership of your business through a transfer to an outside third party. These consist of:

1.   Sale to third party financial buyer (financial or strategic).

2.   Sale to the public market.

3.   Sale to a business liquidation buyer.

4.   A partial sale, to a strategic, financial buyer or the public, or through a joint venture or franchise.

According to Roger Winsby, president and co-founder of Axiom Valuation Solutions of Wakefield Massachusetts, a third of affluent business owners plans to sell their company to an outside buyer. Another third plans to sell to family members. About a fifth of business owners plan to sell their company in some manner to current employees. The balance will liquidate and close the doors. *Sacramento Business Journal* (March 28, 2005).

We've found that most business owners have some idea about who might be a potential outside purchaser of their business. Rarely, however, does a business owner have a good assessment of the full potential market. That's because unless you are actively studying this market on a frequent basis, you simply don't know its reach. This is why we include in the Transition Growth and Exit Planning process the option to pursue an Outside Route Assessment by an M&A advisory firm.

One of the primary reasons business owners have reported dissatisfaction with their exit is that they didn't understand their alternatives. Until you know the actual market outlook for your business, it's difficult to select the best exit route for you and your family. You may prefer to transfer the business to a key employee group and you may feel so strongly about this that an outside sale simply isn't an option for you.

However, we've found that business owners normally want to know what they are leaving on the table by excluding one or more options. An Outside Route Assessment will look at your value strengths and detractors and recommend specific value and marketability enhancements. It will detail the best routes to pursue to target the best potential type of outside buyer. And it will detail an expected sales price range based on specific sale transactions for similar companies in your industry.

Private Equity Groups As An Exit Strategy

Due to the existence of several thousand Private Equity Groups ("PEG") which possess several billion dollars of funding for the purpose of purchasing companies, the potential often exists for a sale to a PEG. Not all companies are attractive to the PEG community. Generally, PEGs find the following characteristics to be appealing.

- Predictable, steady revenue stream. This is preferably generally insulated from market cyclicality.

- Profitability in excess of industry norms. This includes profit margin and other financial ratios.

- A significant level of Earnings Before Interest, Taxes, Depreciation and Amortization ("EBITDA"). A minimum EBITDA of $2 million is generally needed to attract meaningful interest attention from PEGs, though many will consider a lower level.

- Strong Growth Potential. This should be evidenced by a track record of profitable growth and/or an ability to grow with an infusion of outside capital.

- Unique Products, Services, Technical Skills and Customer Bases. PEGs prefer companies with defensible niches with high barriers to entry.

- Strong Management Team With A Deep Bench. PEGs do not want to manage routine operations and want a seasoned and committed management team which can assist them in growing the business.

Being Prepared With The Right Attitude

The eventual exit from active duty and ownership will typically be a major event in the life of a business owner, after which some will transition well and some not so well. Some owners will take a sneak-preview of life after business by taking an extended vacation before reaching the decision to sell, to, in essence, experience a taste of retirement to see how well it suits you.

Once you decide its time to sell and begin the actual sale process, it's best to be both prepared to leave and prepared to not leave – that is, be prepared to stay on if the transaction can't be completed. Unless you maintain the ability to walk away from any deal, you will lose negotiating leverage.

The sale of a business can be a very trying time for a business owner. The transaction intermediaries will tell you that unless a deal has been in the ditch at least a half dozen times, it's not a real deal. Have your S.W.A.T team (exit advisors, transaction intermediary, M & A attorney) assembled well in advance to help pull the deal out of the ditch and keep it on track. But be prepared to walk away from any deal that you find will not meet your objectives.

The Competition For Quality Buyers

Various organizations have projected a substantial, baby boom driven increase in the number of businesses being offered for sale in the next fifteen years. This increase in competition for quality buyers raises the need to develop a Transition Growth Plan with an understanding of the business sale process.

Chapter 52

Understand The Business Sale Process

Are You Ready To Let Go?

Understanding the business sale process isn't limited to just learning the technical aspects. It's important to first address your planned readiness to sell. Entrepreneur Jimmy Calano and author of "Make Your Move" provides a good insight into the mental steps an owner should walk through when approaching the sale of your company. He was co-founder and former CEO of CareerTrack, an international training company. This was an organization he helped grow to 700 employees and $82 million in revenue, conducting business in 24 countries. After heading the company for 13 years, he sold it to a multinational company.

His advice as you contemplate the sale of your company is to first take some time to decide if you are ready, willing and able to let go. He suggests that you do this by first listing out: your reasons for selling, your fears about selling, what could go wrong, your deal team, how you will mentally prepare yourself, the things that you won't miss, your "Dream List" of what you'll do with your days after you've sold, the positive habits and routines you promise to develop, and the goals you plan to achieve after the sale.

You Can't Win If You Don't Know The Playing Field

Just as it's difficult to be successful in running a business without understanding the playing field, it is difficult to be successful in selling your business if you don't understand the field of play. One of the objectives of the Transition Growth and Exit Planning process is to provide the business owner with enough understanding of the business sale process to be able to prepare appropriately and to engage the right expertise at the right time to help accomplish a profitable exit through the sale of your business.

Many business owners fail to build the optimal position for profitably selling their business. Often this results in leaving large amounts on the table. This can arise because of any number of reasons, including the failure to properly design or place your business into a position to be ready for sale, as well as a failure to properly approach the buyer's marketplace.

Understand The Business Sale Process

The business sale process typically consists of four principal stages, including:

- Pre-Sale Planning.
- Marketing The Business.
- Negotiating The Sale.
- Completing And Closing The Transaction.

Pre-Sale Planning

The Next Move Transition Growth Plan, when designed and implemented according to the Action Plan, will accomplish your pre-sale planning (whether for a sale to an outsider or to an insider). Not only will it help in making sure you have properly structured your business organization, but it will also help you focus on growing the value of your business, protecting it through the date of your sale, as well as putting you in a position to be able to sell your company. Approximately 70% to 80% of businesses which are put on the market do not sell. Pre-sale planning will help increase your odds.

In planning the sale of your company, it's important to keep in mind the factors which determine what a buyer is willing to pay. These include (i) the return on investment the buyer expects on the purchase of your business (vs. other investments), (ii) the buyer's expectation of your business' future performance (e.g. predictable, growing future cash flow, management capabilities, proprietary technology and products), (iii) the buyer's own objectives and needs, and (iv) the then-present economic factors affecting the M&A market (e.g. interest rates, capital availability, industry economic cycle).

Marketing The Business

Building Block 1 involved a review of your potential Exit Routes. This included a review of your potential third-party buyers, whether financial or strategic. Depending on the industry within which you operate, you may well possess the best working knowledge of the potential financial and strategic buyers for your type of business. If not, then we would typically work with our business owner clients to engage a transaction intermediary to assist in marketing the business: a business broker (for smaller companies), a middle-market transaction intermediary (for mid-size businesses) or an investment banker (for larger companies).

In each instance, the transaction intermediary will work with us and the business owner to help develop a buyer profile as well as a company information or offering memorandum, which will describe the salient features of your business. This may be known by other names, such as a business description report.

In addition, the transaction intermediary will typically prepare some form of a "teaser sheet", which is a document which contains enough information to test a buyer's interest. Once the intermediary has developed a list of potential buyers, the "teaser sheet" can be distributed to potential buyers to determine an indication of interest. This teaser sheet will typically not contain enough information to identify the specific seller. In addition, depending on the various locations of the intermediary, this might be sent from an office of the intermediary not located in the same general vicinity as the seller.

Once an indication of interest is received from one or more potential buyers, a Confidentiality Agreement will be executed on behalf of the seller, assuming that the buyer is of interest to the seller. At this point, the business description report can be provided for a detail review of interest by the potential buyers.

Depending on the circumstances, some form of "auction" will typically be developed. A "true auction" may be counterproductive due to its inherent time constraints and requirements. Therefore, many intermediaries will engage in what is in effect a limited auction in order to involve multiple potential buyers during the same time process.

A transaction intermediary will typically negotiate a retainer for its fee to engage in this process, coupled with a "success fee" if and when the sale is concluded. Often the success fee will be set at a fixed percentage of a given expected value and a somewhat higher percentage as to that portion of the selling price achieved in excess of that. This has the effect of acting as a motivator to the transaction intermediary to obtain the best price possible.

A seller engaging a transaction intermediary to sell his or her business should anticipate giving the transaction intermediary an exclusive term for a period of time (e.g. 12 months), followed by a cancellation option by either party. An intermediary is also likely to expect a tail period for a certain period of time after termination of the agreement (e.g. for 2 years) in the event a sale transaction is actually consummated with a buyer which the intermediary brought to the table. If the seller brings certain potential buyers to the table, then a discounted success fee may be negotiated or a temporary exclusion may be negotiated with respect to a sale to that buyer.

Negotiating The Sale

The bidding process ends when the seller has selected one of the buyers with whom to complete the transaction. Typically, the parties will then enter into a "Letter of Intent" which will include the key terms of the transaction. This will detail the proposed purchase price, the particular business being sold, the method of payment, a proposed closing date, the expected contingencies to closing (such as completion of financing and the due diligence process), and such other factors as the parties determine. The Letter of Intent can also include provisions which provide for a period of time (known as a standstill) during which the seller cannot market the business to another buyer. The Letter of Intent can also contain further details regarding confidentiality requirements and press release requirements. The Letter of Intent creates the framework for an agreement, but it is not intended to be a legally binding document (other than with respect to certain terms, such as the standstill and confidentiality terms).

Following the execution of a Letter of Intent, the buyer will, with the cooperation of the seller, typically engage in a very comprehensive investigation of the business, known as the due diligence process. Both the transaction intermediary, as well as transaction legal counsel for both the buyer and the seller, are typically involved in the Letter of Intent preparation as well as management and review of the due diligence process.

Following this, assuming that the parties are both in agreement on proceeding, then a "Definitive Purchase and Sale Agreement" will be prepared by transaction legal counsel and further negotiated by legal counsel, the buyer, the seller and the transaction intermediary. The initial draft of the Definitive Purchase and Sale Agreement is typically prepared by the buyer's legal counsel. It will contain the terms of the deal, along with various representations and warranties to be made by both parties, as well as certain covenants regarding actions to be taken or not taken between the date of the agreement and the closing of the transaction. During this process, the buyer will also be negotiating its own financing for the transaction as well.

Completing And Closing The Transaction

Following execution of a Definitive Purchase and Sale Agreement, the buyer will typically engage in additional due diligence to confirm that the representations made in the agreement have been complied with. In order to complete and close the transaction, a number of additional documents will be prepared by transaction legal counsel in order to actually carry out and implement the completion of the sale.

The overall timing for this process can vary greatly from transaction to transaction. Following initial engagement of a transaction intermediary, you can expect a time period of at least four to six weeks in order to develop the business description report and teaser sheet, and then approximately another six to eight weeks in order for the transaction intermediary to be in a position to have developed the potential buyers and be prepared to begin marketing the business. Once a buyer is identified, the parties may take another month to two months to agree to the terms of a Letter of Intent, followed by another sixty to one hundred twenty days to actually complete and close the transaction. Overall, the time period involved from first engaging the transaction intermediary to closing of the transaction could be expected to take from nine months to two years.

The process of selling a business can typically be very complex and can also involve a lot of time by the seller and the company's key employment staff. It's important to involve professionals who have demonstrated experience in the process, both as to the business marketing capabilities of the transaction intermediary as well as the merger and acquisition experience of the transaction legal counsel.

Chapter 53

Plan For An Outside Route Exit

Once you've decided that your primary or backup exit route includes the future sale of your business to an outside third party, it's important to start to consider the terms under which you will be willing to sell by developing an Outside Route Exit Plan. Such a plan would address:

1. **Who will you sell to?** Do you have specific buyers you do or don't want to consider?

2. **What is sold?** What are you selling and what are you keeping?

3. **What is received?** What overall financial package are you willing to receive to accommodate your needs and the buyer's objectives?

Tax Efficient Terms

Many third party outside buyers will prefer to purchase the assets of your business rather than to buy your stock. There are a couple reasons for this. First, it helps them to avoid the risk that they are "inheriting" potential, unknown liabilities that were not reflected on your balance sheet. Second, it helps them to obtain a depreciable tax basis in your assets equal to the price they paid (rather than your typically lower depreciated tax basis).

The tax impact of this asset purchase preference on you is as follows. If your corporation is a "C" corporation or an "S" corporation that converted to "S" status within 10 years of the sale, then when it sells its assets, it owes a tax on the gain (or on the "built-in gain" portion of such a converted "S" corporation). Then, when your corporation distributes the sale proceeds to you, you owe a tax on your gain. So, you've effectively been taxed twice on the sale.

This double tax can be reduced to a single tax if your business is held in an "S" corporation or in a limited liability company. To move from being a "C" corporation to a limited liability company typically produces a tax on the conversion. However, you can become an "S" corporation simply by filing an election with the IRS. The decision to become an "S" corporation involves at least a dozen factors, which are reviewed in the Transition Growth Planning process to help determine if you should make the election.

If you've been a "C" corporation, then to fully realize the "S" election benefit on your sale, you need to make the election at least 10 years before your sale.

The "S" election benefit can be illustrated as follows. Assume that your company's value is $1 million and you have an asset and stock basis of $200,000. The difference in tax cost would be as follows (assuming combined federal and state corporate tax rates of 40% and personal tax rates of 20%):

	"C" Corporation Asset Sale	"S" Corporation Asset Sale
Price		
Sales Price	$1,000,000	$1,000,000
Basis	- 200,000	- 200,000
Taxable Gain	$800,000	$800,000
Seller Tax		
Corporate	320,000	-0-
Personal	100,000	160,000
Total Tax	$420,000	$160,000
Net Proceeds		
To You After Tax	$580,000	$840,000

Obtaining A Higher Stock Tax Basis

Another benefit of the "S" election is that your tax basis in your stock can increase annually, resulting in a lower taxable gain if you (a) sell your stock instead of your assets or (b) sell your assets and distribute the proceeds to yourself in liquidation of the corporation. This is because your stock basis in an "S" corporation increases annually by the excess of the company's income over the amount of dividend distributions.

Assuming the same facts as in the previous illustration, along with a stock basis increase of $250,000 ($50,000 per year for 5 years), the impact would be as follows:

	"C" Corporation Asset Sale	"S" Corporation Asset Sale
Price		
Sales Price	$1,000,000	$1,000,000
Basis	- 200,000	- 450,000
Taxable Gain	$800,000	$550,000
Seller Tax		
Corporate	320,000	-0-
Personal	100,000	110,000
Total Tax	$420,000	$110,000
Net Proceeds		
To You After Tax	$580,000	$890,000

Actual results of course depend on your personal situation.

Tax Efficient Sale To Outsider - Exit Structure Alternatives

Business owners and buyers have a number of alternatives for structuring the transfer of a business. The choice of structure depends on a number of factors, including the parties' objectives and relative negotiating leverage, the seller's present corporate structure and tax attributes, and the nature of the buyer. Some alternatives for you as the business owner (shareholder) include the following:

- **Double Taxed Asset Sale**. The buyer purchases the assets of your "C" corporation (which distributes the sale proceeds to you). Both your corporation and you as a shareholder are taxed on the gain.

- **Almost Double Taxed Asset Sale**. The buyer purchases the assets of your "S" corporation which within 10 years of sale was a "C" corporation. Your "S" corporation will be taxed on the "built in gain" that existed at the time of the "S" election and you as the shareholder will be taxed when the (after tax) sale proceeds are distributed.

- **Single Taxed Asset Sale**. The buyer purchases the assets of your "S" corporation which has either been an "S" corporation since its inception or for at least 10 years. You as the shareholder are taxed once on the gain.

- **Single Taxed Stock Sale**. The buyer purchases the stock of your "C" corporation. You are taxed on the gain, but the buyer doesn't receive a tax basis step-up in the company assets (unless buyer makes what is called a "338 election" to treat the transaction as a taxable asset sale, resulting in taxable gain and basis step-up).

- **Partly Taxed Stock Sale**. The buyer purchases the stock of your "S" corporation. You are taxed on the gain, but the taxable gain may be significantly less depending on how long you've been an "S" corporation, since time builds tax-reducing basis in your stock.

- **Tax Deferred Reorganization**. The buyer purchases the stock or assets of your corporation in exchange for stock of the buyer's corporation in a transaction that qualifies as tax free under the Internal Revenue Code. Tax on your gain is deferred until you sell the buyer's stock.

- **Tax Deferred Installment Sale**. The buyer purchases your stock or the assets of your corporation in exchange for an installment promissory note payable to you over time. This can defer some or all of the tax on the transaction until payments are received.

- **Tax Deferred ESOP Sale**. You sell some of your stock to an outside buyer and some of your stock to an Employee Stock Ownership Plan. This can defer the tax on that stock sold to the ESOP, if you invest the proceeds in qualified securities.

- **Partial Equity Rollover.** Here you will retain partial equity in your business by receiving a portion of the ownership (e.g. 20%) in the entity which is set up to be the buyer. To avoid capital gain taxation on the retained equity, an LLC "drop-down" or an S corporation "inversion" transaction may be utilized.

Summary

These exit structure alternatives illustrate only some of the options available for structuring a sale to an outsider. Other more involved alternatives, as well as tax efficient choices within each alternative, also exist, which can be addressed in the Transition Growth and Exit Planning process. Each proposed sale of a business provides its own set of business, financial and tax planning opportunities.

The Next Move Transition Growth Plan

Chapter 54-   Create Your Next Move
                   Transition Growth Plan

Create Your Next Move Transition Growth Plan

Just as a profitable business bases its success on using an established process, so does our Transition Growth and Exit Planning approach. While some business owners engage us to address specific transition and exit planning strategies that they want to address initially, others prefer that we provide a full plan. We do this through the 12 Building Block process described in this book, resulting in the Transition Growth Plan.

The Transition Growth Plan is a roadmap intended to help a business owner to successfully chart a course for his or her eventual exit. It needs to address business, personal, financial, legal, contingency and tax matters which typically impact the exit process. It presents a proactive plan for your transition and exit. It also addresses contingencies for early death, disability, divorce or burnout. The objective is to maximize your net value, minimize taxes, maintain your control of the process and help assure your personal and financial objectives are met.

Next Move Transition Growth Plan™

A properly prepared Transition Growth Plan is equivalent to a "briefback" – a U.S. Forces plan which outlines a specific proposed mission down to the last detail. The Transition Growth Plan provides a comprehensive plan that will help you accomplish your mission to successfully exit (and pass on) your privately held company on your timetable and your terms. The plan needs to address key questions which you (and your advisors) must address before and when you exit your business.

The military briefback will contain the objectives of the mission, a description of the expected roadblocks facing the successful completion of a mission and the specific details of the means by which the mission will be accomplished. The means for accomplishing any mission include the steps needed for mission approval and mission planning, along with the personnel and tools necessary to carryout the mission. The mission plans need to include steps for dealing with mission financing, responding to unexpected contingencies, appropriate assignments pursuant to an action plan, a detailed timetable and plans for dealing with expected and unexpected contingencies.

Without intending to be overly dramatic in comparing an owner's exit from his or her business to that of a full scale military operation, the two events, while different in order of magnitude, are very similar in terms of the need for the same level of detail which would go into a military briefback. The military plan of action needs to incorporate various types of personnel expertise, levels of command and personnel teamwork, as well as various types of military technology and tools (weaponry, transportation, communication, logistics, etc.) in order to accomplish the mission. What military commander would attempt even an isolated air strike without having the proper personnel experts on board, including a pilot, navigator, and other specialized crew.

Many Miss The Mark

Yet, all too often, equally accomplished business owners are attempting to navigate their exit from their business based on the advice of one or possibly a couple of narrowly specialized professionals who often are operating in an uncoordinated manner at different times attempting to carryout different objectives. Over the years, we have often seen a business owner who will have implemented certain tax advice from his or her CPA one year, executed a Buy-Sell Agreement prepared by his or her legal counsel in another year, purchased some type of life insurance policy at yet another time, perhaps had discussions with a business broker or investment banker at some other time, all after the execution of an estate plan several years prior to all of this through their estate planning attorney.

Each of the professionals may well have provided good separate results for accomplishing certain objectives. However, we have found that these objectives and actions are uncoordinated, inconsistent and incomplete. Like attempting to carry out a military action without yet knowing the target or timetable, these uncoordinated "exit" efforts typically fail to hit the mark. They result in frustration to the business owner and an eventual exit which is less than successful.

A Coordinated Process And Deliverable Are Needed

The purpose of the Transition Growth Plan is to provide a coordinated process and a coordinated deliverable to assist a business owner in planning for and implementing a successful, eventual exit from active duty and/or from ownership in his or her business. Most business owners have become accustomed to seeing such a coordinated effort in other areas, such as computer system development, product research and development, marketing campaigns, building construction, and business site selection processes. No less of an effort is needed to plan for a successful business owner exit.

Addressing 12 Building Blocks

The Transition Growth Plan addresses the 12 Building Blocks that need to be addressed to help assure the successful exit that you are looking for, whether this exit arises on account of your carefully laid out timetable or whether the exit occurs because of an unexpected mishap (death, disability, divorce, dispute or business down grade) or an unexpected opportunity (such as an early opportunity to sell). Each of these 12 Building Blocks, in turn, contains a number of key transition and exit strategies. These are summarized in this book.

All Plans Are Firm Until Changed

In our firm, we operate on a simple principle that "All plans are firm until changed." In the context of Transition Growth and Exit Planning, this means that while a Transition Growth Plan has been prepared, the plan needs to be adjusted and adapted as your objectives, and the facts which impact your objectives, change into the future.

Without a plan at all -- or with an insufficient plan -- there is no real basis for implementing the tools and steps which can help with a successful, eventual exit. However, the intention is never to let the existence of the plan stifle the need to be flexible and adaptable going forward.

Transition Growth Plan Implementation

Once a Plan has been developed, it needs to be implemented. A good Transition Growth Plan will include an Action Plan Checklist along with an Action Plan Timeline. This would be similar to architecting a building. The plans should include not only the design of what the building is going to look like, but also a checklist of who is going to do what in the timeline for accomplishing this.

Our Transition Growth Planning Program for business owners described at the beginning of this book has been specifically designed to help you accomplish your transition and exit successfully.

Transition Growth Plan Implementation

Chapter 55 – Implement Action Plan Checklist

Implement Action Plan Checklist

Once you have designed and prepared your Transition Growth Plan, a number of items typically remain to be implemented before your actual exit. This is regardless of whether your exit is simply from active duty, simply from ownership, or both. In this respect, a Transition Growth Plan is much like a Business Plan or a Strategic Plan. Each involves an analysis of the options available to you for accomplishing a given set of objectives. However, when the Plan is written, it still needs to be implemented.

Some of the common actions remaining to be completed, after your Transition Growth Plan is written and before your actual exit occurs, are summarized on the pages that follow:

Building Block 1 – Decide What I Want

Some actions which may yet need to be implemented under Building Block 1 – "Decide What I Want", include the following:

- **Financial Needs Analysis.** This is a more detailed review of your actual expected future financial needs post-exit. The "cash-in-pocket composite index" provided an estimate. This estimate can be further refined with your financial advisor.

- **Family Retreat or Conference.** You will hold a family retreat or conference with your family to further determine and synchronize your personal, financial and exit objectives.

- **Engage Team.** Engage the Transition Growth Advisor Team that you have selected.

Building Block 2 – Decide What I've Got

Some actions which may yet need to be implemented under Building Block 2 – "Decide What I've Got", include the following:

- **Business Appraisal.** Obtaining a full business appraisal will help solidify a more accurate business valuation. This can also provide a useful tool as part of the negotiation process with either an outside third party or an inside purchaser. The appraisal may also be needed to establish the price under a Buy-Sell Agreement.

- **Normalized Adjustments Confirmation.** In normalizing an income statement, it is necessary to have a good understanding of actual fair market value rental rates for real estate and equipment being leased between related parties, fair market value royalty fees for license agreements between related parties, and fair market value compensation payable to key employee family owners. Each of these amounts are typically estimated in the Transition Growth Plan process but can be more firmly established through CPA and third party consultant reviews.

- **Cash Flow Projection.** Depending on expectations, you may need to have your CPA assist you in developing a more detailed, reliable cash flow projection, on which valuation expectations can be reasonably based.

- **Personal Financial Statement.** This will provide a snapshot of your assets, liabilities and financial net worth.

Building Block 3 – Protect My Family

Some actions which may yet need to be implemented under Building Block 3 – "Protect My Family", include the following:

- **Basic Estate Plan Upgrade.** Your basic Estate Plan is your cornerstone from the standpoint of your family protection and personal financial planning. The elements identified in your Transition Growth Plan to be upgraded need to be reflected in revised Wills, Living Trusts, Health Care and Financial Powers of Attorney, and the Asset Retitling documents identified in your Transition Growth Plan.

- **Owner Exit Estate Plan.** Your Transition Growth Plan should have identified the specific estate planning applicable to you as a business owner. This may include, for example, amendments to your Living Trusts, which should be implemented prior to your unexpected demise.

- **Pre-Fund Personal Financial Gaps.** Your Transition Growth Plan would have identified your personal contingency financial gaps. This would include those areas to be addressed through life insurance and disability insurance products, which should be reviewed in detail with your financial advisor and implemented with the appropriate insurance tools.

- **Charitable Plan.** If you have identified charitable objectives, this may require added steps to implement.

- **Education Plan.** Education funding for children or grandchildren typically calls for specific documents to be established and funded.

- **Asset Protection.** Personal asset protection elements of your Transition Growth Plan typically require specific implementation steps.

Building Block 4 – Protect My Business

Some actions which may yet need to be implemented under Building Block 4 – "Protect My Business", include the following:

- **Business Risk Protection.** This step can include an assessment of your present casualty risks compared to your casualty insurance coverage, as well as a corporate reorganization to provide better corporate limited liability protection.

- **Intangible Asset Protection.** This step would have identified specific intangible asset protection tools which should be implemented to preserve the value you have built with regard to your intangible assets.

- **Pre-Exit Dispute Avoidance.** If your Transition Growth Plan has identified potential family, key employee, customer, vendor or other third party potential areas of dispute which would be caused by your exit, then these should, where feasible, be addressed.

Building Block 5 – Protect My Ownership

Some actions which may yet need to be implemented under Building Block 5 – "Protect My Ownership", include the following:

- **Business Continuity Agreement.** The items outlined in your Transition Growth Plan under this step are the key features that need to be addressed to help provide business continuity in the event of your (or a co-owner's) unexpected death or disability, your (or a co-owner's) divorce, and to help avoid and resolve co-owner disputes. These items need to be reflected in an actual Business Continuity Agreement which is discussed amongst co-owners and family members and executed.

- **Buy-Sell Agreement.** Your Transition Growth Plan would have identified the types of provisions to be included in a Buy-Sell Agreement. This agreement needs to be discussed among co-owners, agreed to and executed.

- **Pre-Fund Business Contingency Gaps.** Your Transition Growth Plan would have identified those areas which call for special funding in the event of the death or disability of yourself or a co-owner under your Buy-Sell Agreement. These are typically handled through life insurance and lump sum disability insurance products which should be implemented ahead of an unexpected exit.

Building Block 6 – Grow My Investments

Some actions which may yet need to be implemented under Building Block 6 – "Grow My Investments", include the following:

- **Comprehensive Wealth Plan.** This is a detailed review of your business and non-business investment plan, to determine if you are investing through the right tools and the right investment firms to optimize your investment growth.

- **Economic Alternative Simulations.** You may find that you've achieved the value you need, but for any of several reasons you aren't yet in a position to sell. You may also be considering whether, from purely an investment standpoint (e.g. due to future concerns about your company or industry or place in the business or economic cycle), you could now do better by selling or investing in a more diversified investment strategy. In these situations, financial managers can provide economic alternative simulations specific to your industry to address potential hedging and investment diversification alternatives.

Building Block 7 – Grow My Business

Some actions which may yet need to be implemented under Building Block 7 – "Grow My Business", include the following:

- **Business Model Innovation Program.** This will enable you to continuously improve the business logic of your Company and its products and services, which is key to remaining profitable and in business.

- **Benchmark Outcome.** The business benchmarking which occurred in this step is comparable to a blood test. It will identify problem areas which need further analysis and corrective measures, as applicable.

- **Strategic Growth Plan.** This plan will address the business plan for how you will profitably grow what you make and sell and would demonstrate how the business will do this without you.

Building Block 8 – Prepare My Management

The actions needed to further implement Building Block 8 – "Prepare My Management", can include the following:

- **Management Recruiter Engagement.** Whether or not you have an adequate depth chart from which to build key management successors, it is usually recommended that you have an ongoing engagement with a good executive or management recruiting firm specializing in your area. Your top management team member working for you today might be working for a competitor tomorrow leaving a gap in your plans which can set you back significantly from your overall objectives if that person cannot be timely replaced. A present, ongoing relationship with a management recruiting firm, who is familiar with your business, provides you with the opportunity not only to replace top performers more quickly, but also to identify top performers whom you may want to hire as you grow your business.

- **Leadership Team Development Program.** This consists of selected programs and tools to develop your key employee leadership skills.

- **Management Duty Transition Program.** Your business growth, as well as your future exit, are dependent on how well you continually transition (delegate) your duties to someone else. It is key that you develop a program to do this.

- **Key Employee Incentive Agreement.** Your Transition Growth Plan would have identified cash and equity compensation incentive alternatives for helping you to keep and attract a key management team and your potential ultimate successor. This will typically be in the form of a written agreement, and may also include stock transfer documents, which need to be discussed with your management team and executed as appropriate.

- **Key Employee Retreat.** To review your transition plans with your key employees, this action involves holding one or more key employee retreats to review the transition terms you propose.

Building Block 9 – Prepare My Company

The actions needed to further implement Building Block 9 – "Prepare My Company", can include the following:

- **Entity Restructuring.** If your Transition Growth Plan calls for restructuring your business entities (for example dividing the company into two companies based on divisions or placing your real estate into a separate limited liability company), then the actual steps for accomplishing this restructuring need to be taken before your exit.

- **Accounting Systems.** If your Transition Growth Plan calls for changes in your accounting system in order to increase its credibility in the eyes of a buyer, or if it requires more formalized financial statements, or requires a change in accounting method (e.g. from cash to accrual), then these changes need to be made in advance of your exit. Ideally these types of changes would be made at least 3-5 years ahead of your exit in order to provide a consistent, credible track record to enable a buyer to review your financial results with the degree of confidence that a good buyer would expect.

- **Pre-Exit Consents.** If your Transition Growth Plan has identified outside third party consents which are needed for your exit, (such as from a lender, franchisor or government licensing agency), then these consents should be discussed well in advance with the person from whom the consent is needed, to identify any terms or conditions which need to be met in advance of your exit.

Building Block 10 – Prepare My Tax Savings Plans

The actions needed to further implement Building Block 10 – "Prepare My Tax Savings Plans", can include the following:

- **Estate Tax Plan.** These recommendations will typically require additional steps to be taken.

- **Federal Income Tax Plan.** If your Transition Growth Plan calls for implementing certain tax elections (such as a subchapter "S" election or a change in certain other tax accounting methods), then these steps typically should be taken in advance of your exit. For example, in order to maximize the benefit of a subchapter "S" election, the election should typically be made at least 10 years before your exit.

- **State Income Tax Plan.** If your Transition Growth Plan calls for steps to avoid State Capital Gain taxes on the sale of your business, certain actions are generally needed at least a year before your sale.

- **State Incentive Growth Plan.** This may entail tax incentive negotiation and application steps to reduce your state taxes.

Building Block 11 – Plan My Inside Route Exit

The actions needed to further implement Building Block 11 – "Plan My Inside Route Exit", can include the following:

- **Banker Review.** If a transfer to insiders is a feasible alternative for you, this will typically involve either third party bank financing to help support the sale or seller-financing, in which you carry back a promissory note to be paid off by the insider over time. If the latter is not your preference, you should plan to pursue a discussion early on with your banker to determine on what terms and circumstances the banker is willing to provide third party financing. This helps provide a reality check as to the feasibility of a transfer at your expected price. It also helps outline some of the specific terms and conditions that the banker would expect, which gives you adequate time ahead of your exit to plan accordingly.

- **Implement Initial Inside Ownership.** While you might anticipate transferring your business to one or more insiders (whether a co-owner, family member or key employee group), those insiders may have a completely different plan in mind, which may or may not include ultimately owning your business. Besides learning whether such a purchase is on their radar screen, early communications with your potential inside buyers will let them know of your interest in the role they play in the future of the company and the future of your transition, which may also help in your retention efforts to keep them as key employees of the company. Once this is agreed to, the actual documentation to carry this out should be dealt with in advance of your actual exit.

- **Complete Inside Sale.** If you are ready to complete your ownership exit, transaction legal counsel should be engaged to help accomplish this.

- **Implement ESOP Study.** This is to be done to determine if you are an ESOP candidate.

Building Block 12 – Plan My Outside Route Exit

The actions needed to further implement Building Block 12 – "Plan My Outside Route Exit", can include the following:

- **Transaction Intermediary Engagement.** While a transaction intermediary may be consulted during the Transition Growth and Exit Planning Process to help evaluate or to test the market outlook for a sale to potential outside third party buyers, a transaction intermediary might not have yet been engaged to be actively pursuing or monitoring the buyers market on your behalf. This type of engagement can be negotiated and arranged. Depending on the nature of the engagement, a retainer fee may be appropriate.

- **Offering Memorandum.** Based on the concept that you should always have your business ready for sale, it is helpful to have a standby offering memorandum prepared. This reflects a summary of the key features of your business as well as a summary of the transaction terms if you were to sell to a third party today. The process of preparing this will help further identify potential weaknesses.

- **Due Diligence Report.** A potential buyer will do a thorough due diligence study. To the extent you do this before a potential sale, you will spot those specific areas a buyer will uncover, allowing you to address them ahead of time.

- **Implement Outside Sale.** If your anticipated exit is now, then you need to engage transaction legal counsel to proceed.

Completing The Transition Growth and Exit Planning Process

The Transition Growth and Exit Planning process will walk you through the questions, alternatives and answers you need to address to keep your business successful and growing during your remaining tenure and to enable you to successfully transition from your business on your timetable and on your terms.

Upon completion of this program, you will have a personal Roadmap which will help you successfully chart a course for your eventual exit from your business. This process provides a proactive plan for your transition. It also addresses contingencies for possible early death, disability, departure, divorce or burnout. The objective of this process is to maximize the net value you can realize from your business, minimize taxes, maintain your control of the process and help assure your personal, financial and legacy objectives are met.

By accomplishing this Action Plan you will be as prepared as reasonably possible for your planned or unexpected exit. After this step, you should re-take the Pre-Exit Fitness Test to chart your progress and to determine whether you've covered the areas that you responsibly want to address.

Looking Forward

Chapter 56 -   Visualize The Legacy You
                Want To Leave

Visualize The Legacy You Want To Leave

As Stephen Covey has reminded us, we should "Begin with the end in mind." In the Transition Growth and Exit Planning context, you need to begin with an understanding of the legacy you want to leave. How do you want to be remembered by your family, your business and your community? What do you want to be able to look back upon as a particular accomplishment you achieved or as a particular good you provided for someone else?

If you have been a long-time owner of your business, then the day-to-day operation of your business has become your way of life. Like many business owners, you are probably largely known or identified with the business that you have built and the success you have achieved in doing so.

In a very real sense, your business is like a child to you. You've nourished it, you've toiled through years of blood, sweat and tears with regard to it. You've seen it through the bad times and you've rejoiced during the good times. Although you've probably had more than your share of days when you've wanted to just walk out, lock up the doors and never return, for the most part, leaving your business can just be plain hard to want to do.

Your Exit Is Not The End – It's Just The Beginning

Many business owners would probably be content to work until their dying day and be carried out boots up. However, it becomes necessary to consider whether that's the best result, whether for you, your spouse, your children, your key employees and the other constituencies affected by what you do through your exit or non-exit from your business.

Legacy Thoughts

My father, Ferd Niemann, was a good example of someone who loved his business and loved his family. He and my uncle owned and successfully exited from a number of businesses throughout their careers. This included the restaurant business, real estate development, retail merchandising, retail gasoline, horse ranching and poultry. However, their mainstay business was the supermarket business. This business began in 1917 as one corner grocery store owned by my grandfather and his brother. Over the years they added several corner grocery stores, before consolidating these into a couple of supermarkets in the 1940's. By the time of my grandfather's death in 1969, he was in partnership with my dad and my uncle. The Company owned and operated six supermarkets.

My dad and uncle spent the next 25 years after my grandfather's death continuing to grow and expand the supermarket operations. Retail, especially supermarket retail, involves a lot of work, long hours and very slim margins. It's a business which my father loved, especially on account of the love and respect which he always held for his father and a clear mission in life to be able to hand the family business down to his children as his father had handed it down to him. However, while we all worked in the grocery business growing up, neither myself nor my other six brothers and sisters felt the supermarket business was our calling.

My dad had always felt that he would never retire from the business he loved. However, as he approached age 65, he began to consider how this would impact his other passions in his life. He and my mother loved to travel, but found it nearly impossible to do on a regular basis given the demands of helping to run a full-time retail supermarket operation. My dad was a Korean war veteran, a former professional baseball player and an avid horseman. He remained active in professional baseball circles and Korean war veteran affairs throughout his life, as well as continuing to own and breed horses.

After a lot of thought and a lot of discussion with my mother, they decided it was time to move on. He had accomplished more than most in his business career. It was finally time to have some fun with his other passions in life. So he did what he previously thought would be unthinkable – he sold his interest in the supermarket business and he retired at age 70.

He hadn't regretted it for one moment. Over the ten years since his retirement, he and my mother had opportunities to travel, to visit family and friends, to spend some time at their favorite destinations, to sleep in, to take drives through the countryside, even to travel across the country at their leisure on a train rather than trying to meet crammed travel deadlines.

A couple years before this book went to print, my father passed away. No one was more thankful than he and my mother that they made the move ten years earlier to retire and enjoy the time together that they have had.

My father's real legacy, however, isn't the supermarket chain he helped build. His legacy was apparent to everyone he met, as illustrated in a story from a couple of years ago. I was on a family trip almost a hundred miles from my hometown of Quincy. Along the way I stopped in a restaurant for a quick lunch. We always kidded my father how he could never leave a restaurant without first learning the life story of the waiter or waitress.

I must have inherited some of his genes, because in talking to the waitress that day, I learned she was the owner. I soon asked how she started the business. Before she knew my last name, she told the story how she had bought some used restaurant equipment from a man in Quincy, Illinois about twenty-five years earlier by the name of Ferd Niemann. She recalled that he had given her a fair deal, but mostly she recalled that "He was a man who loved people."

What is it most about a man's presence that would leave this memorable impression for twenty-five years. That's the legacy my seventy-hour per week working businessman father left. I had seen this in my father for years and this restaurant owner had summed it up. No matter how busy my father was, he always found the time to talk to people – employees, customers, friends, business associates, family - for the simple reason that he loved people.

You Absolutely Won't Achieve The Legacy You Don't Pursue

There's an old saying to the effect that no one on their deathbed ever wished that they had spent more time at the office. For most of us, our business is a means to an end – it at a minimum provides us with a livelihood to support our families.

For many, our business may also be an end in itself as well. However, most business owners whom we know have a vision which extends beyond simply being known as a business owner.

Achieving Your Legacy

As we began this Transition Growth and Exit Planning discussion, we focused on your personal and financial objectives. If you keep the vision of those objectives in the forefront as you embark on the Transition Growth and Exit Planning process, your likelihood of successfully completing a successful transition exit mission will be substantially increased and your happiness with this process will be more thoroughly realized.

That's why the final strategy in the Transition Growth and Exit Planning process is to first look forward as you begin the process to the end result you're trying to achieve, visualize the legacy you want to leave, and then find the time to relax and, simply, enjoy the rest of the ride.

What is the legacy you want to leave?: _____
_____
_____
_____
_____

What is the next move you are going to take to help achieve this?: _____
_____
_____
_____
_____

Appendix

Sampling Of Recent
Transition/Exit Planning
Articles

Recommended Reading

Sampling of Recent Transition/Exit Planning Articles

1. **"Who Will Replace Me?"**
   CNNMoney.com; September 5, 2008.

2. **"Why Succession Planning Matters"**
   Forbes.com; January 7, 2008.

3. **"Success – And Succession – Takes Planning"**
   Forbes.com; July 19, 2007.

4. **"Better Business – Planning Your Exit Strategy"**
   Printweek; November 9, 2006.

5. **"Prepare For The Handoff: Planning For Succession"**
   Accounting Today; November 6, 2006.

6. **"Business Succession That Builds The Value Of Privately Held Companies"**
   Valuation Strategies; November/December, 2006.

7. **"Do You Have An "Exit Plan" For Your Business?"**
   Reed Business Information; October 1, 2006.

8. **"Eyeing Exit Strategies; More Owners Will Need Advice On How To Best Position Their Business for Their Departure"**
   Practical Accountant; October, 2006.

9. **"Why Business Owners Need Exit Planning"**
   Contractor; September 1, 2006.

10. **"Are You Prepared To Exit Your Business? Succession Planning Ensures The Continued Viability Of Your Vision And Should Be A Key Part Of Your Business Plan"**
    Supply House Times; June 1, 2006.

11. **"Making Succession A Success: Perspectives From Canadian Small And Medium-Sized Enterprises."**
    Journal of Small Business Management; April, 2006.

12. **"Reaching The Decision To Sell."**
    Rough Notes Co., Inc.; April, 2006.

13. **"Sound Succession Planning Begins With A Fresh Definition."**
    ABA Banking Journal, April, 2006.

14. **"How To 'Back Away' From A Business Without Selling."**
    San Fernando Valley Business Journal; March 13, 2006.

15. "Always Have An Escape Plan."
    Financial Adviser; January 26, 2006.

16. "There are 8 Exit Strategies for Owners – But Know the Steps."
    San Fernando Business Journal; January 16, 2006.

17. "Walk Away From Everything Without Leaving Anything Behind: Creating a Business Exit Plan."
    Agency Sales; November 1, 2005.

18. "Succession Planning Needs A Wider Definition – Exit Planning."
    MANAGEMENT Keeping Good Companies; October 1, 2005.

19. "Business Owners Need An Exit Strategy."
    OPINION Business Record (Des Moines, IA); September 12, 2005.

20. "Keeping The Engine Running - Finding an Exit Strategy for a Family-Owned Manufacturer."
    Star Tribune (Minneapolis, MN); August 15, 2005.

21. "Owners Who Put Off Planning an Exit Strategy Risk Losing Their Business."
    The Daily Telegraph (London), July 4, 2005.

22. "Exit Strategies; Planning And Common Sense Can Ease The Pain Of Selling A Business."
    Sun-Sentinel (Fort Lauderdale, FL); June 13, 2005.

23. "Smart Owners Plan Their Exit."
    The Dominion Post (Wellington, New Zealand); June 6, 2005.

24. "Parting Company: The Time To Start Planning Your Exit Strategy Is Now."
    Restaurant Hospitality; June 1, 2005.

25. "Know When To Give Up: It's Hard To Call It Quits."
    The Wall Street Journal; May 9, 2005.

26. "Developing Exit Strategies For The Closely Held Business."
    Journal of Financial Service Professionals; May 1, 2005.

27. "Raising Capital And Developing Exit Strategies For The Closely Held Business Owner: A Tutorial For Financial Professionals."

Journal of Financial Service Professionals; May 1, 2005.

28. "What's Your Exit Strategy?"
    Business and Management Practices Reeves Journal,
    May 2005.

29. "Best Way To Make Your Exit – Entrepreneur."
    The Australian; April 29, 2005.

30. "Building Continuity Into Strategy."
    Journal of Corporate Real Estate, April 1, 2005.

31. "Baby Boomers Plan For Life After The Rigors of Business";
    Sacramento Business Journal, March 25, 2005.

32. "New Ending: Succession Plot At Bookstore Took A Surprise
    Twist."
    The Wall Street Journal; March 21, 2005.

33. "Planning A Successful Exit Strategy."
    Business and Management Practices; March 1, 2005.

34. "Eight Different Approaches To A Winning Exit Route."
    Business and Industry Leisure Report; March 2005.

35. "Developing An Exit Strategy: There Are Several Viable Ways
    To Leave Your Business."
    Roofing Siding Insulation, February 1, 2005.

36. "Effective Succession Planning: Should You Keep Leadership
    In The Family?"
    Franchising World; February 1, 2005.

37. "All Business Owners Should Have An Exit Plan; Here's How
    To Put One Together."
    Industrial Distribution; February 1, 2005.

38. "What's Your Exit Strategy? Timing Is An Essential
    Consideration For A Profitable Restaurant Sale."
    Restaurant Hospitality, January 1, 2005.

39. "Helping The Business Owner To Exit."
    National Underwriter Life & Health, November 1,
    2004.

40. "Small Business Owner Needs An Exit Strategy."
    The Toronto Star; October 17, 2004.

41. "The Family Business: Continuity Just May Be More Challenging Than You Think."
   Plain Dealer (Cleveland); September 19, 2004.

42. "Get Out While You Still Can."
   Australian CPA; July 1, 2004.

43. "Plan Well, Early For An Exit Strategy."
   Business Journal; June 4, 2004.

44. "When The Time Comes To Hand Over The Reins Of Your Business—What Is The Best Exit Strategy?"
   NZ Business; June 1, 2004.

45. "Family-Run Operations Must Plan For Succession."
   Commercial Motor; May 27, 2004.

46. "Exit Doors Open Wider For Smaller Businesses."
   Minneapolis St. Paul Business Journal; April 30, 2004.

47. "Exit Planning A Requisite As Owners Eye Retirement."
   The Business Journal; January 23, 2004.

48. "How to Plan Your Exit Strategy."
   Financial Adviser; October 30, 2003.

49. "Business Owners Need An Exit Strategy, Too."
   Newsday (New York); October 25, 2003.

50. "Exiting Gracefully."
   CircuiTree; September 1, 2003.

51. "Profiting Today By Planning For Tomorrow's Succession."
   Journal of Financial Planning; September, 2003.

52. "Sell-Side Trends-The Business Transition Tidal Wave";
   ACG Hub News; August 27, 2003

53. "Transitioning (And Succeeding) In The Closely Held Business Market."
   MarketFacts Quarterly; Summer 2003.

54. "End Games: For Many Builders, Finding A Tolerable Path Into Retirement Is The Toughest Management Challenge Of All. Here's How To Get Started."
   Professional Builder; July 1, 2003.

55. "Boss's Exit Strategy Essential."
   The Orlando Sentinel; March 12, 2003.

56. "Start Planning Before You're Ready to Leave."
   Orlando Sentinel; March 3, 2003.

57. "Exit Strategy; Leaving Your Business."
    Restaurant Hospitality; March 1, 2003.

58. "Family Businesses Should Plan For Next Generation Of Ownership."
    Orange County Register (California); June 22, 2002.

59. "Make A Plan For Your Exit."
    Rocky Mountain News; April 5, 2002.

60. "Exit Strategy: What You Need To Know When You Sell The Business."
    The Wall Street Journal; April 17, 2000.

Recommended Reading

Exit On Your Terms, Nicholas K. Niemann

How To Run Your Business So You Can Leave It In Style, John Brown

The Psychology of Winning, Denis Waitley, Ph.D.

Built To Last – Successful Habits Of Visionary Companies, Jim Collins and Jerry Porras

Blink – The Power of Thinking Without Thinking, Malcolm Gladwell

Make Your Move – And Make The Most of Your Life, Jimmy Calano

The E Myth Revisited – Why Most Small Businesses Don't Work and What To Do About It, Michael Gerber

Good To Great – Why Some Companies Make The Leap ... And Others Don't, Jim Collins

Follow This Path – How The World's Greatest Organizations Drive Growth By Unleashing Human Potential, Curt Coffman and Gabriel Gonzalez-Molina

First, Break All The Rules: What The World's Greatest Managers Do Differently, Marcus Buckingham and Curt Coffman

Confronting Reality – Doing What Matters To Get Things Right, Larry Bossidy and Ram Charan

How Full Is Your Bucket – Positive Strategies For Work and Life, Tom Rath and Donald O. Clifton, Ph.D.

Beyond The Grave – The Right Way and The Wrong Way Of Leaving Money To Your Children (and Others), Gerald Condon and Jeffrey Condon

Index

Key employee valuations, 74
Know-How, 91